We Can't Lead Where We Won't Go

About the Cover

For many years Gary Howard has invited educators on 8-day white water equity workshops on the Colorado River. These adventures are co-led by his son, Benjie, who has been a boatman in the Grand Canyon for more than 20 years. Benjie's friend and fellow canyon traveler, Jason Poole, is an exceptionally talented photographer who captured this image from a high vantage point on a hike at Nankoweap. The awesome immensity and powerful demands of this landscape offer an apt metaphor for the work of committed social justice educators. Here, as in the complex environments of our schools, we are challenged to do more than we know how to do, and travel farther than we think we could ever go.

We Can't Lead Where We Won't Go

An Educator's Guide to Equity

Gary R. Howard

CORWIN
A SAGE Company

FOR INFORMATION:

Corwin
A SAGE Company
2455 Teller Road
Thousand Oaks, California 91320
(800) 233–9936
www.corwin.com

SAGE Publications Ltd.
1 Oliver's Yard
55 City Road
London EC1Y 1SP
United Kingdom

SAGE Publications India Pvt. Ltd.
B 1/I 1 Mohan Cooperative Industrial Area
Mathura Road, New Delhi 110 044
India

SAGE Publications Asia-Pacific Pte. Ltd.
3 Church Street
#10–04 Samsung Hub
Singapore 049483

Acquisitions Editor: Dan Alpert
Associate Editor: Kimberly Greenberg
Editorial Assistant: Cesar Reyes
Production Editor: Amy Schroller
Copy Editor: Gillian Dickens
Typesetter: C&M Digitals (P) Ltd.
Proofreader: Jen Grubba
Cover Designer: Rose Storey
Marketing Manager: Stephanie Trkay
Senior Manager,
Multimedia Product
Development: Barbara De Hart

Printed in the United States of America

A catalog record of this book is available from the Library of Congress.

ISBN 978-1-4833-5241-1

This book is printed on acid-free paper.

14 15 16 17 18 10 9 8 7 6 5 4 3 2

Contents

Handouts related to *We Can't Lead Where We Won't Go* are available
on the companion website.

http://www.corwin.com/guidetoequity

List of School Video Clips (SVC) Located on the DVDs

Orientation to the Professional Development Process		
SVC #	*Title*	*Video Length*
1	**How One School Implemented the PD Process** Jenni Jones, Intern Assistant Principal at Northdale Middle School, describes the process her school went through to implement the Gary Howard work. She provides commentary on the stages of the implementation and the steps they took to guarantee its success.	2:11
2	**One District's *Right* Response to Changing Demographics** Dennis Carlson, Superintendent Anoka-Hennepin School District, explains the way in which their work with Gary Howard provided a positive, systemic response to the rapidly changing demographics of their students and community. He describes how it helped to address increasing issues with racism and sexism and taught the district how to respect, honor, and celebrate the diverse community they are so quickly becoming.	4:22
3	**All Students College, Career, and Culturally Ready** Nancy Chave, Principal Crossroads Alternative High School, describes how her school has fully integrated the principles of cultural competence in order to create a safe, supportive, and inclusive school community.	1:21

(Continued)

(Continued)

SVC #	Title	Video Length
4	**Looking at the Data** Jinger Gustafson, Associate Superintendent Anoka-Hennepin School District, describes how the data is showing the district has made positive gains in overall student achievement and how they have drastically closed the achievement gap because of the systemic work they have done with Gary Howard.	2:01

Phase One: Tone and Trust		
SVC #	Title	Video Length
5	**Relationships are the Key to Tone and Trust** Anthony Luckey, Paraprofessional Crossroads Alternative High School, describes the benefits he has experienced from taking the time to build relationships with the students.	3:15
6	**Victor's Pantry: Creating a Welcoming School Climate** Jenni Jones, Intern Assistant Principal at Northdale Middle School, describes how her school created an on-site food pantry to meet the needs of their growing homeless student population.	3:38

Phase Two: Personal Journey and Personal Culture		
SVC #	Title	Video Length
7	**Student Voices: I Am From Poems** Two students, Laquan and Cocoa, read their I Am From poems that poignantly describe their lives and their cultures.	2:23
8	**Affirming Students' Cultural Connections: I Am From Poems** Tina Tamura, 6th Grade Teacher Northdale Middle School, shares her own I Am From poem and describes how she has her students write their own poems as a way to affirm their cultural backgrounds.	2:14

SVC #	Title	Video Length
9	**Olabisi Isaac Ewumi: A Student's Journey** Olabisi Isaac Ewumi, Former Student Blaine High School, describes his own personal journey of being from Nigeria and becoming American and the tension he feels from experiencing a blend of these cultures.	1:30
10	**Jinger Gustafson: An Associate Superintendent's Journey** Jinger Gustafson, Associate Superintendent Anoka-Hennepin School District, describes her personal journey growing up in a rural area and the ways in which her education and experience in the military have forged the person she is today.	2:10
11	**Cassidy Pohl: A Student Advisor's Journey** Cassidy Pohl, Student Achievement Advisor Blaine High School, describes her experience growing up in a multi-racial family and how feeling like she doesn't distinctly belong in one racial group has caused her to form her own identity.	2:23
12	**Alicia Moore: A Teacher's Journey** Alicia Moore, Social Studies Blaine High School, explains how her experience growing up poor and feeling different than her peers affects her teaching and how she goes out of her way to make all students feel comfortable and safe.	2:30

Phase Three: Social Dominance to Social Justice		
SVC #	Title	Video Length
13	**Getting Others to See the Problem** Dennis Carlson, Superintendent Anoka-Hennepin School District, describes how issues of privilege and power can get in the way of meeting the needs of all students.	2:03
14	**Student Voices: Understanding Changes Your Perspective** Gary Howard leads a discussion with a group of high school girls. They describe how issues of race come into their lives and discuss how other aspects of their schools' culture either help or hinder their learning.	4:02

(Continued)

SVC #	Title	Video Length
15	**Student Voices: Boy's Group Talks About Racism** Gary Howard leads a discussion with a group of high school boys. They discuss how racism influences their lives both in school and in their community.	5:47
16	**Student Voices: Racism** Gary Howard leads a discussion with a group of middle school girls. They discuss ways in which these students experience racism in school and in their community.	4:41
17	**Student Voices: "I Feel Kind of Weird that I'm Different"** Gary Howard leads a discussion with a group of middle school boys. They discuss ways in which these students experience racism in school and in their community.	6:39
18	**Student Voice: Students with Diverse Backgrounds Feel the Tension** Olabisi Isaac Ewumi, Former Student Blaine High School, describes the racial and socio-economic tensions that existed at his high school. He also describes the ways in which students with different sexual orientations commonly experienced discrimination and bullying.	2:18

Phase Four: Classroom Implications and Applications		
SVC #	Title	Video Length
19	**Helping Students Find Their Voice** Julie Davis, 5th Grade Teacher Monroe Elementary School, reflects on her classroom practices and the ways in which she tries to be a culturally responsive teacher.	2:54
20	**A Model Lesson: A Blend of CRT Principles** Holly Clark, 7th Grade English Language Arts Teacher, describes how her lesson integrates and reflects four different culturally responsive teaching principles.	3:58
21	**Little Details Make a Big Difference** Alicia Moore, Social Studies Teacher Blaine High School, describes how she blends and integrates the principles of culturally responsive teaching.	2:11

SVC #	Title	Video Length
22	**Bringing in Students' Lives** Megan Hendrix, 10th Grade English Teacher Crossroads Alternative High School, describes how she attends to the principles of culturally responsive teaching in her lessons related to reading *The Crucible*.	3:02
23	**Student Voices: Changing the Way You Look at School** Gary Howard leads a discussion with high school boys who describe what teachers do that help and support their learning.	6:56
24	**Student Voices: Middle School Boys Talk About What Gets in the Way of Their Learning** Gary Howard leads a discussion with middle school boys who describe the ways in which teachers hinder their learning.	5:21
25	**Student Voices: Middle School Boys Talk about How Teachers Help Their Learning** Gary Howard leads a discussion with middle school boys who describe the ways in which teachers help and support their learning.	3:18
26	**Student Voices: Middle School Girls Talk About What Helps and What Hinders Their Learning** Gary Howard leads a discussion with middle school girls who describe the ways in which teachers help and hinder their learning.	6:46
27	**The Achievement Triangle: Incorporating Relationships and Rigor** Nancy Chave, Principal Crossroads Alternative High School, describes how using the Achievement Triangle helps her teachers increase the rigor throughout the curriculum in all classes and at all grade levels.	2:10
28	**The CRT Principles Breakfast** Jenni Jones, Intern Assistant Principal at Northdale Middle School, describes how her school instituted a Principles Breakfast, which is a way to focus on each of the 7 principles of culturally responsive teaching one at a time, and provides ongoing professional learning for the teaching staff.	3:03

(Continued)

\multicolumn{3}{c}{Phase Five: Systemic Transformation/Planning for Change}
SVC #	*Title*	*Video Length*
29	**A Superintendent Makes the Case for Systemic Change** Dennis Carlson, Superintendent Anoka-Hennepin School District, describes how the Gary Howard work that his district initiated over a five-year period was the key to finding common ground for all stakeholders and allowed the district to make unprecedented progress in boosting student achievement and closing the achievement gap.	5:09
30	**Walking a Political Tightrope** Dennis Carlson, Superintendent Anoka-Hennepin School District, describes the political tensions he needed to navigate within the district's community and with his staff as he instituted the systemic work with Gary Howard.	3:15
31	**A Superintendent Talks About the Power of Student Voices** Dennis Carlson, Superintendent Anoka-Hennepin School District, explains the importance of training students to be leaders now so that they can help create safe environments in all the places that adults cannot access, such as social media sites, so that what happens after school does not spill over and infect the school climate for the most vulnerable students.	3:52
32	**Empowering Students: New Wilderness Project** Cassidy Pohl, Student Achievement Advisor Blaine High School, describes the parallel process her school went through teaching the five phases of Gary Howard's word with students and the impact this learning has had on the culture of the school.	2:43
33	**Assessing Student Outcomes in a Large Urban System** Aukram Burton, Multicultural Education Specialist, describes the way in which a large urban school district measured the effectiveness of the systemic work it did with Gary Howard.	3:28

About the Author

 **Gary R. Howard** has more than 40 years of experience working with issues of civil rights, social justice, equity, education, and diversity, including 25 years as the Founder of the REACH Center for Multicultural Education. He is a keynote speaker, writer, and workshop leader who has traveled extensively throughout the United States and Australia. Mr. Howard completed his undergraduate work in Cultural Anthropology and Social Psychology at Yale University and did graduate work in ethics and social justice at Yale Divinity School. He has served as an Adjunct Professor at both Western Washington University and Seattle University.

Mr. Howard has provided extensive training in cultural competence and culturally responsive practice to schools, universities, social service agencies, and businesses throughout the United States and Australia. He is the author of numerous articles on race, justice, and multicultural issues and has developed collections of curriculum materials that are being used internationally. His landmark book, *We Can't Teach What We Don't Know: White Teachers/Multiracial Schools* (Second Edition, 2006), published by Columbia University, is considered a groundbreaking work examining issues of privilege, power, and the role of White leaders and educators in a multicultural society.

The central focus of Gary Howard's current work, which is documented in this publication, is leading intensive Equity Leadership Institutes that provide educational organizations with the internal capacity to deliver high quality professional development for social justice and systemic change. Mr. Howard is frequently asked to deliver keynote addresses at regional and national conferences. In these presentations he draws on a wide range of experiences and travel exploring diversity and social justice issues with leaders from many cultures around the world. Mr. Howard's speeches employ rich imagery and stories drawn from his annual white water equity workshops on the Colorado River in the Grand Canyon.

To all of the teachers and school leaders who have been in my workshops over the past 40 years. You have touched my heart, informed my thinking, and always kept it real. Thank you for the good work you do every day in our nation's schools.

Tribute

The title for this book is inspired by a statement from Malcolm X: "You can't teach what you don't know, and you can't lead where you won't go." That admonition shook the foundation of my preconceived reality in the 1960s, turned my head and heart toward the path of seeking justice, and set the tone for a lifetime of work.

Introduction
to the Manual

This Leadership Manual addresses the most persistent and problematic challenge facing American public education today: how to get the demographics of race and social class out of the business of predicting academic outcomes. In other words, how to create schools that do a better job with more students across more differences more of the time. The systemic professional development process provided here is based on the belief that real school improvement for equity and social justice is best generated at the building level, created and sustained by principals, teachers, and support staff and informed by the students and their families. In my four decades of working on school change efforts, I have found it is often difficult and usually ineffective to attempt to take "proven practices" from one school setting and export those practices to another setting. Why? Because the activities that were created and implemented in the original school grew from the unique struggles, collaborative energies, and localized real-life experiences of those educators and their students. We can mimic the practices in a new context, but it is almost impossible to export the sense of purpose and moral passion that went into creating them in the first place. Passion for change must be locally grown, rooted in specific school environments, and nurtured in the hearts and minds of the people actually doing the work.

The top-down, externally driven, test-centered approach to school reform that we have experienced over the past two decades, along with the punitive consequences for failure to comply, has significantly affected educators' passion and enthusiasm for the work of real reform. Too many good teachers and leaders have been worn down, burnt out, discouraged, and often enraged by the imposition of countless scripted mandates impacting almost every dimension of professional life (Byrd-Blake et al., 2010). Whereas the required disaggregation of data has been effective in exposing long-term disparities in educational outcomes, the prescribed methods of addressing those inequities have often alienated the very people we need to have most engaged. Ironically and too frequently, the externally imposed pressure for change has seriously depleted the internally generated passion for that change.

All of this has created a profound need for healing among teachers and school leaders. The professional development process provided in this manual is part of the healing response. It offers an approach and a strategy that has proven effective in reengaging educators in the real work of improving their schools, particularly in those settings with a high percentage of racially and economically marginalized students. At its heart, this process is about authentic educational change and bottom-up school reform. Despite all the time, money, and political and professional angst that have gone into top-down accountability and high-stakes testing, we are still not doing well by our nation's most vulnerable student populations (Casey Foundation, 2014; Darling-Hammond, 2010; Meier, 2012; Noguera, 2008; Tienken & Orlich, 2013).

In places where good things are happening for urban, racially diverse, poor, and other marginalized students, the focus has been on the core elements of quality schooling:

- Leaders who are collaborative, courageous, and visionary
- Teachers who are skilled, passionate, and culturally competent
- Students who are challenged, engaged, and culturally affirmed

The professional development activities, concepts, and strategies presented here are designed to support you as a school leader and your faculty and staff in strengthening each of these core elements of authentic school improvement.

KEY CONCEPTS

As you engage in the work outlined here, it is important to use language that frees both you and your faculty to think and act in refreshing and creative ways. I have found in my interactions with educators throughout the country that the old language of "diversity" and "multicultural education" has worn thin. When teachers hear these words, they think, "Here we go again." Too often, their past experiences with "diversity workshops" have been negative, coming from a place of shame and blame rather than mutual exploration and genuine growth. This is not true for all educators or for all past approaches, but the baggage is significantly heavy and prevalent for us to find a different way.

For this reason, I have chosen to focus here on a different set of concepts: inclusion, equity, and excellence. Our schools are *diverse* and our nation and world are *multicultural,* yes, but the critical thing is not the existence of these differences; the issue is what we *do* with them. Inclusion, equity, and excellence are about action, about our practices, about the kind of cultures that we create in our schools. Diversity is a given, but inclusion, equity, and excellence require focused intentionality and hard work. No leader and no teacher can do this alone—thus collaboration becomes our central guiding principle throughout the manual.

Each of these key concepts is defined and discussed in the **Orientation to the Professional Development Process** and the accompanying Video Introduction. I encourage leaders and facilitators of this process to familiarize yourselves with these materials and that section of the manual before engaging the work with your colleagues.

AFFIRMATION BEFORE REFORMATION

Two additional concepts that form the central focus for this professional development process are Cultural Competence and Culturally Responsive Teaching. As you begin the work, it is important to communicate to your staff that you are *not* assuming they are deficient in these capacities. This work is about good people doing hard work, not about bad people messing up. Too much of the politics and past rhetoric of school reform has been anti-teacher and anti–public education. As a result, teachers and school leaders are hungry for affirmation, for recognition of the difficulty and worth of their work. Many of the activities in this manual are designed to create a trusting environment where educators can talk with each other, not in overly scripted and controlled ways, but in an authentic environment of mutual respect and support. This affirmational tone makes it more likely that teachers will be willing to critically reflect on their practice, share their struggles and their strengths, and be more open to shifting their beliefs and behaviors in the service of their students. As Geneva Gay reminded me years ago, if we are serious about growing our people and transforming our schools, then it is critical that we put "affirmation before reformation" (personal communication, March 1997).

LEVELS OF ENGAGEMENT

The professional development process provided here is designed to promote change in three dimensions: the personal, the professional, and the organizational (see Figure 1). We cannot transform our schools without transforming our practices, and we cannot transform our practices without transforming ourselves.

Figure 1   Levels of Engagement

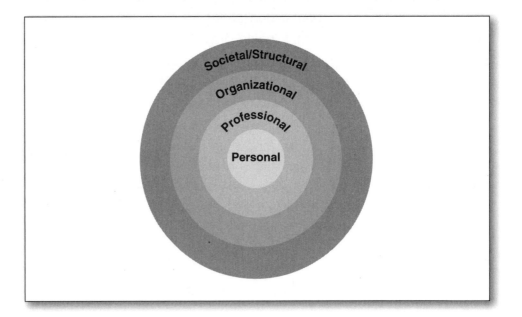

Changing systems requires changing people, and changing people requires changing systems (Fullan, 2009). Thus, in relation to Figure 1, our work must flow across all three dimensions and in both directions, from the outside in and from the inside out. Achieving a greater degree of inclusion, equity, and excellence in our schools requires transformative work that is both multidimensional and multidirectional.

Herein lies one of the more dysfunctional aspects of the top-down approach to school reform. Both No Child Left Behind and Race to the Top were planned and executed from the sociopolitical arena (see the outer circle in Figure 1) and were heavily influenced by the business community, as well as major foundations and think tanks, without meaningful participation of actual teachers and school leaders. The resulting mandates were then imposed monodirectionally and monodimensionally on the schools. The assumption, based on a corporate business model, has been that these externally driven incentives and punitive consequences would lead to positive change in school outcomes, professional practices, and the personal buy-in and motivation of educators. This market-driven approach has clearly not worked (Gorski, 2013; Ravitch, 2013; Schniedewind & Sapon-Shevin, 2012). With tragic predictability, race and poverty continue to determine dropout rates, discipline referrals, and learning outcomes for far too many of our nation's most marginalized students.

The professional development process presented in this manual turns this corporate dynamic on its head, starting from the inside out with actual school people doing their professional work in actual schools. As seen in Figure 1, the personhood of the educator is at the core of the transformative work. If we as teachers and school leaders are not willing to critically examine our own beliefs, personal behaviors, and professional practices, then nothing will significantly improve in the outcomes for our students. The truly courageous part of the work involves asking ourselves, "What might I be doing, or not doing, that is getting in the way of my students' engagement and success?" Externally imposed mandates do not encourage this kind of courageous self-reflection.

Borrowing from the language of brain research, we want our teachers and ourselves as leaders to arrive at a place of *neuro-plasticity* (Wexler, 2006), which is a state of mental and emotional flexibility that allows us to examine how we think and act relative to our professional practices and to consider alternative approaches. The activities, discussion, and conceptual frameworks in this Leadership Manual have proven effective in inviting educators to willingly, not coercively, enter this courageous self-reflective space. This state of *self-generated neuro-plasticity* provides the productive foundation from which to critically assess how we relate to our students across the many dimensions of difference, including race, culture, language, gender, sexual orientation, social class, and special needs. This manual offers many strategies for moving the work from the personal to the professional and from the professional to the organizational levels of engagement. As school leaders, our responsibility is not only to guide our faculties and staffs into the process of personal and professional growth but also to create the kind of school culture and organizational practices that will support and sustain them in their transformative work. And, as is suggested by the title of this manual, we cannot lead our colleagues into this new space without having the will and the courage to go there ourselves.

PHASES OF THE WORK

To support the multidimensional and multidirectional change described above, the Leadership Manual is organized around five Phases of the Work. These phases will be described in the Video Introduction, and once again, it is important for you as leaders and facilitators to get your own feel for the language and structure of the work before you lead others into the process.

Phase One: Tone and Trust. The activities and discussions offered in Phase One are designed to assuage the defensiveness and resistance people often bring to equity work, as well as to prevent the kind of "here we go again" responses that were discussed above. We want our participants to feel that the work is real, that it is not coming from a place of shame and blame, and that they can bring their truth to the conversations, rather than their cynicism or political correctness. We want the work to feel fresh, interesting, and both personally and professionally challenging. We want to create an environment that is safe enough for folks to risk moving past their edges. We want them to be intrigued without being overly threatened. Our goal is for participants to be able to say what I often hear in my workshops: "I look forward to these sessions because we get to talk honestly with each other about what's really happening in our schools."

Phase Two: Personal Culture and Personal Journey. This phase is closely related to the Tone and Trust work. Activities in this section of the manual are intended to recognize and honor the personal racial and cultural narratives of each member of your staff. Everybody has multiple and complex stories and experiences related to the many dimensions of difference. It is not only our students who bring diversity to our schools; every adult in the building also has a unique journey that deserves to be recognized and valued.

This phase of the work is particularly important for white folks, who often do not see themselves as racial or cultural beings. Since the overwhelming majority of teachers in American public schools are white, it is essential that white folks be engaged in exploring their own experiences of race and other differences, even if that story, like mine, involves periods of ignorance, bias, or dis-consciousness (G. R. Howard, 2006). One of the comments I hear most frequently from white educators who have been involved in this process: "This is the first time as a white person that my own story has been recognized, and that I haven't felt blamed."

For people of color and members of other marginalized groups, this phase of the work is also particularly significant. Because the activities in this section of the manual are invitational and not coercive, there is no pressure for people of color to share things they prefer to keep private. However, if we can establish the appropriate level of trust and safety, people will choose to share powerful stories about their own experiences of prejudice and discrimination, stories that many of their colleagues have never heard. In a recent workshop, an African American elementary school principal said, "After sharing here some of my own struggles and tears of pain about race, I have been thinking more deeply about what my students are going through. It's not that it hasn't always been on my mind, it's just that it went to a more personal level."

As the adults in your school grow in their capacity to share and hear each other's stories, they will be more able to attune their personal and professional attention to the many narratives that your students bring with them into the school experience. The more you and your faculty are attuned in this way, the greater will be your capacity to respond effectively to your students' needs. This is the power of Cultural Competence and Culturally Responsive Teaching; it is all about our capacity as adults to be real in the presence of our students.

Phase Three: From Social Dominance to Social Justice. The goal of our overall work is to create schools where more of our students, across more of their differences, are achieving at a higher level and engaging at a deeper level, without giving up who they are. In other words, our purpose is to eliminate educational inequities based on race, economics, and other dimensions of difference, without requiring that our students assimilate to a dominant cultural identity. In Phase Three of the work, we go deeply into those historical and contemporary dynamics that have created and sustained systems of oppression, marginalization, and inequity for far too many of our students and their families. We look at the roots of the so-called "achievement gap," which would be more accurately described as an *opportunity* gap, a *social justice* gap, or a *privilege* gap.

The assumption underlying this part of the work is that we cannot eliminate inequities without first understanding the causes of those inequities. And we cannot understand the causes without talking about issues of race, class, gender, sexual orientation, language diversity, and special needs, as well as racism, classism, sexism, and heterosexism. It is not sufficient to provide teachers and leaders with a solid foundation of instructional strategies, powerful curriculum, and a Common Core focus on outcomes. Even with these interventions in place, systemic inequities will persist unless they are addressed consciously and directly. As James Comer (2013) states, "Even sincere efforts to close the academic achievement gap in education do not address the consequences of a difficult history; indeed, the latter is at the root of the former" (p. xii).

The strategies and activities in Phase Three are designed to engage you and your faculty in authentic conversations about issues of difference and discrimination, privilege and power, and social dominance and social justice that function at the structural and societal levels (see Figure 1). The work is not only theoretical but moves directly to the ways these realities are functioning on a daily basis within the culture of your school, within classroom practices, and within individual belief systems. There is no comfortable way to have these conversations. In fact, if we are overly comfortable in the process, we're probably not having the necessary conversations (Singleton, 2013). Even though the real work requires some degree of unease, the discussions here are intentionally structured to avoid unnecessary levels of shame, blame, finger pointing, and guilt. The activities unfold gradually and lead to increasingly deeper levels of self-reflection and group interaction. As one white participant stated after participating in several Phase Three discussions, "I'm beginning to understand what white privilege is about, and I see it everywhere I look." Another teacher said, "I am going to pay a lot more attention to how my kids are experiencing pressures around their differences in my classroom."

Phase Four: Classroom Implications and Applications. This is where the work moves directly into professional practice, how we bring cultural competence and culturally responsive teaching into the classroom and the culture of the school. This is the largest section of the manual and will be the focus for most of your work. School leaders and teachers are understandably tempted to begin with this phase of the work, going directly into classroom practice and staying there, not taking the time to engage Phases One through Three as described above. My experience working in hundreds of schools, with thousands of educators, has taught me not to give in to this temptation. Teachers need a reason to reflect on their practice and a solid motivational foundational from which to consider changing their strategies and interactions with students. Phases One through Three are designed to build the *passion* for change, while Phase Four provides the *conceptual framework* and the *strategies* for that change.

At the center of the Phase Four content and process are the Seven Principles for Culturally Responsive Teaching, a set of professional guidelines and behaviors that your teachers can connect to the many research-based instructional practices you may already be implementing. Whether it is differentiation, Response to Intervention, Positive Behavioral Interventions and Supports, guided reading, Charlotte Danielson's framework (2007), Robert Marzano's model (2007), Professional Learning Communities, or any of the other initiatives presently being implemented in your school and district, teachers need an integrative structure to bring these things together and make sense of their work. This integrative structure needs to account for the racial, cultural, socioeconomic, linguistic, and other differences your students bring to the classroom. The Seven Principles for Culturally Responsive Teaching provide that structure.

Most of the schools I have worked with around the country, particularly those with large populations of racially and economically marginalized students, are suffering from a particular disease brought on by school reform efforts. This disease I call MIS: multiple initiative syndrome. Although each of the many interventions named above can provide valuable instructional and classroom management resources and skills, teachers often experience these approaches as "one more thing" added to an already overwhelming set of mandated expectations. Refreshingly, I have not found this to be true for the Seven Principles for Culturally Responsive Teaching. The Principles serve as the connective tissue that allows teachers to make sense of their work and bring together all other classroom initiatives. When I ask my participants whether they find this set of teacher guidelines to be a helpful tool, their response is an overwhelming and almost universal "yes." Some sample comments: "I think the Seven Principles provoke great reflection among teachers." "They are practical and simple—teachers can understand them and apply them." "They are a nonthreatening way to identify areas of strength and needed growth." "They are directly applied to acknowledging and appreciating cultures." "I love that these Principles make you realize you may not be doing as good a job as you think you are." And, "They link to the other programs/interventions already taking place in our school."

Phase Five: Systemic Transformation and Planning for Change. This section of the manual provides tools and strategies for reinforcing the growth of your school at the organizational level (see Figure 1). You are given a three-stage model for understanding and assessing the movement of your school culture toward greater inclusion, equity, and excellence, as well as a process for tracking your victories and struggles along the way. There are planning guides to support you and your leadership team in mapping out the multiyear implementation of this professional development process. And there are ideas for integrating the Cultural Competence and Culturally Responsive Teaching work with other instructional and school improvement initiatives you may already have in place. In addition, Phase Five offers strategies for engaging student voices as an integral part of your school improvement efforts. Finally, you are given a model research and evaluation design that demonstrates how this professional development process leads to positive student outcomes related to school engagement, academic achievement, and reduction of discipline referrals.

Team Building and School Improvement. As you engage your faculty in the discussions and activities related to Phases One through Five, one of the corollary benefits will be the team-building aspect of the work. Your people will be talking with each other in new and deeper ways, and they will be reflecting on their practices as individuals and as a school. Some of the comments made by educators related to this aspect of the work include the following: "We are moving forward and not afraid of taking risks as a staff." "We are building cohorts within our school to begin to have the tough conversations." "We have taken ownership of the achievement gap and have a plan for moving forward." And, "I am proud of my team and my school for the work we are doing."

This level of engagement and team building will naturally and positively reinforce your building level goal setting and school improvement processes. As leaders and facilitators, it is important to consciously use this opportunity for thoughtful input into your systemic change strategies. The entire professional development process outlined in this manual is designed to inform and support your collective school improvement efforts. For the greatest benefit, it needs to be intentionally and consistently linked to those efforts.

GUIDELINES FOR USING THE LEADERSHIP MANUAL AND VIDEOS

Organization of the Manual

The main body of the manual is divided into five sections, one for each Phase of the Work. The Introduction to each section provides an overview of the activities, discussion, and videos included in that Phase. Following the introduction, you are given the Facilitator Directions and Video Viewing Guide for each activity. This is where you will find the step-by-step detail for planning and implementing each piece in that Phase of the Work. The final section of the manual includes several articles by Gary Howard that can be used as group readings to support each Phase. Also included in this section is a Discussion Guide to support your group conversations.

Equity Leadership Institutes

Corwin Press offers Leadership Institutes and consulting services led by Gary Howard and his colleagues to support school districts in the use of these materials. You and your Facilitation Team could attend one of these Institutes in your region of the country, or you could commission an Institute to be held specifically for your district or in collaboration with neighboring school systems. Whereas the Leadership Manual and accompanying videos provide sufficient support for you to implement the professional development process on your own, it would be optimal for your team to have an opportunity to work through the entire design in the Institute setting before leading others in the many activities and discussions included here. For information about the Corwin Institute process and supportive consulting services, please visit their website: http://www.corwin.com/institutes/.

Getting Started

Begin your work by either attending a Leadership Institute with Gary Howard or reading through the Leadership Manual with your Facilitation Team. Previewing the Introductory Videos for each Phase of the Work would be helpful as an overview for the entire process. As you are preparing to do this work, pay particular attention to the materials in the last half of Phase Five, beginning with the Video Introduction for Facilitators and continuing on with Video Segments 5:6 through 5:9. Here you are given the tools and ideas for planning your overall systemic professional development efforts. Your primary planning tool is the Implementation Planning Guide in Phase Five (see Handout ST-11). This guide provides an overview of all the materials, activities, and videos included in the manual. On this form, you are given space to plan the projected dates for each activity and to check off items as they are completed. The Video Segments in the last half of Phase Five are addressed particularly to your Facilitation Team. These are informal talks by Gary Howard engaging your team in reflective conversations about the process. These video clips ought to be viewed before you initiate the PD process with your staff.

Video Support

Every aspect of the work is supported by video presentations. In the video, **"Orientation to the Professional Development Process,"** you will hear from teachers, school leaders, and students in schools who have been engaged in the work for over 5 years. You will also hear Gary Howard describe the overall rationale and approach for the professional development process. Then, each Phase of the Work begins with an Introductory Video highlighting teacher, leader, and student experiences and perspectives related to the specific activities and content of that Phase. For each of the 33 activities and discussions included in the manual, your Facilitation Team will have video support from Gary

Howard, providing the key content and setting the context and process for each of your activities you facilitate with faculty and staff. Finally, interspersed throughout the manual, you are provided with School Video Segments featuring teachers, administrators, support staff, and students as they engage in conversations about the work and demonstrate Cultural Competence and Culturally Responsive Teaching practices in actual school settings.

Accessing the Video Segments, School Video Clips, and Handouts

All of the Video Segments and School Video Clips are available to you on the DVDs included with this manual. In addition, Corwin provides each manual owner with online access to the Handouts. Your purchase of the manual provides you with a license to show the videos and copy the handouts for use in your school building. For multiple sites or districtwide use of the materials, leaders should discuss with Corwin the purchase of a site license.

Selecting Your Facilitation Team

Although as school leaders, you could implement much of the professional development process on your own, it is highly recommended that you bring together a Facilitation Team to support you in the work and collaborate in planning and leading sessions with staff. Following are suggested guidelines for selecting members of your Facilitation Team:

- People who have demonstrated a strong commitment to equity and social justice
- People who have earned the respect of their colleagues—who are opinion leaders among their peers
- People who are good stand-up presenters and facilitators of reflective conversations
- People who represent the diversity of your school in terms of race, gender, age, grade level, role, department, specialty, classified and certificated, and other dimensions of diversity you feel are salient
- People who can help you connect with different constituencies or opinion groups within your staff, particularly those who could be resistant to the work
- People who will support you in the implementation of a systemic change process related to cultural competence and culturally responsive practice

Sequence and Customization

In most school districts using Gary Howard's approach, the materials in this manual have supported 3 to 5 years of professional development work. As you do your planning, it is important to keep in mind a long-term systemic perspective; this work is not something to be rushed or short-circuited. It is also important to customize your timing and sequencing of events to fit the unique needs, strengths, and culture of your school and district. You don't need to do every activity in the manual, but it is essential to engage each of the Phases. The tone and trust work in Phase One and the personal culture focus in Phase Two provide critical grounding and preparation for the analysis of social dominance in Phase Three and the transformation of professional practice in Phase Four. Having said this, it is not necessary to move through the Phases in a lock-step sequence. Once the professional development process is in place, you may choose to move back and forth between the Phases to address issues and concerns as they emerge in your actual work with faculty and staff.

Timing the Reflection

Each activity in the manual is accompanied by a suggested time frame for implementation, both for the entire activity as well as each step in the process. You can customize the amount of time given to each activity by either shortening or lengthening the number of minutes given to small-group conversations and large-group share-out sessions. At a minimum level, however, it is always important to allow people an opportunity to reflect on the video segments and make meaning of the different activities. The benefits from this professional development process flow primarily from the engagement of your people with each other, not merely from viewing the videos.

Thoughts on Grouping

For many of the conversations in the professional development process, it is best to organize your staff into max-mix small groups, which means that each group represents as much of a mix as possible of age, gender, race, grade level, specialty, department, political perspective, and other factors you deem important. In this way, you break up any cliques or pockets of ingrown cynicism or resistance to professional development in general, or to equity discussions in particular. Other activities and conversations in the process will be most productive in work-alike groups, where people are talking with colleagues who share the same arena of professional responsibilities. At other times, your Facilitation Team can allow people to set with whomever they choose. The Facilitator Directions will often suggest the optimum grouping for each activity, but it is ultimately a matter of choice for your team.

Gathering Evaluation Feedback

As stated above, Phase Five includes a model district-wide research and assessment design for tracking outcomes resulting from the professional development process. (See Video Segment 5:9.) For gathering more immediate feedback from faculty and staff, Phase Five also includes a set of sample Evaluation/Reflection forms that can be adapted for use at selected times during your implementation (see Handouts ST-13a through 13c). These data will be valuable for you and your Facilitation Team, allowing you to check in from time to time with the feelings, thoughts, and responses of your faculty and make adjustments as needed.

Student Voices and Youth Equity Leadership

Phase Five of the manual also provides materials and strategies to include students in your school district's equity efforts. Student engagement is an integral part of any effective school change process. Video segments show high school students experiencing each of the five Phases of the Work and designing creative action strategies for addressing issues of bullying, discrimination, and oppression in their schools. (See Video Segment 5:8) Gary Howard strongly recommends that you review this section of the manual before implementation and consider how and when to empower your students as essential participants in the systemic change process.

Including Support Staff

It is also strongly suggested that you include your support staff in as much of the professional development work as possible. Your secretaries, instruction support people, custodians, food service workers, security personnel, bus drivers, and any other adults who connect with students and families are essential resources in creating a culture of inclusion, equity, and excellence. The more your support staff are included, the greater will be your impact.

Final Thought

No matter how the politics of school reform may change over the years, those of us working in schools know that our primary accountability is to our students. Their rich diversity, amazing gifts, humor, resilience, and deep needs are always on our minds. The work of Cultural Competence and Culturally Responsive Teaching is at the heart of everything we do. It's not that we aren't already good at this work; it's just that we need to get better. The professional development process presented in this manual is offered in a spirit of deep respect for the good work you and your colleagues are presently doing and with an equally profound hope that, for the sake of our students, we will all continue to grow.

Orientation to the Professional Development Process

Begin your work by using the **Video Orientation to the Professional Development Process** and related discussion activity. This video and conversation will set the context for the entire professional development process related to Cultural Competence and Culturally Responsive Teaching. Here Gary Howard introduces the three core concepts of **Inclusion, Equity, and Excellence;** provides a brief description of the five **Phases of the Work;** and describes the four **Levels of Engagement** that were discussed in the Introduction to your manual. This Video Orientation features comments and perspectives from teachers and school leaders who have worked extensively with this professional development process in their own settings. Your faculty and staff will have an opportunity to reflect together on ideas and experiences presented in the video and share their thoughts in conversations with colleagues.

The central point of this introductory activity is as follows: If we are to create schools that serve all of our students well, then we must do the necessary transformational work at the personal, professional, organizational, and societal levels. With this idea and the foundational concepts in hand, your faculty will be ready to launch into the Phase One activities.

Facilitator Note: *As was stated in the Introduction to this Leadership Manual, before implementing any of these activities or discussions with your faculty and staff, it is important for your Facilitation Team to review the items in the* *second half of Phase Five: Facilitation Team Resources for Planning, Integrating, and Sustaining the Work. These materials will give you the necessary overview of the entire professional development process, and provide the planning tools for organizing your work. If you haven't already done so, view Gary Howard's Video Introduction for Facilitators, which is an informal conversation addressed directly to your leadership team, not intended for your larger audience.*

Orientation to the PD Process		
School Video Clips (SVC)		
In addition to the Phase One Introductory Video, you can show the following segments to show how the adults in one school worked together to create a welcoming climate for their students.		
SVC #	*Title*	*Video Length*
1	**How One School Implemented the PD Process** Jenni Jones, Intern Assistant Principal at Northdale Middle School, describes the process her school went through to implement the Gary Howard work. She provides commentary on the stages of the implementation and the steps they took to guarantee its success.	2:11
2	**One District's *Right* Response to Changing Demographics** Dennis Carlson, Superintendent Anoka-Hennepin School District, explains the way in which their work with Gary Howard provided a positive, systemic response to the rapidly changing demographics of their students and community. He describes how it helped to address increasing issues with racism and sexism and taught the district how to respect, honor, and celebrate the diverse community they are so quickly becoming.	4:22
3	**All Students College, Career, and Culturally Ready** Nancy Chave, Principal Crossroads Alternative High School, describes how her school has fully integrated the principles of cultural competence in order to create a safe, supportive, and inclusive school community.	1:21
4	**Looking at the Data** Jinger Gustafson, Associate Superintendent Anoka-Hennepin School District, describes how the data is showing the district has made positive gains in overall student achievement and how they have drastically closed the achievement gap because of the systemic work they have done with Gary Howard.	2:01

ACTIVITIES, FACILITATOR DIRECTIONS, AND VIDEO SEGMENTS

Activity: Video Orientation and Discussion	
Orientation to the Professional Development Process	
Purpose:	• Establish the context and rationale for the overall systemic professional development process • Introduce the concepts of Inclusion, Equity, and Excellence • Describe the five Phases of the Work • Provide an overview of the four Levels of Engagement • Demonstrate how the professional development process has been applied in actual school settings • Connect this professional development (PD) process to the needs and culture of your school
Suggested Time:	45 minutes
Materials Needed:	Video Segment: Orientation to the PD Process Handout IN-1: Inclusion, Equity, and Excellence Handout IN-2: Phases of the Work Handout IN-3: Levels of Engagement
Advanced Preparation:	• Review the Facilitator Directions. • Preview the Video Orientation to the PD process. • Prepare your comments connecting this professional development process to the needs, culture, and realities of your school.

Facilitator Note: *Before you share the Video Orientation with your staff, it would be good to engage in some thinking and conversation with your leadership team regarding why you are choosing to implement this professional development process.*

1. Set the Focus   5 Minutes

Before showing the Video Orientation, share some of your rationale for implementing this professional development process with your staff. Connect your comments to your school's unique issues, opportunities, data, and challenges. Describe your personal reasons for doing this, how you came to this work, and why you are excited about moving forward with it. Distribute copies of Handouts IN-1, IN-2, and IN-3.

2. View the Video Orientation to the PD Process, Part 1   13 Minutes

Gary describes the rationale for the overall professional development process, using language similar to that in the Introduction to your

Leadership Manual. Some of the key points presented in this video segment include the following:

- You will hear from teachers, school leaders, and students who have implemented the professional development process in their own settings. They share highlights illustrating how the process has affected professional growth, school climate, and student outcomes in their classrooms and schools.
- Gary emphsizes that the real work of school reform and school improvement has to be done at the school level, trusting in the skill and professionalism of teachers, leaders, and staff. The professional development process we are beginning here is built around bottom-up school reform, rather than top-down mandates.
- Real school change is about good people doing hard work, not about bad people messing up.
- Three key concepts will drive the work we are going to be doing together: Inclusion, Equity, and Excellence. Our work is much deeper than mere cultural awareness or adding multicultural content to the curriculum. It includes these things but is primarily concerned with our own beliefs and relationships with our students and their degree of academic engagement and success in our classrooms.

3. Pause the Video for Pair-and-Share Discussion   5 Minutes

Graphics on the screen will prompt you to stop the video and ask people to talk in pairs about the following topics:

- What stood out for you as you listened to the opening comments from teachers, administrators, and students?
- What are you thinking so far about Gary Howard's perspective on school reform and his approach to professional development?
- Share your thoughts about the three concepts of Inclusion, Equity, and Excellence. How do these apply in the context of your work.

Give people about 4-5 minutes for these conversations, then restart the video.

4. Restart the Video Orientation to the PD Process, Part 2   9 Minutes

In this part of the video, Gary Howard will continue his introduction to the key concepts underlying the PD design:

- Our conversations and activities will be focused on five Phases of the Work:

1. Tone and Trust
2. Personal Culture and Personal Journey
3. From Social Dominance to Social Justice
4. Classroom Implications and Applications
5. Systemic Transformation and Planning for Change

- These five Phases of Work will be approached at four Levels of Engagement:

1. The Personal
2. The Professional
3. The Organizational
4. The Social/Cultural

5. Personal Reflection   2 Minutes

The Video Segment will end with three reflective questions. You will **pause the video** and give people a couple of minutes to reflect on what they have just seen and heard.

1. What is one thing that stimulated your thinking?
2. What are you excited about?
3. What is a concern or question you have about this process?

6. Small-Group Conversations   10 Minutes

Form small groups of five to seven people each, and ask each person to share their response to at least one of the reflective questions.

7. Sharing Out   10 Minutes

Ask each small group to share one thought from their discussion. This is not meant to be a summary of everything that was said, just one idea or concern or perspective that they would like to share with the large group.

8. Final Comments   2 Minutes

Thank everyone for their comments and share a few thoughts of your own about your responses to what has been said. Acknowledge any concerns people have about moving into this professional development process, and encourage everyone to continue to be open about their experiences as you move forward. Give your staff a sense of what is coming next, reinforcing the idea that this is a long-term process, not just a one-off event.

Inclusion, Equity, and Excellence

▶ **Inclusion:**

Students and employees feel welcomed, seen, respected, understood, cared for, and safe.

▶ **Equity:**

Educational disparities based on race, economics, and other dimensions of difference are reduced and eliminated. Positive school outcomes are distributed equitably across all demographic and identity groups. Negative outcomes are reduced for all groups.

▶ **Excellence:**

We keep the bar high in all we do. We educate students for life and for reflective citizenship. We empower students and employees in the preservation of their identity and culture. Substance, depth, and critical thinking are more important than either compliance or test scores.

Phases and Objectives of the Work

Phase One: Tone and Trust
- Forming a community of engaged adult learners
- Building a climate of constructive collaboration
- Overcoming past resistance to "diversity" work
- Transcending the rhetoric of shame and blame

Phase Two: Personal Culture and Personal Journey
- Acknowledging each person's unique cultural narrative
- Providing a functional definition of cultural competence
- Clarifying the process of growth toward cultural competence
- Connecting adult cultural competence with student outcomes

Phase Three: From Social Dominance to Social Justice
- Exploring issues of privilege, power, and difference
- Understanding the dynamics of social dominance
- Linking issues of dominance to current educational inequities
- Creating strategies for moving from dominance to social justice

Phase Four: Classroom Implications and Applications
- Reinforcing adult–student relationships as the key to achievement
- Acknowledging classroom successes, challenges, and roadblocks
- Applying the Seven Principles for Culturally Responsive Teaching
- Implementing action research for inclusion and equity

Phase Five: Systemic Transformation and Planning for Change
- Identifying organizational barriers to equity and inclusion
- Applying a three-stage model for organizational transformation
- Creating a holistic integrated approach to school improvement
- Assessing outcomes related to the professional development process

For a discussion of this work in actual school settings, see Gary Howard's article, *As Diversity Grows, So Must We*, in the Selected Articles section of the manual.

Levels of Engagement

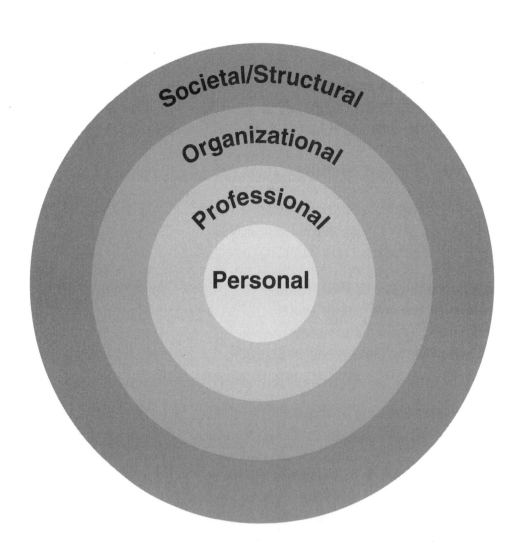

Phase One: Tone and Trust

Goals for Phase One:

- Forming a community of engaged adult learners
- Building a climate of constructive collaboration
- Overcoming past resistance to "diversity work"
- Transcending the rhetoric of shame and blame

RATIONALE AND OVERVIEW OF ACTIVITIES

Phase One is designed to bring your faculty and staff into deeper engagement with equity and school improvement conversations in an authentic and nonthreatening way. Each of the activities in this section establishes an open-ended context wherein individuals are invited to share their perspectives and experiences without judgment from others or preconceived notions of who's right and who's wrong. By setting this invitational tone, it is sometimes possible to engage even those individuals who may be coming to this work with some trepidation, cynicism, resistance, or history of negative experiences in diversity workshops.

You also want to make the conversation real and relevant to teachers who are working their hearts out but may feel overwhelmed by the demands of their job and the pressures of school reform mandates. As a leader in your building, you already have a sense of the capacity and readiness of your faculty and staff to engage in meaningful conversations about the kinds of equity issues they face in their classrooms. If your people are struggling in this arena, or perhaps have a history in the building of tensions and divisiveness among the adults, the Phase One activities will be particularly important. If you presently have a comfortable climate of engagement among your staff, then this phase of the work will help deepen the conversations and the connections.

Begin by showing the **Phase One Introductory Video,** which provides an overview of the purpose and focus of this part of the professional development process. Your faculty will have an opportunity to hear from other educators who have extensive experience with the process and who share their impressions and real-life experiences of working with Tone and Trust issues in their own schools.

The Phase One activities then begin with a set of **Working Agreements**, or ground rules, for creating an invitational tone and a climate of low fear and high trust. These Working Agreements have proven effective for many schools and educators in guiding authentic adult conversations about difficult and complex topics related to race, class, gender, sexual orientation, religion, and other dimensions of difference. They are also an excellent set of ground rules for teachers to use while facilitating discussions in their own classrooms.

The **Questions to Consider** activity creates an open-ended conversation about why we are doing this work. This guided small-group discussion invites participants to share their diverse perceptions and understandings of the long road to social justice. Why has it taken so long? What is in the way of achieving real educational equity that embodies our national vision of freedom, justice, and opportunity for all? What will it take to move us forward on this journey? The perspectives and ideas that flow from this conversation will provide a fruitful backdrop for much of your ongoing work within this professional development process.

Cultural Bingo is a get-up-and-move activity that will be fun for your faculty and help them get to know each other at a deeper level. The Cultural Bingo card has 24 squares describing different cultural experiences, or asking questions about cultural knowledge. Participants move around the room with their cards in hand, asking their colleagues if they can fill in any of the boxes. Inevitably, people learn new things about even those colleagues they have known for 20 years. They also discover, in a gentle way, that there is much cultural knowledge they have yet to acquire. This activity can also be beneficially adapted for use in the classroom.

The **¿Quiénes Somos?** activity (Who Are We?) is designed to introduce and personalize the concept of cultural competence. All members of your group are asked to think of someone in their life who is a role model for cultural competence, someone who has a positive and respectful interest in cultural differences and is good at getting along with people who are not like them. Participants engage in one-on-one interviews describing their cultural competence role models and identifying the behaviors and personal qualities exemplified by these individuals. Following the interviews, the large group generates a list of "Cultural Competence Qualities." This list will be a helpful reference point when you introduce the Seven Principles for Culturally Responsive Teaching during Phase Four of the work.

Phase One culminates with a **Tone and Trust Assessment,** which is a quick and powerful tool for checking the temperature of the interpersonal climate among the adults in your building. On a 1–10 scale, each individual anonymously rates the climate related to the question: "To what extent have we established the necessary tone and trust among the adults in our building to be able to have real and authentic conversations about difficult topics related to equity, diversity, social justice, and improving our professional practice?" The responses are charted, and the resulting profile of your tone and trust environment will provide a provocative snapshot to stimulate and guide further work and school improvement planning.

Phase One: Tone and Trust		
School Video Clips (SVC)		
In addition to the Phase One Introductory Video, you can show the following two segments to show how adults work to create a welcoming climate for their students.		
SVC #	*Title*	*Video Length*
5	**Relationships are the Key to Tone and Trust** Anthony Luckey, Paraprofessional Crossroads Alternative High School, describes the benefits he has experienced from taking the time to build relationships with the students.	3:15
6	**Victor's Pantry: Creating a Welcoming School Climate** Jenni Jones, Intern Assistant Principal at Northdale Middle School, describes how her school created an on-site food pantry to meet the needs of their growing homeless student population.	3:38

Facilitator Note: *Before initiating these activities with your staff, show them the Phase One Introductory Video.*

PHASE ONE ACTIVITIES, FACILITATOR DIRECTIONS, AND VIDEO SEGMENTS

Activity: Working Agreements	
Phase One: Tone and Trust	
Purpose:	• Provide ground rules for authentic conversation • Establish an invitational tone • Create a climate of low fear and high trust
Suggested Time:	30 minutes
Materials Needed:	Phase One Introductory Video Video Segment 1:1 Handout TT-1: Working Agreements Flipchart with pens or other visual recording device
Advanced Preparation:	• Review the Introduction to Phase One in your manual • Preview Video 1:1 and the Introductory Video • Read through the Facilitator Directions

Facilitator Note: *This activity is good to use early in the process, so you can refer back to these Working Agreements as you navigate any difficult moments that may emerge in your future conversations. If you and your faculty have already established a set of protocols or ground rules for guiding meetings and conversations, you may want to skip this activity. Another option would be to share these Working Agreements with your staff and have them discuss how these guidelines intersect with what you already have in place. How are these ground rules the same or different from your protocols?*

1. Set the Focus   10 Minutes

If you haven't already done so, begin this session by showing the Phase One Introductory Video, where your staff will hear educators from other schools talk about their experiences with the Tone and Trust aspects of the work.

Then, before you show Video Segment 1:1, ask your staff to consider what kind of ground rules or community agreements they would like to have in place to help create productive conversations about difficult issues related to equity, school improvement, and professional practice. Elicit their responses and record them on a flipchart or screen. Distribute copies of Handout TT-1.

2. View Video Segment 1:1   **8 Minutes**

Gary describes the overall purpose and rationale for this set of Working Agreements, and then discusses the meaning and implications of each item. He emphasizes that these agreements are designed primarily to support faculty and staff in their conversations about issues of equity and social justice, but they can also be helpful as guidelines for student and teacher interactions in the classroom.

3. Pair-and-Share Discussions   **5 Minutes**

At the end of the video, Gary will prompt people to pick a partner and share their ideas related to these two questions:

1. What would you like to see added to this list of Working Agreements?

2. Which item on the list presents the greatest challenge for you?

4. Closing Comments   **7 Minutes**

Give people a signal to bring their pair-and-share conversations to a close. As the large group comes back together, ask if there are any suggestions for additional Working Agreements, things that your staff members would like to see added to this list. Record these and ask everyone to keep these agreements in mind as you move further into the professional development process. You may want to ask for a show of "thumbs up" to publicly acknowledge that everyone is on board with your Working Agreements.

Working Agreements

▶ *Participate fully*

▶ *Speak for yourself*

▶ *Listen for understanding*

▶ *Take some risks*

▶ *Support risk takers*

▶ *Say "ouch" so we all can learn*

▶ *Encourage participation of others*

▶ *Recognize the right to pass*

▶ *Share the "air" time*

▶ *Ask questions*

▶ *Be clear about language*

▶ *Honor confidentiality and privacy*

▶ *Start and end on time*

▶ *So that:*

We create a high-trust, low-fear climate

Activity: Questions to Consider	
Phase One: Tone and Trust	
Purpose:	• Create an engaging open-ended conversation • Recognize and respect multiple perspectives • Stimulate thinking about the long road to equity and social justice • Move beyond the shame and blame approach
Suggested Time:	40–45 minutes
Materials Needed:	Video Segment 1:2 Handout TT-2: Questions to Consider Flipchart with pens
Advanced Preparation:	• Review the Introduction to Phase One in your manual • Preview Video 1:2 • Read through the Facilitator Directions

Facilitator Note: *This activity provides a good opening conversation, focusing on the large end of the funnel regarding issues of equity and social justice. It is designed to allow for maximum participation and sharing of ideas, with minimum allegiance to political correctness or notions of right and wrong opinions. It is best to do this activity in max-mix small groups.*

1. Set the Focus   2 Minutes

This will be one of the first engagement activities you will do with your staff as part of the overall professional development process. Highlight the open-endedness of this activity, and make a couple of comments about why you look forward to hearing their responses. Distribute copies of Handout TT-2.

2. Start Video Segment 1:2   8 Minutes

Gary sets up the conversation with a historical quote and a question: "Who said this in 1965?" The video prompt will ask you to **pause for a minute** to allow people to share their ideas about who the speaker was. When you **restart the video,** Gary will name the speaker, give some context for the quote, and provide three questions to guide the next part of the conversation:

1. Why so long?

2. What's in the way?

3. What will it take?

You will be prompted to **pause the video** once again, and allow people some personal think time to ponder how they would answer at least one of these questions.

3. Restart the Video: Small-Group Conversations   **10 Minutes**

Gary will introduce the small-group conversation, reinforcing the ground rules of no right or wrong answers and maximum respect for different perspectives. **Pause the video** when prompted to do so, and the groups will begin their discussions. While the groups are talking, prepare three flipchart pages with the headings of the three questions: Why so long? What's in the way? What will it take? Toward the end of the 10-minute conversation period, give a 1-minute warning and go around to the different groups and prompt them to be ready to share some of their answers with the large group.

4. Large-Group Share-Out   **10 Minutes**

Take the questions one at a time, and gather three to five different answers to each question. One member of the Facilitator team will record the answers while another leads the group. Post each chart on the wall as it is completed, so everyone can see the range of answers. Before you finish each chart, ask if anyone has a different answer to that question, something that has not been said so far. By the time you finish all three questions, make sure you have recorded at least one response from each small group. If some of the answers seem directly contradictory to each other, remind the group that you are not looking for a single truth here, but respecting the many different ways people see these questions.

5. Restart the Video: Closing Conversation   **10 Minutes**

Return to the final section of Video 1:2, where Gary provides some concluding comments and asks the group to consider what they learned from this conversation. You will be prompted to **stop the video** and gather a few responses from the group before you close.

Questions to Consider

GIVEN ALL OF OUR EFFORTS TO ACHIEVE EDUCATIONAL EQUITY:

▶ *Why so long?*

▶ *What's in the way?*

▶ *What will it take?*

Activity: Cultural Bingo	
Phase One: Tone and Trust	
Purpose:	• Provide a fun team-building activity for the adults in your school • Reinforce the idea that everyone has cultural knowledge • Encourage your staff to learn more about each other and about the cultures of their students • Model an activity that could be used in the classroom
Suggested Time:	30 minutes
Materials Needed:	Video Segment 1:3 Handout TT-3: Cultural Bingo Activity Sheet Handout TT-4: Cultural Bingo Answer Sheet Handout TT-5: Blank Cultural Bingo Template
Advanced Preparation:	• Preview Video 1:3 • Read through the Facilitator Directions • Prepare a customized version of Cultural Bingo (optional)

Facilitator Note: *This is an engaging get-up-and-move activity. It could be used at a back-to-school session in August or as an icebreaker and refresher activity at any professional development workshop. It is designed to be fun and to connect the adults in your school with each other in a way they haven't in the past. And it is a good introduction to discussions about personal culture.*

Create Your Own Version: Your manual contains a generic version of Cultural Bingo that was designed by Gary Howard and in some ways reflects his West Coast coming-of-age-in-the-1960s experiences. While this version has worked well with all audiences, it would be more fun and engaging for your staff if you create your own version of the Activity Sheet, including items that relate to the specific cultures, events, places, and experiences that may be familiar to them and come from your region of the country. One way to do this would be to ask different members of your staff to provide one item for the Bingo card. A blank Cultural Bingo Template (Handout TT-5) is included later in this section for this purpose.

1. Set the Stage   2 Minutes

Distribute copies of the Cultural Bingo Activity Sheet, either Handout TT-3 or your customized version, and let everyone know they will have an opportunity to share their own experiences and learn new things about their colleagues during this activity. Do not give out the Answer Sheet at this time.

2. Show Video Segment 1:3   3 Minutes

Gary sets up the activity, has everyone write their name in the center square of their Cultural Bingo Sheet, describes the process for gathering answers, and gets the group up and moving around the room. He emphasizes that this is not competitive Bingo, just an opportunity to learn as much as possible from your colleagues in the time allowed. You will be prompted to stop the video and allow time for the Cultural Bingo game.

3. Cultural Bingo Interaction   10 Minutes

People will be up and moving around the room, gathering signatures from their colleagues, trying to fill in all 24 squares on the Bingo card. You and your Facilitator team should participate along with everyone else, but don't give away all of the answers from the Answer Sheet. Just fill in squares that are part of your prior knowledge. Allow about 10 minutes for the interaction, then give a 1-minute warning and ask people to return to their seats.

4. Large-Group Conversation   10 Minutes

Ask if there is anyone who was able to get signatures in all of the squares. Only one left blank? Only two? Were there any squares nobody was able to sign? Then open it up for anyone who wants to ask about any of the squares. When they ask their questions, see if somebody in the room can provide the answer. If nobody can, then read the answer from the Answer Sheet. Let them know they will be receiving a copy of the Answer Sheet at the end of the activity (Handout TT-4). Complete the large-group conversation by asking for responses to the following questions (which will appear on the screen when you advance the video a few seconds):

1. What did you personally learn from this activity?

2. What was the value or lesson of Cultural Bingo for the group as a whole?

3. How might this activity be adapted for use in the classroom?

5. Restart the Video: Closing Comments   5 Minutes

Gary makes a few summary comments. He will acknowledge that some people can feel inadequate during this activity, judging themselves for not having enough cultural knowledge. Other people may feel pride that their culture or experiences were included in the items on the Bingo card. The game is a reminder that there is always more to learn about different cultures, that nobody has all of the knowledge, and our colleagues can be a great source of information. Hopefully, the Cultural Bingo experience will prompt teachers to ask, "What don't I know about the cultures of my students?" When the video ends, hand out copies of the Answer Sheet.

Cultural Bingo

Who has attended a potlatch?	Who has traveled overseas at least twice?	Who speaks and understands two or more languages?	Who has hosted or recently met someone from another country?	Who is wearing something made in a foreign country?
Who has relatives living in another country?	Who has attended Bon O Dori?	Who has read a book by Alice Walker?	Who knows dances from 3 different cultures?	Who has lived on a farm?
Who has participated in the bone game?	Who has been to both Canada and Mexico?	**Put Your Name Here**	Who makes good Italian food?	Who has a Spanish surname?
Who has lived in more than 5 states?	Who can name 3 Motown hits?	Who has been to Lucia Bride Festival?	Who knows why the Ethiopian New Year is on a different date?	Who has participated in a Seder celebration?
Who has worked for a woman supervisor?	Who is a first-generation immigrant to the U.S.?	Who comes from a family of seven or more children?	Who has attended a Cinco de Mayo celebration?	Who can name at least 10 American Indian tribes or nations?

Answer Sheet For Cultural Bingo

Who has attended a potlach?

A potlach is a celebration of primarily Northwest Coastal tribes, throughout the Pacific Northwest and British Columbia. Usually given by a prominent member of the village for a special reason—birth, death, marriage, etc. The member and his family recognize others by giving away many, if not all, of his possessions to honor others. The current adaptation of the potlach used by many tribes throughout America is known as a "giveaway". People are honored by receiving gifts from their hosts, rather than giving gifts to the host.

Who has attended a Bon O Dori?

A Bon O Dori is a Japanese American celebration and dance honoring ancestors.

Who has read a book by Alice Walker?

Two of her books are: *The Color Purple* and *In Search of My Mother's Gardens*

Who has participated in the bone game?

The bone game is a Native American gambling game where there is singing and drumming. The basic idea is to guess which hand holds the marked bone. Also known as a stick game or hand game by some tribes. In other cultures, dominoes and dice are known as bone games.

Who can name 3 Motown hits?

A few by the Jackson Five, The Temptations, The Supremes, and The Four Tops:
- "Stop in the Name of Love"
- "Tears of a Clown"
- "Ain't No Mountain High Enough"
- "My Girl"
- "You Can't Hurry Love"

Who has been to a Lucia Bride Festival?

This festival is a Scandinavian celebration held during the Christmas season where the eldest daughter serves special food to her family. The eldest daughter wears a white dress and a crown of candles on her head.

Who knows why the Ethiopian New Year is on a different date?

It operates on the Coptic calendar, an older calendar than the Gregorian calendar.

TT-4 Answer Sheet For Cultural Bingo

Who has participated in a Seder Celebration?
Jewish celebration held at Passover that involves a meal with symbolic foods served, which represents the exodus of the people of Israel out of Egypt.

Who has attended a Cinco de Mayo celebration?
Cinco de Mayo is the Fifth of May—the celebration of the victory of the Mexican people over the French during a major battle. (Not to be confused with Mexican Independence Day on September 16th.)

Who can name at least 10 American Indian tribes or nations?
Navajo, Hopi, Seminole, Ojibwe, Iroquois, Cree, Shoshone, Delaware, Yakima, Warm Springs, Comanche, Blackfeet, Nez Perce, Choctaw, Cheyanne, Pima, Klamath, Assiniboin. (There are more than 500 additional American Indian tribes.)

Blank Cultural Bingo Template

Cultural Bingo				
		Put Your Name Here		

Activity: ¿Quiénes Somos? Who Are We?	
Phase One: Tone and Trust	
Purpose:	• Personalize the concept of Cultural Competence • Strengthen relationships among staff members • Identify Cultural Competence behaviors and qualities
Suggested Time:	30 minutes
Materials Needed:	Video Segment 1:4 Handout TT-6: ¿Quiénes Somos? Activity Sheet Flipchart or other visual recording device
Advanced Preparation:	• Preview Video Segment 1:4 • Read through the Facilitator Directions

Facilitator Note: *Before your staff is given a formal definition of Cultural Competence (coming later in Video Segment 2:3), the ¿Quiénes Somos? activity asks them to work with their own understanding of what that term means. They will do this by identifying a person in their own life who exemplifies what they consider to be Cultural Competence. This is an energizer activity, since it requires people to get up and move, find a partner whom they are not presently sitting with, and share information about their Cultural Competence role models.*

1. Set the Stage   2 Minutes

Distribute copies of the ¿Quiénes Somos? Activity Sheet (Handout TT-6), and inform everyone that this activity will be exploring the meaning of Cultural Competence.

2. Start Video Segment 1:4   5 Minutes

Gary will initiate the activity, describing what it means to be a Cultural Competence role model and asking each person to think of someone in his or her life who fits this description. Once they have had a chance to choose their role models, he will prompt everyone to find a partner in the room and spend a few minutes interviewing each other, describing their role models by identifying the behaviors and qualities that exemplify these people. You will be prompted to **pause the video** when the interview process is about to begin.

3. Role Model Interviews in Dyads   8 Minutes

As people get up to find their partners, you and your Facilitator team can help the process by joining with anyone who has not found a partner. If you don't have an even number of people in the group, one of the facilitators can step out for this part of the activity. About 1 minute before the end of the interview session, remind everyone to make a note of the behaviors and qualities that describe their Cultural Competence role models.

4. Small-Group Conversations   5 Minutes

Return people to their tables or small groups. Give them 5 minutes to share what they learned from their partners during the interviews. What were the Cultural Competence qualities and behaviors that were mentioned in their interviews? Ask someone in each group to make a list of these.

5. Large-Group Sharing and Recording   5 Minutes

Pull their attention back to the large group. Go around to each table or small group and ask for one quality or behavior that was listed during their small-group discussion. One of the Facilitators will record these on chart paper or another device, while another leads the large-group share-out. The title of the chart will be "Cultural Competence Qualities and Behaviors."

6. Restart the Video: Final Comments   5 Minutes

Gary provides summary comments regarding what has been learned about Cultural Competence. He will ask people to look over the list of behaviors and qualities and consider which of these are present in their own teaching and leadership. For whom are you a role model? What are your students learning about Cultural Competence by observing you?

7. Distribute the Notes Follow-Up

Soon after completing this activity, transcribe and distribute the list of Cultural Competence Behaviors and Qualities to your staff. You may want to revisit this list from time to time, especially when you are working with the Seven Principles for Cultural Responsive Teaching in Phase Four of the work.

¿Quiénes Somos?
Who Are We?

CHOOSE A PARTNER AND INTERVIEW HIM/HER WITH THE FOLLOWING QUESTIONS:

▶ Who is a cultural competence role model for you (someone who knows how to be respectful and inclusive with people from a broad range of different cultures and backgrounds)?

▶ What personal qualities and behaviors are demonstrated by your role model?

▶ Remember your partner's responses to these questions and ask permission to share them in the large group discussion.

Activity: Tone and Trust Assessment	
Phase One: Tone and Trust	
Purpose:	• Assess how staff presently view the quality of tone and trust among adults in your school • Stimulate a conversation about what needs to happen next to improve your climate • Provide baseline data from which you can measure your progress over time
Suggested Time:	30 minutes
Materials Needed:	Video Segment 1:5 Handout TT-7: Tone and Trust Assessment Flipchart or other visual recording device showing a 1–10 scale
Advanced Preparation:	• Preview Video Segment 1:5 • Read through the Facilitator Directions • Organize people into max-mix groups

Facilitator Note: *This activity is the culmination of Phase One of the work. After participating in the other Phase One activities, your faculty and staff are asked to give their perceptions of the quality of tone and trust among the adults in your school. You can use these data to stimulate discussions of school climate and to plan for what steps can be taken next. It is best to do this assessment conversation in max-mix groups of five to seven people each.*

Optional Method: The process described below asks people to share their personal assessments in small-group discussions at a faculty meeting. As a more anonymous alternative, you could distribute the Tone and Trust Assessment tool in hard copy or electronically to your staff and ask them to return it without names attached. You could then post the range of responses at a faculty meeting and have the discussion at that time. In this case, you would follow Steps 1 to 3 below at one meeting, then ask people to send in their responses over the next day or two, and begin with Step 5 at a later meeting.

1. Set the Stage   2 Minutes

Get everyone organized into max-mix small groups. Inform them that this is the final activity in Phase One of the professional development process. We will be participating in an assessment of how well we feel we are doing in creating an open and welcoming climate among the adults in our school.

2. View Video Segment 1:5   **3 Minutes**

Gary provides a brief summary of the previous Phase One activities and then introduces the Assessment tool. He will ask everyone to think about the question: "To what extent have we established the necessary tone and trust among the adults in our school to be able to have real and authentic conversations about difficult issues related to equity, diversity, social justice, and improving our professional practice?" He will set up the personal think time, and you will be prompted to **pause the video.**

3. Personal Think Time and Distribution of the Handout   **2 Minutes**

While people are thinking about their responses to the assessment question, members of your Facilitation team will distribute copies of Handout TT-7. It is important to remind everyone that this is **not** a time for conversation about the question. That will come later. This is a time to focus on your own thoughts.

Some people may ask for a clarification of the question. Remind them of what Gary says in the video: "Just go with your gut-level feeling about the question. Look at the overall climate among adults in your building, not just the people you are closest to in your arena of work. You don't want to noodle on this too long—just indicate the number that best reflects your perception of the climate."

Make sure everyone has indicated a number on the assessment scale.

4. Restart the Video Segment and Sharing in Small Groups   **7 Minutes**

Gary will ask people to share their numbers with each other in the small groups. Similar to other Phase One discussions, he will emphasize that this conversation should be carried out without judgments or arguments about who is right or wrong. It is all about the range of responses and the overall pattern that will emerge from everyone's perceptions. Each small group will record the numbers as they are shared. You will be prompted to **pause the video** while small groups have a brief discussion about the different responses.

5. Charting the Distribution   **7 Minutes**

After a few minutes of small-group conversation, pull everyone back together. Have the 1–10 scale posted in a large enough format for everyone to see. Ask one member of each small group to report out the numbers that were stated by their members. For example, "We had two 4s, one 5, one 6, and two 8s." This way of reporting allows some degree of anonymity—no one is personally connected to a specific number. A member of your Facilitator team records these as they are mentioned. The result will be a chart that looks something like this:

1	2	3	4	5	6	7	8	9	10
	x	x	x	x	x	x	x	x	
		x	x	x	x	x			
		x	x		x	x			
		x		x	x	x			
		x			x				

6. Reflective Conversation   6 Minutes

When the chart has been completed, ask the large group the following reflective questions:

- What meaning do we make from this?
- What are the possible interpretations?
- What are some action implications?

7. Restart the Video:
Closing Comments/Next Steps   3 Minutes

Gary provides some perspective on what might come next. The assessment you just completed is a single marker in time. As you go through the rest of the process, it might be good to check the climate at various time intervals using this tool. Your Facilitation and leadership team could use these data to map out possible next steps for action and conversation, based on the input from your staff. Compare this assessment outcome with other climate data that you regularly gather. What is the overall picture that emerges? What are the lessons?

Tone and Trust Assessment

To what extent have we established the necessary tone and trust among the adults in our school to be able to have real and authentic conversations about difficult issues related to equity, diversity, social justice, and improving our professional practice?

Low									High
1	2	3	4	5	6	7	8	9	10

Note: Each person answers this question independently before talking with others. After each person has recorded his/her own answer, then chart the distribution of responses. Caution everyone from making any judgemental conclusions about the answers. The "truth" is the whole distribution of responses.

Phase Two: Personal Culture and Personal Journey

Goals for Phase Two:

- Acknowledging each person's unique cultural narrative
- Providing a functional definition of cultural competence
- Clarifying the process of growth toward cultural competence
- Connecting adult cultural competence with student outcomes

RATIONALE AND OVERVIEW OF ACTIVITIES

Phase Two of the work invites your faculty and staff into a variety of conversations that acknowledge, honor, and share each person's cultural stories and experiences. With a strong focus on disaggregated data and student diversity, we give considerable attention to student differences in our schools but can often overlook or minimize the importance of the rich and diverse personal backgrounds of the adults. The more opportunities we as adults have to share our own cultural journeys, identifying both the strengths and the limitations of our perspectives and experiences, the better we can understand and empathize with the complex cultural narratives of our students. Said differently, if the adults in your building do not have the willingness and capacity to engage in honest and critical reflection about their own cultural and racial lenses, then you increase the likelihood that those unacknowledged lenses will get in the way of your students' success.

Phase Two provides a definition of cultural competence that emphasizes the importance of building authentic relationships with our students, relationships based on who our students really are, rather than on our adult projections regarding who we think they are or ought to be. Cultural competence is presented here as a *process of growth,* not a fixed or immutable state. Phase Two is based on the assumption that we cannot *train* people to be culturally competent, but we *can* engage them in a dynamic climate of self-reflection, adult interaction, and mutual professional growth. The intent for this phase of the work is for you and your colleagues to achieve that state of *self-generated neuro-plasticity* discussed in the Introduction to this manual, that state of openness and willingness to honestly examine and courageously challenge our own beliefs, interpersonal behaviors, and professional practices. Related to Phase Two, there are two key courageous questions for adults in your building to be asking themselves: What might I be thinking, believing, or doing that could be getting in the way of my students' learning and success? And, what is the next step for me in my own growth toward greater cultural competence?

Begin your work by showing the **Phase Two Introductory Video,** where your faculty and staff will see how this aspect of the work plays out in real school settings.

The first activity in Phase Two is **Sharing Personal Culture,** which is a fun and nonthreatening way to open up the conversation about the diverse cultural journeys of adults in your building. All participants are asked to bring an object, photo, story, symbol, or anything that represents some aspect of their own cultural background, family history, or personal roots. Staff members share these stories and objects with their peers in small-group discussions. This activity usually takes the conversation to a deeper level than you achieved with Cultural Bingo in Phase One, because here people learn more about the nuances and complexities of their colleagues' cultural narratives, discovering new things about even those staff members they have known for a long time. It is an excellent activity for team building during your August back-to-school sessions, and it can be easily adapted for use with students in the classroom.

The **Culture Toss** activity then takes the work to an even deeper level. On a six-windowed grid, participants are asked to name several of their core identities, related to race and ethnicity, language, religion, beliefs, vocation, and possessions. In a simulated oppressive environment, where personal culture becomes targeted by people in power, participants are challenged to give up several of their identities and imagine what it would be like to live without them. In small-group reflective conversations, they share what they learned from this activity and consider how, and to what extent, students in your school experience pressure to *not* be who they are, to give up or hide essential and core aspects of their identity. Valuable lessons about privilege and social dominance emerge naturally from this discussion, lessons that set the stage for your later work in Phase Three. For example, white people often realize how quickly and easily they are willing to give up their racial identity, while many of their colleagues of color would never do so, or only with great reluctance.

The Culture Toss activity sets the stage for your discussion of the **Definition of Cultural Competence,** which is "the will and the ability to form authentic and effective relationships across differences." In the Video Segment for this activity, Gary Howard analyzes each of the key words in this definition, with particular emphasis on the *will* to pay attention to differences. Too many educators, even those working in highly diverse school settings, still see *colorblindness* as their desired state in dealing with students' differences. "I don't see color." "I treat them all the same." Gary shares several striking anecdotes to debunk this mythology and connects cultural competence to student achievement with the following summary "bottom-line" comment: "The more culturally competent we are as adults, the less our students have to play 'give it up' in our presence. And the less pressure they feel to *not* be who they are, the more energy they have available to engage and learn."

I Am From Poems offer another vehicle for your faculty and staff to reflect on and share their own cultural journeys. With the tone and trust you have hopefully established by this point in the work, the I Am From Poems will take the personal sharing to a new level of self-disclosure and collegial conversation. Gary sets up the activity by reading sample I Am From poems from adults and students, and then provides a structure for you and your colleagues to write your own poems. These are read in small groups, and a reflective conversation focuses on the lessons that emerge. The I Am From activity is another powerful tool that teachers can incorporate into the classroom.

The notion of "personal journey" is made explicit and given a research base in the **Stages of Personal Growth Toward Cultural Competence** discussion. In this Video Segment, Gary reviews a compilation of the theoretical work he and others have done related to the significant passages and personal transformations that individuals experience on the journey toward greater cultural competence. Here again, cultural competence is perceived not as a destination but as a lifelong process of learning. Gary describes some of his own experiences in each stage along the way, and participants are invited to share stories related to the various stages in their own lives. What often emerges from these stories is the realization that teaching in a diverse school has been, in itself, a significant catalyst for the personal transformation of many educators, challenging them to rethink old paradigms and belief systems.

Phase Two culminates with **Personal Growth Projects,** which are the personal and professional take-aways from this Phase of the work. All members of your staff are asked to design for themselves a learning goal and a set of activities that will expand their cultural competence over the course of the next year. Participants are asked to identify one of their own personal edges of growth related to cultural competence. What is an area of difference they want to learn more about? What is an arena of unknowing that they would like to explore further? Related to what culture of group of students would they like to expand their own experience and awareness? All members choose a critical friend to support them on their project, and staff members are encouraged to check in with each other to share progress and lessons along the way. By committing to these projects, each member of your team is acknowledging that we are all on a journey of growth; none of us has arrived.

Phase Two: Personal Journey and Personal Culture		
School Video Clips (SVC)		
In addition to the Phase Two Introductory Video, you can show the following segment to demonstrate how the Personal Culture and Personal Journey work has been implemented in several schools. Your Facilitator Directions suggest key places where these SVCs might be most productively shown.		
SVC #	Title	Video Length
7	**Student Voices: I Am From Poems** Two students, Laquan and Cocoa, read their I Am From poems that poignantly describe their lives and their cultures.	2:23
8	**Affirming Students' Cultural Connections: I Am From Poems** Tina Tamura, 6th Grade Teacher Northdale Middle School, shares her own I Am From poem and describes how she has her students write their own poems as a way to affirm their cultural backgrounds.	2:14
9	**Olabisi Isaac Ewumi: A Student's Journey** Olabisi Isaac Ewumi, Former Student Blaine High School, describes his own personal journey of being from Nigeria and becoming American and the tension he feels from experiencing a blend of these cultures.	1:30

10	**Jinger Gustafson: An Associate Superintendent's Journey** Jinger Gustafson, Associate Superintendent Anoka-Hennepin School District, describes her personal journey growing up in a rural area and the ways in which her education and experience in the military have forged the person she is today.	2:10
11	**Cassidy Pohl: A Student Advisor's Journey** Cassidy Pohl, Student Achievement Advisor Blaine High School, describes her experience growing up in a multi-racial family and how feeling like she doesn't distinctly belong in one racial group has caused her to form her own identity.	2:23
12	**Alicia Moore: A Teacher's Journey** Alicia Moore, Social Studies Blaine High School, explains how her experience growing up poor and feeling different than her peers affects her teaching and how she goes out of her way to make all students feel comfortable and safe.	2:30

Facilitator Note: *Before initiating these activities with your staff, show them the Phase Two Introductory Video.*

Suggested Group Readings for Phase Two

- **White Man Dancing: A Story of Personal Transformation.** Chapter 1 in Gary Howard's book, *We Can't Teach What We Don't Know: White Teachers, Multiracial Schools.* New York: Teachers College Press, 2006.
- **Mapping the Journey of White Identity Development.** Chapter 5 in Gary's book.
- *Identity Safe Classrooms: Places to Belong and Learn.* By D. M. Steele and Becki Cohn-Vargas. Thousand Oaks, CA: Corwin, 2013.

PHASE TWO ACTIVITIES, FACILITATOR DIRECTIONS, AND VIDEO SEGMENTS

Activity: Sharing Personal Culture	
Phase Two: Personal Culture and Personal Journey	
Purpose:	• Introduce the idea that culture is something everybody has • Connect faculty and staff with each other at a deeper level through the sharing of personal stories • Model an activity that can be used in the classroom to recognize and honor the many cultures of your students
Suggested Time:	45 minutes
Materials Needed:	Phase Two Introductory Video Video Segment 2:1 Handout PC-1: Sharing Personal Culture Preparation Memo Handout PC-2: Sharing Personal Culture Discussion Guide Handout PC-3: Personal Culture Reflective Conversation
Advanced Preparation:	• Preview the Introductory Video and Video Segment 2:1 • Read through the Facilitator Directions • Send out the Personal Culture Preparation Memo (Handout PC-1) several days ahead of the activity • Organize max-mix groups of five people each

Facilitator Note: *Several days ahead of doing this activity with your staff, send out the Preparation Memo (Handout PC-1). This will allow your people some time to think about what they would like to bring and share with their colleagues. The advanced notice also gets some buzz going about the whole concept of Personal Culture.*

1. Set the Stage   9 Minutes

Begin by showing the Phase Two Introductory Video. Have the room organized into groups of five, with table numbers indicating where each max-mix group will be sitting. Introduce the activity using language from the Preparation Memo. Provide some comfort to people who may have forgotten to bring their cultural item to share. Gary will provide options for them in his introduction to the activity. Distribute copies of Handouts PC-2 and PC-3.

2. Start Video Segment 2:1   5 Minutes

In this opening segment, Gary introduces the concept of Personal Culture and sets up the small-group conversations. For those people who may not feel prepared for sharing, he reminds them that it is not necessary to have a physical object. Any story related to personal history or family background will be fine. He also cautions people to only share aspects of their personal story that they feel comfortable sharing at this time. **Pause the video.**

3. Small-Group Conversations   25 Minutes

At the end of Gary's comments, video prompts will summarize the key points in the Sharing Personal Culture Discussion Guide (Handout PC-2). Just before the conversations begin, it would be good to remind the groups to keep an eye on time. Each person will have a maximum of 5 minutes to share. If a small group finishes early, they can start their Reflective Conversation (Handout PC-3).

During the last 5 minutes of the small-group conversations, members of your Facilitation Team should circulate around the room, identifying groups who have finished the personal sharing. Ask them to pick a spokesperson and be ready to share with the large group one response related to one of the Reflective Questions.

Make sure you have prepared at least one group to respond to each of the four questions.

4. Large-Group Sharing   5 Minutes

Call on your designated groups to share their responses to the Reflective Questions. If you have time, ask for any additional responses from other groups or individuals. If time is tight, you can do this part of the discussion in pair-and-share groups. That would allow more active participation in a shorter time frame.

5. Restart the Video: Summary Comments   3 Minutes

Gary highlights the importance of Personal Culture and reminds your staff that culture is not only related to differences in ethnicity, language, nationality, or religion. Every aspect of our personal histories and family backgrounds, every influence that has made each of us the person we are, is part of our Personal Culture. He encourages faculty and staff members to continue to share their stories with each other and to find ways to bring the rich diversity of their students' Personal Cultures into the classroom.

Sharing Personal Culture

▶ *MEMO TO PARTICIPANTS*

Send out several days before your session:

Part of our focus for our next meeting will include a discussion of Personal Culture, which comes under Phase 2 of the Cultural Competence work we have been doing. For this discussion, we are asking each person to bring a story, object, photo, symbol, or anything else that represents some aspect of your own culture, family history, or personal roots. Another way to describe this is to think of some part of your personal history that has been significant in making you the person you are today. Please reflect on this, decide what to bring or what story to tell, and be ready to share something of your personal culture and/or family history in a small group of your colleagues.

Sharing Personal Culture

▶ *Each person in your small group will have 5 minutes to share something about his/her personal culture with the rest of the group.*

▶ *Listen to each of the stories and look for connections as well as differences related to your personal cultural story.*

▶ *When everyone has finished, move on to consider the Reflection Questions on the next page.*

▶ *Have a spokesperson ready to share some of your responses/insights.*

Personal Culture Discussion

▶ What similarities and differences among the members of your small group did you notice in your discussion of personal culture?

▶ What did we learn about culture from this activity?

▶ How do the different elements in your personal culture inform / influence / motivate the work you do, how you do it, and why you do it?

▶ Implications for our students?

Activity: Culture Toss	
Phase Two: Personal Culture and Personal Journey	
Purpose:	• Provide an experiential understanding of Personal Culture • Create awareness of the ways that power, privilege, and oppression can impact personal identity • Demonstrate the concept of "negotiating identity" • Reflect on the ways that school culture can cause some students to *not* bring their whole selves to the classroom
Suggested Time:	50 minutes
Materials Needed:	Video Segment 2:2 Handout PC-4: Culture Toss Activity Sheet Handout PC-5: Culture Toss Discussion Guide
Advanced Preparation:	• Preview Video 2:2 • Read through the Facilitator Directions • Organize max-mix groups of five to seven people each

Facilitator Note: *This activity sets the foundation for many conversations to come. It allows the adults in your school to experience how each of us carries our multiple identities, and the powerful ways that school culture impacts our personal cultures, sometimes causing both adults and students to bring less than their full energy to the teaching and learning process. Make sure you allow ample time for reflection and debriefing. The lessons of Culture Toss come not only from the activity itself but also from the conversations that follow.*

1. Set the Stage   2 Minutes

Have the room organized into max-mix groups of five to seven, with table numbers indicating where each small group will be sitting. Distribute copies of the Culture Toss Activity Sheet (Handout PC-4).

2. Start Video Segment 2:2:
Completing the Grid   7 Minutes

In the opening section of this video, Gary introduces the activity and guides the participants in filling out the six boxes on the grid. Facilitators should circulate around the room and encourage people to be filling in their forms while the video is showing. This is not a time for discussion, so keep the interaction to a minimum. You will be prompted to **stop the video** for a brief time to make sure everyone has completed the grid.

3. Restart the Video: Simulated Oppressive Environment

3 Minutes

Gary shifts the tone and creates a simulated police state, where individual identity and culture are targeted, and people feel threatened to express who they are. For their own personal safety and survival, everyone has to give up two aspects of their identity; they have to cross off two of the boxes on the grid.

After Gary has set the tone and required people to cross off two of their boxes, you will be prompted to **pause the video.** Take a minute or so to make sure everyone has completed the task, then restart the video.

4. Restart the Video: Small-Group Conversation 1

7 Minutes

Gary sets the parameters for small-group conversations (Handout PC-5). All participants will take a minute to describe what they have written in each of their boxes, as well as share which two they have crossed off and why they selected those two. **Pause the video** and allow time for the group discussions.

5. Restart the Video: "Things Are Getting Worse"

3 Minutes

Don't worry if not all the small groups have completed their conversations: They will have more sharing opportunities soon. In this section of the video, Gary increases the pressure of the simulated oppressive environment. More police on the streets; more dangerous to be who you are. In this context, everyone must now give up two more boxes. Once again, you will be prompted to **stop the video** and make sure everyone is completing the task.

6. Restart the Video: Small-Group Conversation 2

6 Minutes

Gary introduces the next round of conversation, with each person sharing which two additional boxes they have now crossed off and why. **Pause the video** while groups engage in the conversation.

7. Restart the Video: Posing the Reflective Question

7 Minutes

Gary sets the tone for a reflective conversation: "What did you learn about yourself from this activity?" **Pause the video** and allow time for the reflective conversation.

8. Reflective Conversation   7 Minutes

After about 5 minutes of reflective conversation, Facilitators should go around to each small group and prompt them to select a spokesperson and be ready to share one example of something that was learned from this activity. This can be either a personal lesson from one of the members of their group, or it can be a group lesson that emerged from their conversation as a whole.

9. Large-Group Sharing   5 Minutes

Facilitators bring everyone's attention back to the large group and invite each small group to share one of the lessons that came out during their discussion. If you have a large group and only limited time at this point, you can select only a few groups for their input. Thank each group and acknowledge any themes or generalizations that have emerged from the various comments.

10. Restart the Video: Summary and Application Question   7 Minutes

Gary summarizes some of the key learnings from this activity and plants the seeds for an ongoing conversation about how these lessons apply to the students in your school. One of the central concepts that comes out of the Culture Toss activity is that people in dominant culture groups seldom feel pressure to give up who they are. Members of nondominant or oppressed groups, on the other hand, often feel that the school environment does not fully welcome them, that they must find ways to alter, hide, or negotiate their identity to feel safe or included in the dominant culture.

At the end of the Video Segment, Gary poses the application question: "In what ways are students in your school feeling pressure to give up aspects of their identities, to not be fully who they are?" If you have time left in your session, you can invite a few responses to that question or put people into pair-and-share conversations to discuss their thoughts. In any case, ask your faculty to keep this question in mind as they interact with students, and continue to consider this question in their collegial conversations and other team or department meetings. Ask them to ponder: How do we create a school culture where more of our students, across more of their differences, feel more welcomed and included, more of the time?

Final Note: The Culture Toss activity sets the stage for the next Video Segment, where Gary provides a Definition of Cultural Competence and makes the connection between the level of Cultural Competence of adults in your school and the degree of engagement and academic achievement of your students. It would be helpful to introduce this Definition as soon as possible after completing the Culture Toss activity.

PC-4

Culture Toss

Race / Ethnicity	Religion / Spirituality
Language	Life Value
Vocation	Possession

Culture Toss Discussion Guide

Small-Group Conversation 1:

Which two boxes did your cross off and why?

Small-Group Conversation 2:

Which two boxes did you cross off this time?
Why did you keep the two boxes that are left?

Reflective Question:

What did you learn about yourself from this activity?

Application Question:

How do see the students in your school experiencing pressure to give up aspects of their own identities, or not be fully who they are? Which identities are being targeted?

Note: In what ways are the adults in your school creating this pressure for students not to be who they are?

Activity: Definition of Cultural Competence	
Phase Two: Personal Culture and Personal Journey	
Purpose:	• Provide a functional definition of Cultural Competence • Reinforce the idea that every student and employee brings multiple dimensions of difference into our schools • Establish a direct relationship between the cultural competence of adults and the engagement and achievement of students • Summarize research that establishes the causal link between Cultural Competence and student achievement
Suggested Time:	30 minutes
Materials Needed:	Video Segment 2:3 Handout PC-6: Lenses of Difference Handout PC-7: Definition of Cultural Competence Handout PC-8: Stereotype Threat Research Summary
Advanced Preparation:	• Preview Video 2:3 • Read through the Facilitator Directions • Staple together the three handouts

Facilitator Note: *This Video Segment pulls together the conceptual framework and research base for understanding and working with Cultural Competence. It directly relates the lessons that came out of the Culture Toss activity to the work of eliminating educational disparities. This segment is primarily a talking piece, with some opportunities for small-group reflective conversation. It is best if you use this Video Segment immediately following, or in close proximity to, the Culture Toss activity.*

1. Set the Stage   2 Minutes

Distribute copies of the stapled handout packet: PC-6, PC-7, and PC-8. Inform your faculty that this Video Segment will draw upon the lessons that came out of their Culture Toss discussion. They will be provided with a definition of Cultural Competence and a summary of research that demonstrates the direct relationship between the Cultural Competence of adults and the engagement and success of students.

2. Start Video Segment 2:3   3 Minutes

Here Gary introduces the Lenses of Difference conversation (Handout PC-6). He reminds the participants that the actual diversity that we and our students bring to the school experience is much more complex than the six boxes we worked with in the Culture Toss activity. You will be prompted to **pause the video** and begin the pair-and-share discussion.

3. Pair-and-Share Conversations   5 Minutes

Participants will select one of the Lenses of Difference and talk about how it has been a challenge in their own lives, or in the lives of their students or colleagues. At the close of the pair-and-share conversations, bring the group back together and ask several people to share which lenses of difference were the focus of their discussion. Are there other lenses they would like to add to the list given on Handout PC-6?

4. Restart the Video: Definition of Cultural Competence   10 Minutes

Here Gary provides the definition of Cultural Competence: *the will and ability to form authentic and effective relationships across differences* (Handout PC-7). He shares stories that illustrate the deeper meaning of each key word in that definition. He debunks the notion of "colorblindness" and highlights the essential role of authenticity in our relationships with students. He also connects this definition with the lessons that came out of the Culture Toss activity. You will be prompted to **stop the video** and return to conversations with a partner.

5. Pair-and-Share Reflective Conversation   5 Minutes

Partners will share their responses to the definition of Cultural Competence. Specifically, they will be asked to apply the concepts of authentic relationship and Cultural Competence to the stories they told earlier in their Lenses of Difference conversation. In what ways was Cultural Competence either missing or present in the challenges they have faced related to their own differences, or in the challenges faced by their students and colleagues?

6. Restart the Video: Research Base for Cultural Competence   5 Minutes

Gary reviews the key findings of Stereotype Threat Research (Handout PC-8) and makes the case for a causal relationship between the Cultural Competence of adults and the engagement and success of students. He emphasizes the "Bottom Line" for this entire professional development process:

> The more culturally competent we are as educators,
>
> the less our students have to play "give it up" in our schools.
>
> The less pressure they feel *not* to be who they are,
>
> the more energy they have available to engage and learn.

This presentation provides the evidence-based rationale for why we are doing this work.

Lenses of Difference

Which lens of difference has been the greatest challenge for you in your life?

Age	Gender	Race
Religion	Economics	Language
Disability	Culture	Accent
Values	Role/Position	Status
Appearance	Education Level	Body Size
Personality	Sexual Orientation	Politics
Learning Styles	Family Background	Other?

1. Share a story from your own experience that illustrates how one of these dimensions of difference has created a challenge for you.

or

2. In what ways do you see students or adults in your school experiencing challenges related to their lenses of difference?

3. Are there other lenses of difference you would like to add to this list?

Definition of Cultural Competence

> **The will and the ability**
>
> **to form authentic and effective relationships**
>
> **across differences**

Pair-and-Share Conversation:

1. Share your responses to this definition of Cultural Competence.

2. In what ways were authentic relationship and Cultural Competence either missing or present in the Lenses of Difference challenges you discussed earlier?

Stereotype Threat Research Summary

- The interpersonal and cultural context of learning has a profound impact on students' motivation and performance.
- If students feel:
  - a lack of belonging,
  - a low level of trust in the people around them, or
  - a sense that teachers do not value their intelligence,

  then their feelings of competence, their motivation, and their performance will be lessened.

Aronson, J., & Steele, C. M. (2005). Stereotypes and the fragility of human competence, motivation, and self-concept. In C. Dweck & E. Elliot (Eds.), *Handbook of competence and motivation*. New York: Guilford.

Steele, C. M. (2004). A threat in the air: How stereotypes shape intellectual identity and performance. In J.A. Banks & C.A.M. Banks (Eds.), *Handbook of research on multicultural education* (pp. 682–698). San Francisco: Jossey-Bass.

Steele, D. M., & Cohn-Vargas, B. (2013). *Identity safe classrooms: Places to belong and learn*. Thousand Oaks, CA: Corwin Press.

The Bottom Line

The more culturally competent we are as educators,
   the less our students have to play "give it up" in our schools.

The less pressure they feel *not* to be who they are,
   the more energy they have available to engage and learn.

No person should ever live under a cloud of suspicion just because of what they look like.

—President Barack Obama

Activity: I Am From Poems	
Phase Two: Personal Culture and Personal Journey	
Purpose:	• Take the sharing of Personal Culture to a deeper level • Honor the uniqueness of each adult on your staff • Explore similarities as well as differences • Recognize the many dimensions of culture • Demonstrate a strategy for bringing students' cultures into the classroom
Suggested Time:	50–55 minutes
Materials Needed:	Video Segment 2:4 Handout PC-9: I Am From Writing Prompts Handout PC-10: Sample I Am From Poem Handout PC-11: Blank I Am From Writing Page Handout PC-12: I Am From Reflective Conversation
Advanced Preparation:	• Preview Video 2:4 • Organize max-mix groups of five to seven people each • Staple the four handouts together as a packet • Read through the Facilitator Directions

Facilitator Note: *This activity requires max-mix groups, so have those set up ahead of time. People will be sharing at a fairly deep level, so it is important that you have established the kind of tone and trust that will allow for a climate of emotional safety.*

1. Set the Stage   2 Minutes

Distribute copies of the stapled packet including Handouts PC-9, 10, 11, and 12. Inform your faculty that this activity will allow them to learn more about each other through sharing different aspects of their personal culture. It is also an activity that has powerful applications and implications in the classroom.

2. Start Video Segment 2:4   10 Minutes

Gary sets up the activity, walking people through the writing prompts for creating their own I Am From poems. He illustrates the process using stories and examples from his family and cultural background, and encourages participants to make their own notes on the Writing Prompts page (Handout PC-9). These notes will serve as the raw material for constructing their personal poems. Gary concludes by reading his I Am From poem and sharing a video of two sample student poems.

3. Personal Writing Time   10 Minutes

You will be prompted to **stop the video** and provide time for people to write their I Am From poems, using the blank I Am From page (Handout PC-11). If necessary, remind the group that this is not a time for conversation; that will come later. This is a time for each person to work in silence, drafting verses that respond to the I Am From writing prompts.

4. Restart the Video: Setup
for Small-Group Sharing   2 Minutes

After the group has completed the writing process, Gary provides some guidelines for sharing I Am From poems in small groups. He encourages people to share as much of their poems as possible but also gives the freedom to leave out certain parts that may be uncomfortable to share at this time. This freedom to pass usually opens the door for people to share at a deeper level, without feeling forced to do so. Gary will also point out the Reflective Questions and ask groups to begin that discussion when they have finished reading their poems.

5. Small-Group Reading of
I Am From Poems   15 Minutes

About 10 minutes into the small-group time, Facilitators should circulate around the room. Identify groups who have completed the reading of their poems, and remind them to discuss the reflective questions (Handout PC-12). Ask selected groups to have a spokesperson ready to share one insight or experience that came out of this activity. One option is to select four groups and assign each to respond to a different question on the reflective conversation sheet.

6. Large-Group Sharing   8 Minutes

Bring the group back together and ask selected groups to share their comments and reflections. As time allows, you can also ask for responses to these questions:

- What was difficult about this activity?
- What was the value of this activity?
- How would you adapt the I Am From poem for use in the classroom?
- What concerns would you have about doing this with students?

7. Community Reading   8 Minutes

As a culminating activity, ask each small group to send to the front of the room one person to read his or her poem aloud to the large group. Form a line across the front of the room, and ask people to read their poems as one continuous I Am From. Ask the audience not to applaud or respond between poems, just keep the words flowing from one person to the next. At the end, applaud all of the readers at one time, and thank them for stepping up to be a part of this Community Reading.

8. Show School Video Clip of I Am From Poems

If you have time at the end of your community reading, this would be a good opportunity to show SVC-8. This video clip features a middle school teacher sharing her poem and sample verses from the poems of her students.

I Am From

I AM FROM....

...places

   ...products

      ...food

         ...people

            ...common things

            ...pictures

            ...events

            ...phrases

           ...smells

        ...sounds

      ...sights

   ...touches

I Am From Sample Poem

I am from platanos and sugar canes in the mountains
  I am from coffee beans roasting in the morning
    I am from sandy beaches and clear paradise
      I am from freestyle battles in the corners
        I am from double dutch on a warm afternoon
        I am from rice and beans
          the chewy steak on Sunday nights
          Yuca and salami when the sun is at it's highest
          I am from the palo drums,
          the guitar's song in bachata,
          the beat boxing and struggle
          I am from tios and tias
          from centuries of Spanish-speaking culture
          from endless rivers of family
        I am from baggy clothes and shorts
      I am from years of tambora and guira playing
    from hips that move like the waves of the Caribbean
  I am the Dominican Republic
I am New York
I am Karen

For more ideas about I Am From Poems and other strategies for bringing students' lives into the classroom, see Linda Christensen's book, *Reading Writing and Rising Up: Teaching about Social Justice and the Power of the Written Word* (available from Rethinking Schools).

Blank I Am From Writing Page

My I Am From Poem

I Am From Reflections

► What similarities and differences among the members of your small group did you notice in your discussion of the I Am From poems?

► What did you learn about race and culture from this activity?

► How do the different elements in your personal culture and I Am From inform / influence / motivate the work you do, how you do it, and why you do it?

► How do the many different I Am From experiences of your students and colleagues impact their journeys toward inclusion and success in our schools?

Activity: Stages of Personal Growth Toward Cultural Competence	
Phase Two: Personal Culture and Personal Journey	
Purpose:	• Review research on personal identity development • Introduce seven stages of growth toward cultural competence • Share stories related to the growth journey • Consider the implications of this developmental model
Suggested Time:	40 minutes
Materials Needed:	Video Segment 2:5 Handout PC-13: Stages of Personal Growth Toward Cultural Competence Handout PC-14: Stages of Cultural Competence Discussion Questions
Advanced Preparation:	• Preview Video 2:5 • Read through the Facilitator Directions

Facilitator Note: *For this activity, you can decide whether to set up max-mix groups or allow your faculty and staff to self-select their small groups. Talk with your Facilitator Team to see which format would work best. Whichever way you go, groups of four people would be optimal for this activity, allowing everyone time to talk. Before you implement this discussion, have your Facilitation Team view the School Video segments that highlight the personal journey stories of students, teachers, administrators and student advocates. These include SVCs 9-12. Watch each of these and decide which ones you would like to share and discuss with your faculty and staff.*

1. Set the Stage   2 Minutes

Distribute copies of the two handouts, and inform people that this activity will continue to focus on the Personal Journey aspects of our work. The key question here is: How do we grow toward Cultural Competence?

2. Start Video Segment 2:5   12 Minutes

Building from the early seminal research on racial identity theory by Helms (1994), Tatum (1992), and Carter (1995), Gary describes his perspective on seven stages in the journey toward becoming a culturally competent person. He illustrates each stage with stories from his life journey and invites the participants to be thinking of their own experiences. You will be prompted to **stop the video** and allow time for your faculty and staff to share their stories.

3. Small-Group Sharing of Stories   12 Minutes

In his setup for the small-group conversations, Gary asks each person to share a personal story about one of the Seven Stages of Growth Toward Cultural Competence. Groups should keep an eye on the time, with each person given 2 to 3 minutes to talk.

4. Reflective Conversation   6 Minutes

Toward the end of the small-group conversation time, ask each group to focus on the reflective questions (Handout PC-14). As they engage in this part of the discussion, go around the room prompting several groups to be ready to share their response to one of the questions, or any other comment describing their experience with this activity. If you have a group of people who have been resistant to the work you have done so far, make sure to call on them. This sometimes helps bring greater focus to their thinking.

5. Large-Group Share-Out   7 Minutes

Ask each of your selected groups to share their responses with the large group.

If any of the reflective questions have not been responded to, ask if anyone in the room has something to add related to those questions. If you have time, you can ask for responses to additional reflective questions:

- Which Stages were the primary focus of the stories told in your small group?
- What were some of the commonalities you noticed in the stories?
- Are these Stages experienced differently by people of color as compared to white people?
- Were there generational differences you noticed?
- How do we see our students experiencing these different Stages?

6. Restart the Video: Summary Comments   3 Minutes

In this closing piece, Gary highlights some of the implications of a developmental model of growth toward Cultural Competence. It is not something we either have or don't have. It is a matter of lifelong learning. It is not something we can "train" people to become. It is a matter of consciousness and choice, a choice to critically reflect on our own experiences and reactions, a choice to pay attention.

Stages of Personal Growth Toward Cultural Competence

▶ *Pre-contact*

▶ *Contact*

▶ *Disintegration / Meltdown*

▶ *Reintegration / Retrenchment*

▶ *Pseudo-Independence*

▶ *Immersion / Emersion*

▶ *Autonomy / Authenticity*

Adapted from: Helms, J. E. 1990. *Black and White Racial Identity: Theory, Research and Practice.* Westport, CT: Greenwood Press.

For further discussion of these stages, see Chapter 5 in Gary R. Howard's book, *We Can't Teach What We Don't Know* (Second Edition, 2006), Teachers College Press.

Stages of Cultural Competence Discussion Questions

▶ Share a story about your personal experience with one or more of the stages.

▶ What is the relationship between these stages of cultural competence and our work for diversity, equity, and excellence?

▶ How do the different elements in your personal culture inform/influence/motivate the work you do, how you do it, and why you do it?

▶ How can we support ourselves, our colleagues, our students, and our school community in better navigating the journey toward cultural competence?

Activity: Personal Growth Project	
Phase Two: Personal Culture and Personal Journey	
Purpose:	• Engage individuals in deepening their personal journey • Identify personal growth goals for Cultural Competence • Design personalized action projects • Create a process for sharing and accountability
Suggested Time:	25 minutes
Materials Needed:	Video Segment 2:6 Handout PC-15: Personal Growth Project
Advanced Preparation:	• Preview Video 2:6 • Read through the Facilitator Directions

Facilitator Note: *This is the culminating activity for Phase Two of the work. All members of your faculty and staff will design and commit to carrying out a personalized action/growth project that will expand their own Cultural Competence. It would be good for you and a few members of your Facilitation Team to have your projects ready ahead of time to share as examples. This activity is best done at the same time, or closely following, your work with Stages of Personal Growth Toward Cultural Competence (Video Segment 2:5). Also, you should look ahead and set at least two check-in dates when people will have an opportunity to talk with each other about the lessons that are emerging from their action projects.*

1. Set the Stage   2 Minutes

Distribute copies of the Personal Growth Project planning form (Handout PC-15) and let people know that this activity will serve as their homework assignment to bring the lessons of Phase Two into practical application in their personal and professional lives.

2. Start Video Segment 2:6   10 Minutes

Gary discusses the purpose of this activity and walks people through the planning form, giving several examples of Personal Growth Projects that have been created by participants in his workshops over the years. He will prompt you to **stop the video** and invite members of your Facilitator Team to share their plans.

3. Individual Work on Designing
Personal Growth Projects   8 Minutes

After two or three Facilitators have shared their sample plans, give people time to work on designing their own Personal Growth Projects, filling in the various sections of Handout PC-15. As they work (or don't work) on their projects, remind them that everyone will be checking in with each other at several points in the future to share progress and lessons coming out of these projects. Facilitators can circulate around the room supporting people who may be having trouble designing their projects. Also, encourage people to talk with a friend to get ideas, or even design a team project if that feels more workable.

4. Sharing Examples of Goal Statements   4 Minutes

As people are working on their projects, Facilitators will identify five or six people who would be willing to share their goal statements and a brief summary of their project with the larger group. Make sure you select/recruit people who represent diverse roles and subgroups of your faculty and staff. Bring the large group back together and ask your selected people to share their action plans. After these people have spoken, ask if there is anyone else who would like to share what they have created.

5. Announce the Check-In Dates   1 Minute

Just before you close this activity, give people the dates when you will come together to share progress with these projects. It would be good to have one of these dates within a month or 6 weeks from the time you introduced the activity, and then a second date further out. They can check in with their Critical Friend more often than this, but everyone will have at least these two opportunities to share their progress and lessons, and listen to the experiences of others. Work with your Facilitation Team to plan how you will structure these check-in sessions.

Personal Growth Project

Your Name: Date:

▶ Objective: (Something you will do this year to enhance your own cultural competence.)

▶ Action Steps: (Steps you will take to accomplish this objective.)

▶ Actions:	With Whom?	By When!

▶ Assessment: (How will you know you have accomplished this objective?)

▶ Allies and Critical Friends: (People who can help you accomplish and reflect on this work.)

Phase Three: From Social Dominance to Social Justice

Goals for Phase Three:

- Exploring issues of privilege, power, and difference
- Understanding the dynamics of social dominance
- Linking issues of dominance to current educational inequities
- Creating strategies for moving from dominance to social justice

---

RATIONALE AND OVERVIEW OF ACTIVITIES

Phase Three takes the personal and professional conversations you have had up to this point and moves them into the organizational, societal, and structural dimensions of the work (see Figure 1 in the Introduction). If we are to overcome the educational inequities we see manifested in our schools today, we must understand the causal factors rooted in our history and still deeply embedded in our social and institutional structures. One of the most glaring deficiencies in recent school reform efforts has been the lack of any political or historical perspective on these causal factors. This deficiency in analysis gives rise to the false assumption that we can close educational outcome gaps simply by working within the schools themselves. Related to poverty, for example, a lack of structural analysis has led policy makers to place heavy pressure for testing and accountability on educators working with students in high-poverty schools but allows these same policy makers to do essentially nothing to address the causal factors leading to the growing incidence of childhood poverty in the United States (Gorski, 2013). Likewise, related to race, the lack of an adequate historical and contemporary understanding of the role of racism in determining housing and school assignments patterns has led the Roberts Supreme Court to deny school districts the right to use race as a means of overcoming the re-segregation of our nation's schools (*Parents Involved in Community Schools v. Seattle School District No. 1*, 2007). Concerning both poverty and race, inadequate structural analysis has led to inadequate policy and legal decisions. Educational historian, Diane Ravitch (2013), provides exhaustive documentation of this lack of structural analysis in her critique of the top-down market-driven approach to school reform and concludes,

> The reformers say they care about poverty, but they do not address it other than to insist on private management of the schools in urban districts; the reformers ignore racial segregation altogether, apparently accepting it as inevitable. Thus, they leave the root causes of low academic performance undisturbed. (p. 6)

In focusing on the societal and structural forces that have created and sustained educational inequities, the intent of Phase Three is neither to overwhelm your faculty and staff with the heaviness of our historical burden nor to give them an excuse to explain away the inequities they see in their own classrooms. The intent, rather, is to reinforce the vital importance of the work they are doing and ignite their passion for social justice. Many of your colleagues already embrace this deeper vision and passion for their work. They chose the vocation of teaching precisely because they want to provide their students with the tools to overcome any obstacles that the demographics of birth may have put in their way and give them the full measure of opportunity for creating a good life. These teachers see their work as intimately connected to social justice and the overturning of centuries of racism, classism, and other dimensions of dominance. For other members of your team, however, who may not have made these deeper connections in their own minds and hearts, the Phase Three activities and discussions will hopefully encourage them to see their work in a new light and engage their students with fresh energy and perspective.

In addition to its focus on the historical and societal dimensions, Phase Three also invites you and your faculty to consider how issues of privilege, power, and social dominance function within the culture of your school. Related to race, social class, gender, sexual orientation, religion, language, and special needs, which groups of students in your school are more included, involved, recognized, and rewarded, and which groups are less privileged and more marginalized? What policies, practices, and assumptions get in the way of full inclusion and equity, and which programs and approaches are working to break down these patterns of social dominance? Related to parents and other adult influences within your school's broader service community, what forces are working to strengthen respect and full engagement for all of your students, and what dynamics are creating obstacles? How can you and your team reinforce those things that are strengthening social justice for your kids and diminish the power of things that are not?

After showing your faculty the **Phase Three Introductory Video,** begin with the **We, the People** activity, which directly connects the historical arrangements of social dominance laid down in the founding of our nation with the continuing inequities we see reflected in our schools and society today. The Video Segment for this activity highlights the stark contrast between the broadly *inclusive* language of the Constitution, Declaration of Independence, and Bill of Rights and the narrowly *exclusive* group of white male property owners who were allowed full participation in the new nation. Participants are asked to consider the question: How far have we come since 1787 in actually living the ideals set forth in our founding documents? People place themselves along a continuum from 0 to 100 and discuss why they chose to stand at different points along the line. This discussion demonstrates the value of multiple perspectives and reinforces the notion that "truth" is viewed differently by different people depending on the varied lenses we use to focus our separate realities. Following this discussion of the nation's progress, the focus is shifted to your school, and your team forms a new continuum based on their perceptions of how far you have come in creating a culture of inclusion, equity, and excellence for all of your students. From this exercise, it becomes clear that the very groups that were excluded from full participation in the founding of the nation over two centuries ago are often still marginalized in our schools today. The We, the People activity has "legs" in the sense that you and your colleagues will continue to refer back to these discussions as you move on to the Phase Four and Five exploration of classroom practices, Culturally Responsive Teaching, and school improvement.

The Guessing Game is a simulation that provides an experiential basis for understanding the social and historical dynamics that have created and sustained educational inequities based on race, social class, gender, and other dimensions of difference. This competitive problem-solving activity sets up a mock oppressive culture, wherein some groups are privileged with helpful resources that support them in winning the game, while others are left to struggle with inadequate information that continually causes them to fail. Participants have fun with the over-the-top role-playing that often results from the hyped competition of this activity. Later, the debrief conversation grounds them in the reality that the same dynamics of privilege and dominance that emerged in the game are actually occurring in your school on a daily basis. What happens to children and young people who experience marginalization and failure throughout their years of schooling? To what extent are we as adults complicit in maintaining these systems of privilege that favor some groups of students over others, and to what extent are we consciously working to dismantle these arrangements of dominance?

Following the simulation activity, you will lead your faculty and staff into a discussion of the central conceptual framework for Phase Three: the **Definition and Dynamics of Social Dominance.** Social dominance is defined here as *systems of privilege and preference, reinforced by power, favoring certain groups over others.* The simulation activity described above immerses your colleagues in precisely this kind of a system, causes them to see and feel its impact, and provides an experiential basis for understanding social dominance. Following the definition of dominance, Gary Howard describes the three Dynamics of Social Dominance: *the assumption of rightness, the luxury of ignorance, and the legacy of privilege.* These are the behavioral and attitudinal dynamics that have created and sustained systems of privilege and power over the centuries. People in power usually don't see their "truth" as being relative to other truths, or as being merely one perspective among many. They assume they are right and that theirs is the *only* truth. This assumption of rightness is fueled often by their ignorance of other realities, their lack of exposure to how less dominant people and groups experience and view the world. This ignorance is a luxury because it flows from the social and psychological insulation provided by the unearned legacy of both power and privilege; other people's realities simply don't impact them. Oppressed groups do not enjoy this luxury; their survival depends on understanding how the forces of privilege and power function. In a later activity, you and your staff will consider how and where these dynamics may be functioning in your school and community.

The **From Social Dominance to Social Justice** conversation then provides a sense of movement away from the arrangements of dominance and toward a culture of inclusion, equity, and excellence. In this Video Segment, Gary Howard shares a Definition of Social Justice: *systems of equity and fairness, reinforced by respect and shared power, favoring* *the inclusion and well-being of all groups.* He also sets forth a description of the Dynamics of Social Justice: *the assumption of multiple perspectives and truths, the luxury of being heard and understood, and the legacy of our shared human destiny.* The parallel language here provides a counterbalance for the definition and dynamics of social dominance and also articulates a vision for where we want to be moving in our school improvement and social change efforts.

We want teachers and school leaders to see their work in this broader and deeper context, to honor the transformative power of public education as a force for social justice, and to transcend the simplistic notion that our work is only about raising test scores. This is the level of awareness and the affirmation we are attempting to reinforce in Phase Three of the work.

The **Privilege and Power School Assessment** activity gives you and your team an opportunity to view your own school through the lens of the social dominance and social justice conceptual framework presented in the earlier activities. In small-group conversations, teachers and staff members consider where and to what extent they see "systems of privilege and preference" functioning within personal interactions, professional practices, or organizational policies within your school or district. They also look for evidence of the dynamics of social dominance at work in the personal and professional relationships in your school. Where do they see examples of the assumption of rightness, the luxury of ignorance, or the legacy of privilege being played out in their own classrooms or in the culture of your school? Then, most important, they work together to design strategies that will help mitigate against those dynamics of dominance they have identified, moving your school forward on its journey of becoming a system of equity and fairness, reinforced by respect and shared power, favoring the inclusion, well-being, and success of all groups. This is the key take-away activity for your work with Phase Three.

This section of the manual also offers an opportunity for your faculty to focus specifically on the issue of race. Since 85% to 90% of teachers in the United States are white, and students of color are rapidly becoming the majority in our nation's schools, it is imperative to consider how race is impacting classroom culture and outcomes. Undoing race-based inequities is a central priority for any meaningful school improvement plan, and we are never going to get to our desired results without honest and real dialogue and action related to race. The **Focus on Race Conversation** engages your faculty in sharing their own experiences of racial identity development and provides them with the White Identity Orientations model as a conceptual framework for understanding the different ways that white people deal with race and the reality of their own whiteness. For people of color, this conversation is often a welcomed shift in focus, away from the race conversation always being about them, and instead looking at racial healing via a consideration of the changes needed in the dominant group. It is important to look at how white educators deal with the dynamics of their own racial dominance and how they can grow toward a more informed, authentic, and effective role in dismantling the legacy of racism in our nation's schools. To deepen and extend the conversation about race, you are encouraged to view two excellent films from Shakti Butler: *Mirrors of Privilege: Making Whiteness Visible* and *Cracking the Codes: The System of Racial Inequity.*

The final piece in Phase Three is a short conversation about **Shifting the Emotional Paradigm.** As you and your faculty work through the Phase Three activities and struggle with issues of privilege, power, and social dominance, both in their historical context and in their current influence on educational inequities, some challenging emotions will inevitably emerge. You will be confronting issues of racism, sexism, classism, homophobia, and other difficult realities. Feelings of guilt, shame, anger, denial, or fear often accompany these discussions, both for those individuals who are members of dominant social groups and for those who have been excluded and oppressed because of social dominance. It is important to acknowledge the presence and legitimacy of these feelings but not to leave people stuck in a negative place. Just as we are attempting to move away from systems of social dominance and toward a culture of social justice, so we need to support ourselves and our colleagues in moving through and away from these "zinger emotions" and toward what Gary Howard calls the "responses that heal." In this Video Segment, he describes a broad range of emotional responses that can accompany this work and encourages participants to see these difficult feelings as a natural part of a journey that can lead to greater humility, honesty, empathy, advocacy, and creative action.

	Phase Three: Social Dominance to Social Justice School Video Clips (SVC)	

The following video segments can be used to initiate reflective conversations about issues of social dominance, privilege, power, and oppression as experienced by students and administrators in actual school and community settings. View these with your Facilitator Team and decide which SVCs would be most appropriate for use with your faculty and staff.

SVC #	Title	Video Length
13	**Getting Others to See the Problem** Dennis Carlson, Superintendent Anoka-Hennepin School District, describes how issues of privilege and power can get in the way of meeting the needs of all students.	2:03
14	**Student Voices: Understanding Changes Your Perspective** Gary Howard leads a discussion with a group of high school girls. They describe how issues of race come into their lives and discuss how other aspects of their schools' culture either help or hinder their learning.	3:56
15	**Student Voices: Boy's Group Talks About Racism** Gary Howard leads a discussion with a group of high school boys. They discuss how racism influences their lives both in school and in their community.	5:47
16	**Student Voices: Racism** Gary Howard leads a discussion with a group of middle school girls. They discuss ways in which these students experience racism in school and in their community.	4:41
17	**Student Voices: "I Feel Kind of Weird that I'm Different"** Gary Howard leads a discussion with a group of middle school boys. They discuss ways in which these students experience racism in school and in their community.	6:39
18	**Student Voice: Students with Diverse Backgrounds Feel the Tension** Olabisi Isaac Ewumi, Former Student Blaine High School, describes the racial and socio-economic tensions that existed at his high school. He also describes the ways in which students with different sexual orientations commonly experienced discrimination and bullying.	2:18

Facilitator Note: *Before initiating these activities with your staff, show them the Phase Three Introductory Video.*

Suggested Group Readings for Phase Three

- **Decoding the Dominance Paradigm.** Chapter 3 in Gary Howard's book, *We Can't Teach What We Don't Know: White Teachers, Multiracial Schools.* New York: Teachers College Press, 2006.
- **Whites in Multicultural Education: Rethinking Our Role.** See Gary Howard's articles in the back of the manual.
- **How We Are White.** See Gary Howard's articles in the back of the manual.

PHASE THREE: FROM SOCIAL DOMINANCE TO SOCIAL JUSTICE

	Activity: We, the People
	Phase Three: From Social Dominance to Social Justice
Purpose:	• Explore the historical roots of educational inequities • Consider how far we have come in dismantling the arrangements of dominance, both as a nation and as a school/district • Create an interactive experience of multiple perspectives and multiple truths • Emphasize why strategic initiatives related to race, gender, class, and other differences are critically important in today's schools
Suggested Time:	60–70 minutes
Materials Needed:	Phase Three Introductory Video Video Segment 3:1 Handout SJ-1: We, the People Handout SJ-2: We, the People Discussion Three flipcharts and easels
Advanced Preparation:	• View the Introductory Video and Video Segment 3:1 • Review the Facilitator Directions • Locate a space to do "the line" • Place number signs on the wall from 0 to 100 (increments of 10)

Facilitator Note: *This activity can take longer than 60 minutes, or it can be shortened, depending on the flow of your session and how much time you have available. Areas of facilitator discretion include how much time you allow for small-group sharing and how many voices you invite to share as you process the line. Watch your time to make sure you allow for the school/ district application and for the small-group debrief. The central point of We, the People is to demonstrate that the issues of equity and diversity that schools and other organizations are dealing with in the 21st century are directly connected to the arrangements of dominance that were established over two centuries ago in the founding of the nation. It is particularly important for your Facilitation Team to view the Video Segment and discuss the Facilitator Directions before implementing We, the People with your faculty* *and staff. This is a rather complex activity to facilitate, but the video prompts and directions will guide you step-by-step through the process. It is also essential to create time for reflection after the activity, so your participants will be able to make meaning from their experience.*

1. Set the Stage   8 Minutes

View together with your faculty the Phase Three Introductory Video. This clip includes many educator comments that will help make the case for dealing with issues of social dominance and social justice in school settings.

Have three flipcharts set up side-by-side in the room, with the heading "1787" on the left-hand chart, "We, the People" on the middle chart, and "Ideals" on the right-hand chart. Distribute copies of Handouts SJ-1 and SJ-2, and announce to your faculty and staff that you are now going to introduce Phase Three of the work. By looking at the roots of our country's system of government, you will be exploring what was happening around issues of inclusion and equity when the country was very young.

2. View Video Segment 3:1   3 Minutes

In the first section of the video, Gary Howard sets up the activity by asking the question: Who were "We the People" in 1787? In other words, who were the people who had full rights of participation under the Constitution of the new nation? He will list "white, male, property owners" on his video flipchart. One of your Facilitators will write these same words under "1787" on the left-hand chart in your workshop room.

Gary will then ask participants to think about the other groups of people who were living in the country at that time but were not included in the full rights of citizenship. You will be prompted to **stop the video** and allow time for your group to ponder that question.

3. Large-Group Brainstorming: Who Else Was Here?   3 Minutes

One of your Facilitators will elicit answers from the audience and another will record the names of groups on the middle chart under the heading, "We, the People." After each group is mentioned and listed, repeat the question: "Who else was here?" When considering this question, you will ask people to think of the whole land base that was to become the United States as we know it today, not just the original 13 states.

4. Restart the Video:
The Founding Ideals   4 Minutes

Gary reviews his list of the groups that were excluded from full participation, acknowledging that these people represent the vast majority of folks living here at the time. He also points out that there were conversations and consciousness about including women, about the status of African Americans, and some of the structures of the new American democracy were based on the governing arrangements of Native tribes. However, none of these groups were allowed to participate in the new nation. He writes the word "Exclusion" on the 1787 chart, and you can do the same on yours.

Gary then transitions to a consideration of the ideals that were written down in the founding documents: the Constitution, the Bill of Rights, and the Declaration of Independence. He will prompt you to **stop the video** and allow time for your group to brainstorm a list of these founding ideals.

5. Listing the Founding Ideals   3 Minutes

One of your Facilitators will lead the brainstorming session, while another records the group's responses under the heading "Ideals" on the right-hand chart.

6. Restart the Video: Setting Up "the Line"   6 Minutes

Gary goes over his list of the founding ideals and writes the word "Inclusion" on this chart. He describes the tension that was created in the founding of the nation, a tension between these inclusive ideals, on one hand, and the narrowly exclusive reality of who was actually allowed to participate fully in those ideals. This is the "American Dilemma" discussed by Gunnar Myrdal (1944) in his classic study of American democracy.

Gary then asks the groups to consider how far we have come in actually living the ideals that were laid down in the founding documents. He gives some personal think time for everyone to choose a number, from 0 to 100, to reflect their perception of how far we have come as a nation. It is not an issue of whether we *believe* in these ideals; it is a question of how far we have come in actually *living* them. After the personal think time, he invites everyone to move to the number line that has been posted in the room and stand under the number that corresponds to their perspective on the question. He prompts you to **stop the video** and encourage people to move to the line.

Facilitator Note: *Some people may want more clarification of the question before they feel able or willing to select a number. Other folks may want to overthink the question, bringing in complexities that have not been mentioned in the video. Don't spend much time on this kind of discussion. Gently move people through their decision-making process, reminding them that we are only asking for a gut-level response, not a scientifically validated analysis.*

7. Processing the Line   20 Minutes

You will be doing this part of the activity on your own. Here are the key steps and some sample language to guide your facilitation of the line:

Allow a few moments for the line to settle in. Go to either end and determine the highest and lowest number.

Say to the group, "We have a spread from 20 to 85 (or however your line comes out) so we have many different perceptions here. Now I would like you to form small groups of three to five people with folks who are standing right near you. Compare notes with these people and talk about why you are standing where you are."

While they are sharing in their small groups, one of the Facilitators should pick out several small groups at different locations along the line and ask them to pick a spokesperson and be ready to share three reasons why they are standing where they are. Select one group from the 80s, one from the 70s, one from the 60s, and so on, so you have groups representing the highest and lowest numbers and everywhere in between.

Bring the group's attention back, and say, "Now let's hear from several different voices along the line. Remember that this is going to be an actual living experience of multiple perspectives. We're going to be hearing from different witnesses along this line, each having their own set of reasons for standing where they did. There are no right or wrong answers, only different perspectives on the truth. So we're not trying to prove anything here, or compete for the best answer. Just listen and try to understand how and why each person has chosen to stand where they are. There will be no applause or booing, just listening to the different perspectives."

Start with the highest end and move by 10-point increments to the lowest end. Have spokespersons step out in front of the line so they can be seen and heard, and share three reasons their group stood where they did. Keep these comments brief, and don't allow for other feedback or discussion. Just let each group share and then invite the next.

Reinforce the honoring of multiple perspectives.

8. Invite the Guest Sociologist   3 Minutes

(**Note:** If time is short, you can skip this step.)

After you have heard from the witnesses along the line, ask someone who has not spoken to step out in front of the group. Say to this person, "You are our visiting sociologist, and I want you to look at the whole line and see if you see any trends in how we have arranged ourselves in terms of age, gender, race, ethnicity, job title, or other factors." Allow a couple of minutes for this person to share his or her observations, and thank the sociologist. Depending on time, you can ask for any other comments at this point. Do people see any other trends in terms of how we arranged ourselves on the line?

9. The School or School District Line   3 Minutes

You might switch lead Facilitators at this point to demonstrate the transition to a new question. Here are the Facilitator comments for this part of the activity:

"Before we return to our seats, let's look at a different question."

"Instead of thinking about the country, the Constitution, and our democratic ideals, think about your school/district and its stated ideals or goals related to inclusion, equity, diversity, and excellence."

"How far has our school/district come in actually living our ideals related to equity, inclusion, and excellence?"

"Move to that place now and let's see what happens."

Allow people to settle into their new positions. Once they have established the new line, ask the group to look around and see what they notice. How many people moved up and how many moved down? How does this line compare to the one they created for the country?

For the sake of time, you probably won't be able to go through the same sequence of small groups and selected feedback along the line. That is not a problem, because they will be sharing this information during their debrief conversation.

Thank people for their work here in looking at how far we have come both as a nation and as a school/district in attempting to create more inclusive and equitable realities. Remind them that all of the perspectives on this line are part of the larger truth. No single perspective has the whole story. In a sense, the entire extent of the line is "the truth." Even though we have many different perceptions, we all agreed that we have come a ways (if no one stood at "0") and that we still have a ways to go (if no one stood at "100").

Ask the group to remember this school-related line and return to their seats for a debrief discussion of the activity.

10. Debrief Conversation   10 Minutes

Bring everyone's attention to Handout SJ-2, and ask them to begin their small-group conversations. All participants will share where they stood for each of the lines and give a brief explanation of why they stood there. Participants will also be asked to consider what lessons emerge from this activity, related to both the country and to their school. Ask them to focus primarily on the school-based questions, particularly if they did not have time to process those while standing on the line. During the final 2 minutes of the small-group conversation, Facilitators should circulate around the room and assign each of the reflective questions to a different small group. Ask them to select a spokesperson and be ready to respond to their assigned question. If you have a time, you can ask all small groups to be ready to share.

11. Large-Group Share-Out   5 Minutes

Invite each of your assigned groups to share their responses to the reflective questions. If time allows, invite other responses as well.

12. Restart the Video: Summary and Closing Comments   5 Minutes

Gary brings the focus back to issues of inclusion and exclusion, and connects the We, the People activity to the educational disparities that we see in our schools related to race, social class, and other dimensions of difference. The data of inequities in our schools are our history as a nation staring us in the face. The system of social dominance and privilege that was established by the founding fathers, and perpetuated over the centuries, is still living with us in our classrooms. Although it is a harsh reality to acknowledge, the success of wealthy white men in our country, and the marginalization of other groups, is intimately connected to the racism, sexism, genocide, and land theft that were integral to the founding of the nation. Gary will discuss the importance of engaging Phase Three of the work. If we are to overcome and eliminate the inequities we see in our schools, then we must understand the sources of those disparities and courageously challenge the arrangements of dominance that are still embedded in our society and in the culture of schooling. Some of the courageous questions would include the following:

What are we as adults doing in our school to reinforce an equitable and inclusive environment?

What specific behaviors and practices are in place to reinforce equity, and what specific identity groups are benefiting from our efforts at inclusion? Which aren't?

What are the barriers that we as adults are creating, things that get in the way of a welcoming and equitable environment?

What specific behaviors and practices, related to what specific identity groups, may be getting in the way of full equity and inclusion?

What is the unfinished work in our school?

In what ways do we see systems of social dominance and privilege still functioning in our school and in our community?

Phase Three of the work invites us into a consideration of these and other questions related to educational disparities, and into a conversation about what it will take to bring our schools into closer alignment with our ideals.

We, the People

1787 _____   IDEALS _____

0   10   20   30   40   50   60   70   80   90   100

SJ-2

Discussion Questions for We, the People

We, the People Reflective Conversation

Each person takes 2 minutes to share:

1. Where you stood on the line for the United States and for your school/district.

2. Some of the reasons you stood where you did.

Small-Group Reflection:

3. What did we learn from this activity and discussion?

4. What are the implications for the work that needs to be done in our schools going forward?

Large-Group Sharing:

Choose a spokesperson to share one of your ideas or insights from the reflective questions above.

Activity: The Guessing Game	
Phase Three: From Social Dominance to Social Justice	
(Developed by Laura Branca and Kirby Edmonds of TFC Associates. Adapted by them from an activity designed by Peer Educators in Human Relations at Cornell University. Used here with their permission.)	
Purpose:	• Provide a simulated experience of inclusion and exclusion • Examine school culture and outcomes through the lens of privilege, power, and social dominance • Illustrate the behaviors that are created by systems of privilege and preference that favor some groups over others • Acknowledge the deeper dynamics of privilege and power that have created and perpetuated educational inequities • Initiate a conversation about the ways that educators can interrupt the dynamics of exclusion and dominance in their classrooms and schools
Suggested Time:	60–70 minutes
Materials Needed:	Video Segment 3:2 Handouts SJ-3 to SJ-6: Round 1 Guessing Game Clue Sheets Handouts SJ-7 to SJ-10: Round 2 Guessing Game Clue Sheets Handout SJ-11: Guessing Game Answer Sheet Flipchart and easel (multiple sets for larger audiences)
Advanced Preparation:	• View Video Segment 3:2 together with your Facilitation Team • Carefully review the Facilitator Directions • Create your method for getting people into small groups • Think about whether there are individuals who should not be in the least privileged group (Group 4) or should be in the most privileged group (Group 1) • Organize the clue sheets for efficient distribution • Create your scoring sheet out of the view of the participants

Facilitator Note: *This activity creates a simulation in which participants experience how systems of privilege, power, and exclusion operate and affect both individuals and groups, as well as contribute to school inequities. The Guessing Game is a powerful and engaging way to introduce the Definition and Dynamics of Social Dominance, which are the core conceptual framework for Phase Three of the work. The game uses "information" as its primary resource, to which participants have different access. What begins as a fun problem-solving game later leads to a deep conversation about the ways that privilege, power, and varying degrees of inclusion and exclusion operate in school settings.*

You will be facilitating the Guessing Game on your own. In Video Segment 3:2, Gary walks you through the steps in the process. This beginning section of the video is intended for your Facilitation Team only, not for use with your faculty. The Guessing Game is fairly complex to implement but also a lot of fun for your Facilitation Team and the participants, while at the same time making some important and powerful points about the dynamics that create and sustain educational inequities.

Be sure to structure in enough time for the reflective conversation after the game. It is essential that people have an opportunity to make meaning from their experience, to make the necessary connections to your work for inclusion, equity, and excellence. In the final section of Video Segment 3:2, Gary reviews some of the key intended learnings from the Guessing Game. You and your Facilitators can make these points on your own as part of the reflective conversation, or you can play that section of the video for your faculty as a summary of the activity.

1. Set Up the Game   5 Minutes

Have people organized into small groups of five to eight each. Briefly explain how the game will be played. Do not say that there will be points for correct answers. Sample explanation to participants:

> We're going to play a problem-solving game that is simple and fun. We will play two rounds of the game, and each round takes 3 minutes. You will be working together in your small groups. You will be given a sheet of paper with clues for objects. There are four objects with three to five clues for each object. Work together with your team, and when you think you have a correct answer, raise your hand and one of the Facilitators will come to check it and let you know if you are correct.

Facilitator Note: *What the participants are not told is that the clues are different for each group, with varying degrees of difficulty. They are also not told that the Facilitators will play a role, selectively rewarding the groups, enforcing uneven access, and scolding the "limited access" groups for not trying hard enough. All of the Facilitators can be involved in demonstrating different aspects of exclusionary and inclusionary behavior. They should also be circulating and noticing dynamics within the groups to point out during the processing of the activity. Establish the hierarchy of access, inclusion, and privilege by:*

- *Placement of groups nearer to or farther from the Facilitators. The nearest will be the most privileged (Group 1).*
- *Order in which the groups receive their clues (Group 1 always first, Group 4 always last).*
- *Amount of attention Facilitators pay to different groups. Make it harder for the most excluded group to get attention, and so on.*
- *Trainer's tone or attitudes toward each group in terms of praise, encouragement, judgment, support, friendliness, disappointment, scorn, disgust, and so forth.*
- *Unequal clues given to groups, with Group 1 getting the easiest and Group 4 the most difficult.*
- *Number of points awarded to each group. Bonus points can be awarded to the most privileged group for speed, finishing first, and good behavior, and points can arbitrarily be subtracted from other groups for whimsical reasons, like "bad attitude."*

It is very important throughout this activity to maintain a tone of lightness and levity. When the instructions suggest admonishing Group 4, this is done in a lighthearted way, not in a mean-spirited way.

2. Play Round 1 of the Game   5 Minutes

Give each group one copy of the Clue Sheet for their group. There are four objects to be identified for each round. The clues are different for each group, so it is important not to mix them up. Group 1 is your most privileged group, and their clues are the easiest to solve. Group 4 is your least privileged group, and their clues are the most difficult.

A Note on the Clue Sheets: It is important that your participants do not know they are getting different clues in their small groups. When you pass out the clues to the groups, be careful not to show them the Clue Sheets for other groups. It is helpful to copy all of the Round 1 clues on one color of paper and all of the Round 2 clues on a different color, so they all look alike for each round. The following list will help you keep track of the clues:

Round 1 Clues	*Round 2 Clues*
Group 1 gets Handout SJ-3	Group 1 gets Handout SJ-7
Group 2 gets Handout SJ-4	Group 2 gets Handout SJ-8
Group 3 gets Handout SJ-5	Group 3 gets Handout SJ-9
Group 4 gets Handout SJ-6	Group 4 gets Handout SJ-10

For smaller faculties, you can play the game with just four groups. For larger faculties, you will have more than one small group getting the different sets of clues. For example, with a faculty of 96 people, you would divide into 12 groups of 8 people each. For these larger faculties, it works best to have fewer small groups getting the Group 1 and 4 clues, and more small groups getting the Group 3 and 4 clues. With 12 small groups, for example, 2 small groups would get the Group 1 clues, 4 would get the Group 2 clues, 4 would get the Group 3 clues, and 2 would get the Group 4 clues.

Facilitator Note: *Announce the beginning of the round to the whole group as you hand the most privileged group their clues. Tell them that the clock is now running on the 3 minutes they will have to solve the four items. Appear to be handing out the clues in an arbitrary way, but be sure to give the Group 4 clues out last and several seconds after the clock has started. Immediately after the clues are handed out to all the groups, go directly to Group 1 and give them some encouragement and support.*

- The Facilitator should encourage Group 1 to enjoy the game and do well.
- As the Facilitator is spending time with Group 1 explaining the game, members of the other groups will try to get the Facilitator's attention to get instructions.

- When responding to the other groups, particularly Group 4, act slightly annoyed and bothered. Tell them you will get to their questions eventually. The different groups should be treated with varying degrees of hostility and annoyance, with Group 4 eliciting the harshest response and the lowest priority for assistance. The Facilitator must do a good acting job so the participants believe that they are doing something wrong to cause the Facilitator's reaction.

Sample interaction with Group 4:

Facilitator:	Did you figure it out?
Participant:	No.
Facilitator:	Well, don't call on me until you have an answer.
Participant:	But I don't understand what I'm supposed to be doing.
Facilitator:	Well, they (point to the most privileged group) are doing just fine. Maybe you need to work a little harder and stop expecting me to explain everything to you.

With the middle groups, you might say, "Well, you just need to concentrate a little more. Keep trying." The goal is to make them think that they can succeed if they work hard enough.

The point is for the Facilitator to act as if all groups have an equal chance of getting the right answers and to convince them that they must be doing something wrong when they can't. This should be done so that the whole group can observe how the different groups are being treated, but not so obviously that the game seems rigged or people decide to stop playing.

You want to orchestrate the game so that Group 1 comes up with all the answers (even if it means giving them hints) and Group 4 comes up with the least (even if it means misdirecting them).

Group 1 will be finished ahead of time and will have time to socialize. You should use this to make an example of them. ("Look at how well you're doing. Didn't I tell you this would be fun? You can just sit and relax—the other groups are a bit slower.")

A goal is to keep the middle groups and Group 4 wondering what's going on. Act as if you are really trying to get to all the groups but are unable to because of time. You should spend the least amount of time with Group 4. Be accessible to the middle groups, but not overly encouraging. In addition, treat the two middle groups slightly differently (Group 2 more favorably than Group 3 so that a hierarchy is established between these groups as well). Make frequent trips back to the most privileged group to encourage their work and praise their accomplishment, even when they have clearly already got all the answers.

Dynamics to expect during the first round:

- Participants are usually focused on the task and don't consciously pick up on the dynamics in Round 1. Often it happens so fast that the participants are left with feelings for which they cannot quite pinpoint the source.
- Group 1 is unlikely to pay much attention to how others are being treated.
- The middle groups are more likely to be task oriented.
- Group 4 may become loud and protest their treatment (sometimes this doesn't happen until the second round). If this happens, you should ignore them or tell them to get themselves together and focus on coming up with answers.
- Remember to keep time and call out the times as you go (i.e., "Two minutes left"). This adds to the frustration and self-doubt about ability and intelligence of the less privileged groups.

Before the round is over, Facilitators should check in with each group to see how many correct answers they have, so you can quickly transition to the point scoring. It helps if Facilitators have memorized the answers for each round or carry with them a copy of the Answer Sheet (Handout SJ-11). If you have the Answer Sheet with you, make sure the participants don't see it.

At exactly 3 minutes, call time.

3. Record the Scores for Round 1   5 Minutes

Prepare a flipchart ahead of time. If you have only four small groups, your scoring chart will look like the one below. If you have more than four groups, use additional flipcharts to record the scores.

	Group 1	Group 2	Group 3	Group 4
Round 1 Points				
Bonus Points				
Subtotal				
Round 2 Points				
Bonus Points				
Subtotal				
Grand Total				

Tell the groups that you have come to the end of Round 1 and it's time to score the round. Announce that each correct answer will be awarded 20 points.

Facilitator Note: *Start with the most privileged group and "arbitrarily" put their score under Group 1. Record scores in such a way that the least privileged group becomes Group 4. For larger faculties, you will have more small groups, so list their scores in order of their preferred status, manipulating the bonus points to make sure the more privileged groups come out with more total points, in descending order from the most privileged group to least.*

- Although the participants have not been told previously that points are to be given, they accept it when the Facilitator assigns points after Round 1. This is an important dynamic to point out during processing of the game.
- While assigning points, give verbal messages (modeled on examples below) to each group, reinforcing their status.
- Examples of messages from the trainer to the different groups might include the following:

  o Group 1—Reinforce their natural intelligence, their likability; reward them for their success and for not causing problems.
  o Groups 2 and 3—Reassure them that they can succeed if they try harder; suggest they are not working hard enough and tell them you expect better of them.

○ Group 4—Show disappointment and/or impatience, implying that they lack intelligence or are not making a real effort, or in some way are not good enough. Blame them for their failure, especially if they have been acting out at all. Suggest they improve their attitude for the next round.

- To ensure the "correct" hierarchy of points, you may need to assign bonus points (e.g., a speed bonus or team work bonus of 20 points) or point penalties (e.g., minus 5 points for being too loud or distracting others, or bad attitude). At this point, participants may express anger since this is something that was not previously stated. It is important for the primary Facilitator to establish control and move into the next round. Encourage all other groups to work for the time bonus or avoid point penalties in the second round.

4. Play Round 2 of the Game   5 Minutes

- Hand out the clues for Round 2.
- Use the same procedure as for Round 1, starting the round when Group 1 has their clues and giving Group 4 their clues last after the clock has started running.
- By now, everyone should be getting clear about the rules of the game. You should use this to set up the expectation that everyone should do better and admonish them if they don't.
- Continue to use Group 1 as an example of model performance. Display an attitude that, although you don't need to worry about Group 1, you prefer to spend time with them. Immediately go over to them and establish a friendly rapport so that they unwittingly become co-enforcers of the hierarchy by enjoying the game and feeling superior.
- At the same time, because the other groups are trying to succeed, they will quickly try to get your attention. In this round, you will need to spend more time with Groups 2 to 4 setting up and reinforcing certain roles. Group 2 should be treated as they were in the first round (cordial but task focused) to set up the dynamic that they have a hope that they can be as good as Group 1. The dynamic you want to now set up with Group 3 is to get them to stay in the game and feel glad that they are not Group 4, whom you ignore or admonish.

- As Facilitators, you will need to raise your "attitude" level a notch or two. Group 4 will realize that they are in a no-win situation and will exhibit certain behaviors. They may get loud and boisterous and protest or stop participating because they feel hopeless.
- Remember to eagerly check in with Group 1 whenever you have a moment.
- Again, you want to create a sense of time pressure, especially with Groups 3 and 4.
- Before the round is over, check in with each group to see how many correct answers they have so you can quickly transition to the point scoring.
- At exactly 3 minutes, call time.

5. Record Round 2 and Grand Total Scores   5 Minutes

- Again, record the groups' scores, with each correct answer being awarded 20 points.
- Assign bonus and penalty points to reinforce the arbitrary nature of the reward system and keep the hierarchy of success in place.
- Reward a time bonus or good teamwork bonus to Group 1.
- For this round, you can add a bonus for good behavior to Group 2.
- Enthusiastically engage the whole group in congratulating the winners (Groups 1 and 2).
- Praise Group 3 for staying with the game and trying harder. Even though their score is nowhere near the upper two groups, you want to distract their attention from this and make them feel glad that they are not Group 4.
- Group 4 should be admonished in a way that blames them for their failure. You should act as if they had an equal chance to succeed and pretend that you are baffled as to why they couldn't get the answers. This will be a challenge for the Facilitator because the members of this group have essentially "checked out" of the game and will not be paying attention or will be challenging you. You will need to stay in role and keep the game dynamics running.
- Note the body language of the groups at this point—it will reflect their relative privilege—and use this in the processing of the whole exercise.

6. Process the Activity in an Interactive Group Discussion   10 Minutes

Facilitator Note: *In some ways, this is the most challenging part of this activity because the Facilitator who managed the game needs to stay in role and act surprised at people's different reactions to the game.*

- Ask things like:

    o How did you like the game?
    o How did your group feel playing the game? Ask each group to respond to this question.
    o How did your group feel about the Facilitator(s)?
    o What did you think of the other groups?
    o **What do you think accounts for why the groups did so differently?** This is the key question you want to spend some time processing. You might say something like: "You would think that intelligence would be distributed equally among all of the groups. How do you explain the fact that some groups did so well and others so poorly?" Let the group process this question, coming up with different hypotheses for the discrepant outcomes. Some will blame the Facilitators; some will think the answers were different for different groups or that the clues were rigged. If someone wants to read out the clues from the different groups, don't spill the beans right away. Just say, "We'll take a look at that in a minute. What other reasons do you think account for the differences in scores?"

- At some point, someone will want to know the correct answers.
- Invite Group 1 to read their answers.
- Following this, one of the groups will want to see the clues. If they have asked for this earlier, and you have put them off, now is the time to share the clues.
- Invite Group 1 to read their clues for one of the items, and then have Group 4 read their clues for that same item.
- This effectively ends the role-play for the Facilitators. The truth is out and other groups will want to read out their clues, and, of course, Group 4 will want to read more of their clues to show how difficult they were. Group 4 clues for Item 1 in Round 1 and Item 3 in Round 2 are especially fun to share.
- You can also ask Groups 2 and 3 to read some of their clues, to show the increasing levels of difficulty.
- Share the correct answers for all of the items.

7. Large-Group Reflective Conversation   15 Minutes

At this point, announce that the Facilitators are dropping the roles they have been playing and are now moving on to support the group in processing what just happened.

Possible Reflective Questions:

- Were you aware of the nature of the lead Facilitator's role and the difference in how groups were being treated?
- How did this affect your experience of the game?
- What does this remind you of? How does this game reflect the larger society? Who are these different groups in our society?
- Go to Group 1 and ask them how they feel now that they know the game was rigged in their favor.
- **The key question for this Reflective Conversation is: "How is this game like school?** Pause the large-group conversation for a few minutes and ask each small group to talk about that question: "How does this game remind you of the things that happen in our school?"
- After a few minutes of small-group conversation, bring the large group back together and ask each small group to share one of the ways that this game is like school.
- Ask participants to think about the impact of these dynamics in schools.
- Who are the students in each of these groups in our school? If you have time, you can ask each group to talk about who is in their group in your school. Who are the Group 1 kids? Who is in Group 4? etc.

8. Additional Questions if You Have Time   10 Minutes

- Do any of the behaviors exhibited in the game parallel how students and teachers act in your schools?
- What might be "clues" in school and in real life? Clues are the things a person needs to be successful in school.
- What are the "points"? Points are the rewards that come if you are successful.
- What are the "bonuses"? Bonuses are the perks that come from being in a privileged group.
- Different groups have different reactions to the Facilitator. Why? Relate responses to real-life experience in which different groups

of students have different reactions to authority figures in the school.

- If you suspected that the clues were unequal, what kept you from sharing your clues with other groups?

9. Summary and Closing Comments   5 Minutes

Your Facilitation Team can make these points, or you can play the last section of Video Segment 3:2 (beginning at 6 minutes 50 seconds into the video) and have Gary do the summary.

- Point out how quickly people acted out roles in the game that are present in society and in schools. We all know how to play these roles.
- People often get rewarded or punished and perceived in a certain way for certain behaviors that can be predicted based on how they are treated.
- This was just a game. Think about students who actually live it. In real life, they cannot just walk out of the game.
- What must it be like to experience 13 years of schooling as a member of Group 4?
- What are the different coping mechanisms these students develop to deal with the feelings of exclusion and lack of privilege?
- To what extent are racial disparities in discipline referrals related to Group 4 status?
- Issues of differential access to power and privilege are real and impact us and our students as individuals and as groups.
- This game points out the underlying dynamics that produce and maintain educational inequities. If we are going to eliminate racial and economic barriers to student success, we must interrupt centuries of oppression and social dominance that have predetermined that certain groups would have privileged access to success, and other groups would be systematically denied that access.
- Eliminating educational disparities regarding achievement, discipline referrals and suspensions, access to higher level courses, graduation rates, and access to college will require much more than we are presently doing in our school reform efforts.
- Achieving educational equity will require deep structural changes, not only in the educational arena but in the very fabric of our society.

- As we saw in the We, the People activity, systems of privilege and preference based on race, gender, and economic status were institutionalized in the very founding of our nation. Those systems are still functioning in our schools and society.
- Our history of oppression and exclusion is staring us in the face every day in our classrooms.

Next Steps

As soon as possible after completing the Guessing Game, introduce your faculty to the Definition and Dynamics of Social Dominance (Video Segment 3:3), which comes in the next section of your manual. These concepts will help give focus and meaning to the Guessing Game experience. After you have introduced those concepts, you can move to the Privilege and Power Conversation, which will help your faculty examine the ways that systems of privilege and preference are operating in your school.

The Guessing Game

Round 1 Clues

Item 1: Has filament
Pear or globe shaped
Uses electricity
Glass and metal

Item 2: Rectangular object
Handheld
Made of plastic
Has push buttons

Item 3: Used to tell time
Article of apparel
Can be wound up
Some can survive under water

Item 4: Uses mercury
Measures body heat
Made of glass
Found in medicine cabinets

Guessing Game Clues

The Guessing Game

Round 1 Clues

Item 1: Uses electricity

Made of glass

Can be clear or opaque

Can vary in intensity

Item 2: Electronic

Requires dexterity

Battery operated

Item 3: Comes in different sizes and shapes

Can be for men, women, or children

Worn or carried

Item 4: Has numbers

Found inside or outside

Can measure in three ways

The Guessing Game

Round 1 Clues

Item 1: Glows in the dark
Attracts insects
Can help show the way

Item 2: Arouses competitiveness
Often handled by men in household
Can change things

Item 3: Comes in different shapes and sizes
For men, women, or children
Worn or carried

Item 4: May be electronic
Not always easy to read
Can measure in three ways

Guessing Game Clues

The Guessing Game

Round 1 Clues

Item 1:   Pear shape

Prevalent in Las Vegas and Reno

Looks good with shades

Item 2:   Arouses competitiveness

Source of domestic disputes

Often handled by men in a household

Item 3:   Comes in different shapes and sizes

Some can survive under water

Can be slow moving

Item 4:   Contains a dangerous element

May be electronic

Can be found outside

SJ-7

Guessing Game Clues

The Guessing Game

Round 2 Clues

Item 1: Used for cutting

Used in sewing

Has moving parts

Swivels

Item 2: Has a key pad

Uses a password

Dispenses cash

Found in many places

Item 3: Uses alcohol

Comes in glass or plastic containers

Can be sprayed on

Found attractive by some

Item 4: Made of glass or plastic

Needs to be sterilized for use

Has a nipple

Has interchangeable parts

Guessing Game Clues

The Guessing Game

Round 2 Clues

Item 1:   Double-edged

Has holes

Made for right-handers

Item 2:   Uses a key pad

Some are bilingual

Found in many places

Addresses you by name

Item 3:   Can be detected from a distance

Comes in glass or plastic containers

Source of allergies

Requires the right chemistry

Item 4:   Uses a special formula

Source of health and comfort

Made of plastic or glass

Needs to be sterilized for use

Guessing Game Clues

The Guessing Game

Round 2 Clues

Item 1: Hard, cold, dangerous
Sharp and steely
Severs ties

Item 2: Works for a bank
Some are bilingual
Offers many choices

Item 3: Whale by-product
Requires chemistry
Uses alcohol
Can be detected from a distance

Item 4: Has interchangeable parts
Contains liquids
Source of great comfort
Generates gas

Guessing Game Clues

The Guessing Game

Round 2 Clues

Item 1:   Can be pointed, blunt, and cutting
Steely
Hard, cold, dangerous
Severs ties

Item 2:   Uses paper or plastic
Offers many choices
Convenient

Item 3:   Uses alcohol
Can be detected from a distance
Smells and is hard to ignore

Item 4:   Generates gas
Source of great comfort
Has interchangeable parts

Guessing Game Answer Sheet

The Guessing Game

Answer Key

Round 1:

1. Light bulb

2. Remote control

3. Wristwatch

4. Thermometer

Round 2:

1. Scissors

2. ATM machine

3. Perfume

4. Baby bottle

Activity: Definition and Dynamics of Social Dominance	
Phase Three: From Social Dominance to Social Justice	
Purpose:	• Provide a conceptual framework for understanding issues of Social Dominance • Relate the Guessing Game experience and the We, the People activity to the Definition and Dynamics of Social Dominance • Create a systemic foundation for understanding and working with educational inequities
Suggested Time:	15 minutes
Materials Needed:	Video Segment 3:3 Handout SJ-12: Definition of Social Dominance Handout SJ-13: Dynamics of Social Dominance
Advanced Preparation:	• View Video Segment 3:3 • Read the Facilitator Directions

Facilitator Note: *This is a talk piece, with Gary Howard providing the conceptual framework for understanding both the We, the People activity and the Guessing Game experience. It works best to use this Video Segment along with, or soon after, playing the Guessing Game. If your faculty had any difficulty understanding the purpose of that activity, this video will help bridge the gap. If members of your faculty have read Gary's book,* **We Can't Teach What We Don't Know,** *they can refer to Chapter 3 for further discussion of the ideas presented in this video clip.*

This is a relatively short piece, so it could be combined in a single session with Video Segment 3:4, which provides the Definition and Dynamics of Social Justice and gives a multidimensional overview of the work leading from Social Dominance to Social Justice.

1. Set the Tone   2 Minutes

Distribute copies of Handouts SJ-12 and SJ-13. Inform your faculty that this Video Segment will provide them with a conceptual framework for understanding why we did the Guessing Game activity.

2. Play Video Segment 3:3   9 Minutes

Gary presents the Definition of Social Dominance: "systems of privilege and preference, reinforced by power, favoring certain groups over others." He connects this definition to the Guessing Game, which simulated just such a system. He also draws a direct parallel to the We, the People activity, which highlights the systems of privilege and preference based on race, gender, and social class that were built into the founding of the nation.

Next Gary describes the three Dynamics of Social Dominance: the Assumption of Rightness, the Luxury of Ignorance, and the Legacy of Privilege. These dynamics are the personal, professional, and institutional processes whereby Social Dominance plays itself out in our relationships, our classrooms, and the broader society. Gary provides stories and examples to make the Definition and Dynamics real for your faculty, and he continues to bring their attention back to the lessons of We, the People and the Guessing Game.

3. Pair-and-Share Conversations   3 Minutes

You will be prompted to **stop the video** and invite your faculty to form dyads and discuss their thoughts and responses related to the Definition and Dynamics of Social Dominance. The focus questions are as follows:

- How do you respond to the Definition of Social Dominance?
- Have you experienced such a system of privilege and preference?
- What do you think about the Dynamics of Social Dominance?
- Do you see the Assumption of Rightness, the Luxury of Ignorance, or the Legacy of Privilege operating in your school or community?

4. Close the Session   1 Minute

Thank the group for their engagement in this discussion, and remind them that you will continue to work with this information as you go further into Phase 3. In your upcoming sessions, you will be looking more deeply and specifically at how these dynamics are operating in our own school.

If you are combining this session with the next Video Segment, make that transition at this time.

Social Dominance Definition

SJ-12

▶ **Social Dominance:**

 ▶ *Systems of Privilege and Preference*

 ▶ *Reinforced by Power*

 ▶ *Favoring Certain Groups Over Others*

The Dynamics of Dominance

▶ **The Dynamics of Dominance:**

▶ *The Assumption of Rightness*

▶ *The Luxury of Ignorance*

▶ *The Legacy of Privilege*

Activity: From Social Dominance to Social Justice	
Phase Three: From Social Dominance to Social Justice	
Purpose:	• Provide a conceptual framework for understanding Social Justice • Acknowledge that issues of Dominance and Justice play out across multiple dimensions of diversity • Present a multidimensional model for guiding the work from Social Dominance to Social Justice • Place school reform in the context of a movement away from Social Dominance and toward Social Justice
Suggested Time:	25 minutes
Materials Needed:	Video Segment 3:4 Handout SJ-14: Definition of Social Justice Handout SJ-15: Dynamics of Social Justice Handout SJ-16: From Social Dominance to Social Justice Handout SJ-17: Qualities of a Social Justice Ally
Advanced Preparation:	• View Video Segment 3:4 • Read the Facilitator Directions

Facilitator Note: *Here Gary provides the Definition and Dynamics of Social Justice, which closely parallel those presented for Social Dominance in the previous Video Segment. This piece can be used in conjunction with, or shortly following, your discussion of Social Dominance. Video Segment 3:4 has two central purposes: (1) to create an inclusive discussion of dominance that incorporates multiple dimensions of difference and (2) to conceptualize the broader purpose of education as a movement away from Social Dominance and toward Social Justice. Taken together, Video Segments 3:3 and 3:4 provide the foundation for helping your faculty view the work of school reform and school improvement in the larger context of deconstructing and disrupting a deep history of dominance and oppression.*

1. Set the Tone   2 Minutes

Distribute copies of four Handouts, SJ-14 to SJ-17. Inform your faculty that this Video Segment will provide them with a conceptual framework for understanding the movement from Social Dominance to Social Justice.

2. Play Video Segment 3:4   9 Minutes

Gary presents the Definition of Social Justice: "systems of equity and fairness, reinforced by respect and shared power, favoring the inclusion and well-being of all groups." He also describes the Dynamics of Social Justice, which are the ways that justice shows up in our personal and organizational lives: the Assumption of Multiple Truths, the Luxury of Being Heard and Understood, and the Legacy of Our Shared Human Destiny. This conceptual framework provides a stark contrast to the Definition and Dynamics of Social Dominance presented in the previous segment.

After introducing the Definition and Dynamics of Social Justice, Gary describes a set of personal attitudes and behaviors that characterize people who are committed to the work of social justice (Handout SJ-17). These qualities of a Social Justice Ally include the following:

- The good of the many over the greed of the few
- Multiple perspectives over single-dimensional truth
- Humility rather than hubris
- The alchemy of privilege
- The personal and political will to resist oppression

At this point, you will be prompted to **stop the video** and allow people some time in dyads to reflect on this discussion of social justice.

3. Pair-and-Share Conversations   3 Minutes

Video prompts will guide your faculty to share their thoughts and responses related to the Definition and Dynamics of Social Justice, and the set of attitudes and behaviors Gary has presented. Each person is asked to respond to at least one of the following questions:

- Is this how you would define Social Justice? What would you add/ change?
- How do you see the Dynamics of Social Justice operating in your school?
- Which of the qualities of a Social Justice Ally is consistent with your thinking about Social Justice? Which is problematic for you?

4. Restart the Video: From Social Dominance to Social Justice   5 Minutes

Here Gary describes a model for understanding our larger work of school reform as a process of movement away from systems based on

Social Dominance and toward a different set of social arrangements based on Social Justice (Handout SJ-16). This model is presented from the perspective of the multiple lenses of difference that were described in Phase Two. From this perspective, the work of social justice and school change should not be carried out only in relation to single dimensions of difference, like race *or* class *or* gender. Rather, our work must be understood and implemented in the complex interaction of all the intersecting differences that our students bring to school, including race, gender, class, language, religion, sexual orientation, special needs, learning style, personality, home culture, immigration status, and many others.

5. Reflective Conversation in Small Groups of Three   5 Minutes

You will be prompted to **stop the video** again, and allow for some reflective conversation in small groups. Focus questions for this short conversation are as follows:

- Which dimension of difference on the "From Dominance to Justice" chart has been the most influential in your life? Which have you spent the most time dealing with or thinking about?
- In what ways do you agree with Gary's analysis in this model? In what ways do you disagree or hold a different perspective?

6. Closing Comments   1 Minute

Bring the group back together, and inform them that the next step in the process will be to apply the Social Dominance and Social Justice concepts to what is happening in your school. Ask them to be thinking about that and talking with their colleagues in preparation for your next session together.

Social Justice Definition

Social Justice:

▶ *Systems of Equity and Fairness*

▶ *Reinforced by Respect and Shared Power*

▶ *Favoring the Inclusion and Well-Being of all Groups*

The Dynamics of Social Justice

▶ **The Dynamics of Social Justice:**

▶ *The Assumption of Multiple Perspectives / Truths*

▶ *The Luxury of Being Heard and Understood*

▶ *The Legacy of Our Shared Human Destiny*

From Social Dominance to Social Justice

TOWARD A NEW PARADIGM FOR HUMAN COMMUNITY

SOCIAL DOMINANCE PARADIGM

- Human Beings over Nature
- Male over Female
- Whites over Other Races
- Christianity over Other Religions
- Heterosexual over Other Gender/Sexual Identities
- Abled over "Disabled"
- Haves over "Have-nots"
- Youth over Old Age
- "Superiors" over "Subordinates"
- English Only
- Diversity as a Problem

SOCIAL JUSTICE PARADIGM

- Harmony and Sustainability
- Gender Equity
- Racial Understanding and Justice
- Religious/Spiritual Pluralism
- Affectional/Sexual Pluralism and Equal Rights
- Equitable Access & Opportunity
- Distributive Justice
- Honoring All Stages of Life
- Respecting and Including Everyone
- Language Preservation and Respect
- Diversity as an Opportunity

SJ-17

Qualities of a Social Justice Ally

The good of the many over the greed of the few

Multiple perspectives over single-dimensional truth

Humility over hubris

The alchemy of privilege

The personal and political will to resist oppression

Activity: Privilege and Power School Assessment	
Phase Three: From Social Dominance to Social Justice	
Purpose:	• Examine how issues of privilege and preference are functioning in the school setting • Identify the ways in which the Dynamics of Social Dominance may be getting in the way of equitable outcomes • Design strategies for reducing the impact of dominance by strengthening a culture of inclusion, equity, and excellence
Suggested Time:	45 minutes
Materials Needed:	Video Segment 3:5 Handout SJ-18: Privilege and Power Discussion Three flipcharts with easels or other recording device
Advanced Preparation:	• View Video Segment 3:5 • Read the Facilitator Directions • Decide the best way to structure the discussion groups

Facilitator Note: *This is the application piece for Phase Three, the conversation you and your Facilitation Team have been building toward in all of the previous activities. Hopefully, by this point in the process, you have provided your faculty with a solid conceptual grasp and understanding of Social Dominance, and you have established a good foundation of tone and trust. Both of these factors are important catalysts for creating a courageous and real conversation about the ways in which privilege, power, exclusion, and the dynamics of dominance may be getting in the way of your expressed goals of equity and inclusion.*

Talk together with your team about the best way to form the small groups for this discussion. Work-alike teams by grade level or department may be the most practical way to make the conversation real. However, max-mix groups may be better if you have significant levels of resistance showing up in some of your work-alike teams.

It would also be helpful for your Facilitation Team to view SVC-13, where a school superintendent discusses how issues of privilege and power have presented a challenge in his district. This might be a good video clip to share with your faculty before you begin the discussion of privilege and power in your school setting.

1. Set the Tone   1 Minutes

Organize your faculty into small groups of five to eight people each and distribute copies of Handout SJ-18. Let people know that today's conversation will focus on the culture of your school and assessing that culture through the lens of what you have been learning about privilege, power, and social dominance.

2. Start Video Segment 3:5   2 Minutes

Gary establishes a context for the conversation by briefly reviewing some of the key concepts you have covered so far in Phase Three. He asks people to focus on the first two questions on Handout SJ-17, and a video prompt gives them some personal think time to consider their responses. After the think time, Gary invites people to enter this conversation through the lens of multiple perspectives. They will not be looking for a single truth or having a debate about who is right or wrong. Instead, they will be genuinely focused on identifying the different ways that social dominance challenges may be showing up in the culture of your school.

3. Small-Group Conversations: Part 1   10 Minutes

Stop the video and allow time for the small groups to discuss the first two questions. Facilitators can circulate around the room and support any groups that may have questions about the process. This time is also a good opportunity to get a sense of how deeply the groups are engaging with the social dominance issues.

4. Restart the Video   2 Minutes

Call everyone's attention back to the video. Gary brings the conversation to the third question, dealing with strategies for addressing issues of privilege, power, and social dominance in your school setting. He will instruct the small groups to come up with a strategy for how they might address one of the dominance challenges they identified during Part 1 of their conversation. Video prompts will guide them in preparing for the large-group share-out.

5. Small-Group Conversations: Part 2   10 Minutes

Stop the video and allow time for small-group discussions of the third question. Groups will be selecting one of the challenges they discussed in Part 1 and designing a possible strategy for interrupting that particular manifestation of privilege, power, and dominance in your school culture. They will also select a spokesperson and prepare to share the following items with the large group:

- One example of "systems of privilege and preference" present in your school
- One example of the "dynamics of dominance" showing up in the school culture
- One possible strategy for addressing the above issues

Toward the end of this conversation time, Facilitators should circulate around the room and make sure the small groups are ready to share.

6. Large-Group Share-Out   20 Minutes

Pull the large group back together and begin the share-out time. Members of the Facilitation Team can be recording the responses as each group shares. You can create three different lists: one list for "Systems of Privilege and Preference," another for examples of the "Dynamics of Dominance," and a third list for "Strategies for Inclusion and Equity." These lists can be word processed and distributed to everyone after the session.

7. Closing Comments   1 Minute

Thank everyone for their engagement and contribution to the discussion. Mention that the notes from the Large-Group Share-Out will be incorporated into your school planning and school improvement processes. Ask each of the grade level or department teams to keep these things in mind as they teach and do their planning, and continue to look for the ways that issues of dominance, exclusion, and privilege may be getting in the way.

Privilege and Power Discussion

1. Share one example of how "systems of privilege and preference" function within personal interactions, professional relationships, or organizational practices in your school/district/institution.

2. Describe how at least one of the "dynamics of dominance" is at work within personal, professional, or organizational life in your school system/institution/community.

   ▶ *The Assumption of Rightness*

   ▶ *The Luxury of Ignorance*

   ▶ *The Legacy of Privilege*

3. How do we work with these issues of privilege and power in ways that will create a more inclusive and welcoming learning/working environment and better outcomes for our students, colleagues, employees, and community?

Activity: *Focus on Race Conversation*	
Phase Three: From Social Dominance to Social Justice	
Purpose:	• Create an authentic conversation about issues of race • Examine social dominance through the lens of whiteness • Gain an understanding of white privilege • Introduce the White Identity Orientations model • Support people of color and white people in becoming allies for transformative work
Suggested Time:	45–50 minutes
Materials Needed:	Video Segment 3:6 Handout SJ-19: White Identity Orientations Handout SJ-20: Race and Whiteness Conversation Recommended Additional Resources: Two films by Shakti Butler: • *Mirrors of Privilege: Making Whiteness Visible* • *Cracking the Codes: The System of Racial Inequity* Handout SJ-21: *Mirrors of Privilege* Discussion Guide
Advanced Preparation:	• View Video Segment 3:6 • Read the Facilitator Directions • Decide the best way to structure the discussion groups

Facilitator Note: *At some point in your work with Social Dominance, it is recommended that you focus specifically on issues of race and white privilege. This is important precisely because such a large percentage of teachers are white. This Video Segment creates a conceptual foundation and a process for guiding the conversation on race and whiteness. Your Facilitation Team should talk about when might be the best time to initiate this activity and how you want to structure the small groups for discussion. For diverse faculties, it is best to have a mix of white people and people of color in each of your small groups.*

*Shakti Butler's **Mirrors of Privilege** video can serve as a helpful introduction to the Race and Whiteness Conversation, and her **Cracking the Codes** film is an excellent follow-up. Gary Howard strongly recommends that you acquire each of these films and view them together with your Facilitator Team before you initiate any race and whiteness conversations with your faculty. You can access the films, along with discussion guide materials, at Shakti's website: www.world-trust.org. The Race and Whiteness Conversation presented in Video Segment 4:6 and outlined below can be engaged without using these films, but you will have a much richer experience with your faculty if you can include Shakti's work.*

It would also be helpful for your Facilitation Team to preview several of the school-based video clips (SVC-14 through SVC-18), which feature many examples of the ways students experience racism in both school and community settings. These are dramatic stories that clearly demonstrate the realities of race and whiteness in students' lives. Decide which of these videos would be most appropriate for your staff and when might be the best time to show them.

Optional Film Showing

Before you implement the activities described below, it would be good to show your faculty Shakti Butler's film, *Mirrors of Privilege: Making Whiteness Visible.* For discussion purposes, you can use the guidelines available on Shakti's website or a shorter Discussion Guide provided here at the end of this section (Handout SJ-21). You can also use the student video clips mentioned above or launch into the activities below before viewing any of the films or videos.

1. Set the Tone   2 Minutes

Organize your faculty into small groups of five to eight people each and distribute copies of Handouts SJ-19 and SJ-20. (You can copy these back-to-back.) Announce to the faculty that you will be focusing today on one dimension of difference, the dimension of race. If you have previously shown Shakti Butler's *Mirrors of Privilege,* let the group know that today's activity will continue and expand that conversation.

2. Start Video Segment 3:6   12 Minutes

Gary makes the case for talking explicitly about issues of race in our schools, with a particular focus on whiteness. His comments draw connections to several activities you have already implemented with your faculty, including Culture Toss, Stages of Growth Toward Cultural Competence, and We, the People. Using stories from his own experience and research, he describes how white people grow in their understanding of race. As he shares these stories, he describes each of the three stages in the White Identity Orientations model. He also asks people of color to consider how they have experienced white people in each of the Orientations and whether there are similar stages of development for people of color.

3. Small-Group Reflective Conversation   15 Minutes

At the close of Gary's comments, you will be prompted to **stop the video** and invite your faculty to begin their small-group conversations. Handouts SJ-19 and SJ-20 provide them with the White Identity

Orientations model and the focus questions. As people are talking, Facilitators should circulate and check in with the groups. Toward the end of the discussion period, make sure each of the groups is ready to share some insight or observation that has come out of their conversation. Prompt one or two groups to be ready to start the sharing.

4. Large-Group Sharing   10 Minutes

Bring the large group back together, and invite spokespersons from each of the small groups to offer a 1- or 2-minute comment on something that came out of their discussion. Look for trends or themes in these comments, and have one of your Facilitators record these as the discussion continues. Draw any connections you can to other activities you have done with the faculty, particularly the dynamics of dominance issues that were identified in your Privilege and Power School Assessment activity (SJ-18).

5. Restart the Video: Summary and Closing Comments   5 Minutes

Gary provides a few summary comments about the discussion of race and whiteness. His points include the following:

- We were not attempting in this conversation to come to any grand conclusion about race and whiteness, but merely to deepen everyone's thinking and engagement with the realities of race.
- Race is always in the room. Whether you have an all-white student population or a highly racially diverse school, race is present.
- Race and other differences make a difference in the classroom, but they don't have to get in the way.
- The main way race gets in the way is when we pretend it doesn't exist.
- There is not one way of being white, but many.
- We all have a choice to become transformationist educators.

Follow-Up Film Option

Shortly following your Race and Whiteness Conversation, it would be helpful to show Shakti Butler's *Cracking the Codes* video. This film expands the conversation beyond issues of whiteness and is often highly engaging for people of color. It looks at the way that racial inequalities show up in personal, interpersonal, institutional, and structural ways. There are powerful stories from many people of color about their experiences of racial inequality, including that which flows from internalized oppression. Several of the white people who appeared in *Mirrors of Privilege* are also present in this second film and take their analysis to a deeper level. Discussion prompts and guiding questions are built in at selected points during the film.

Facilitator Note: *If issues related to guilt, denial, anger, or other difficult emotions have surfaced in your discussion of race and whiteness, you might want to go immediately to the next and final piece in Phase Three:* **Shifting the Emotional Paradigm.** *In that Video Segment, Gary directly addresses the emotional components related to the movement from Social Dominance to Social Justice.*

White Identity Orientations

Fundamentalist White Identity

Thinking:	Ignorance	Supremacy	Denial
Feeling:	Fear	Anger	Hostility
Acting:	Assimilation	Judgmental	Racist

Integrationist White Identity

Thinking:	Awareness	Curiosity	Dissonance
Feeling:	Defensive	Guilty	Missionary Zeal
Acting:	Paternalistic	Colorblind	Compliance

Transformationist White Identity

Thinking:	Questioning	Self-Reflective	Affirming
Feeling:	Humility	Courage	Respect
Acting:	Advocacy	Anti-racist	Shifting Power

Note: For more detail and discussion related to these White Identity Orientations, please see Chapter 6 in Gary Howard's book, *We Can't Teach What We Don't Know: White Teachers, Multiracial Schools (2006).*

Race and Whiteness Conversation

Directions: Each person in your small group will select *one* of these questions as his or her primary focus. Give 2 minutes for each person's response.

1. **In what ways do you see these three White Identity Orientations (WIOs) showing up in your school, department, or workplace?**

2. **How might people in different WIOs demonstrate either acceptance or resistance to the work of racial equity, inclusion, and social justice?**

3. **How can we interface effectively with people in the different WIOs—to support their growth?**

4. **How do you see your life story reflected in these different WIOs?**

5. **How do people of color experience white folks who are in these three different WIOs?**

6. **Are there similar identity orientations for people of color? For groups of people related to sexual orientation, religion, socioeconomic status, or other differences?**

Report Out:

- What is one idea, insight, or lesson from your conversation you would like to share with the large group?
- Select your spokesperson and be ready to share.

Shakti Butler Video

Mirrors of Privilege: Making Whiteness Visible

www.world-trust.org

Video Discussion Guide

Directions: As you view the film, please take notes on the following questions.

1. Be ready to talk about one scene/person/comment that particularly connected with you at the emotional level.

2. Look for some of the key experiences or catalysts that led to personal change for the people in the video.

3. What is something in the video that challenges your own previous thinking?

Activity: Shifting the Emotional Paradigm	
Phase Three: From Social Dominance to Social Justice	
Purpose:	• Address the emotional component of transformative change • Identify those emotions that can get in the way of personal growth and organizational change • Provide positive alternatives for addressing difficult emotions
Suggested Time:	20 minutes
Materials Needed:	Video Segment 3:7 Handout SJ-22: Shifting the Emotional Paradigm
Advanced Preparation:	• View Video Segment 3:7 • Read the Facilitator Directions • Together with your Facilitation Team, discuss the emotional responses you have observed so far in your work with your faculty

Facilitator Note: *This brief Video Segment can be used anytime in the process when your Facilitation Team decides it would be most helpful. If feelings of guilt, anger, denial, or fear have surfaced during any of your Phase Three conversations and activities, you might want to show this video and talk explicitly about these "Zinger Emotions." It is inevitable that some difficult emotions will emerge while you are dealing with the complex issues addressed within this phase of the work, but it is not our goal to leave people stuck in that place. Sometimes, merely by acknowledging the legitimacy of these feelings, we can open the way to the "Responses That Heal."*

1. Set the Tone   2 Minutes

Distribute copies of Handout SJ-22, and inform your faculty that you will take a few minutes to look at the emotional component of the work you have been doing.

2. Play Video Segment 3:7   8 Minutes

Gary acknowledges that any discussion of Social Dominance issues inevitably takes us out of our comfort zones, precisely because we are being challenged to move beyond our familiar paradigms and personal perceptions of what is real and true. In fact, if we are not experiencing some discomfort, we are probably not having a real conversation. Gary addresses each of the "Zinger Emotions" and gives examples of the way these difficult feelings can emerge as individuals and groups work with the movement from Social Dominance to Social Justice. He then talks about the positive options to each of these challenging emotions, options that he calls the "Responses That Heal." He asks your audience to think about which of the Zinger Emotions they or their colleagues may have experienced during your work together and what they consider to be some options for positive movement and personal growth.

3. Pair-and-Share Conversations   7 Minutes

You will be prompted to **stop the video** and invite people into dyads to discuss their thoughts and responses. The following discussion questions will appear on the screen:

- Which of the "Zinger Emotions" have you experienced or witnessed your colleagues experiencing?
- Are there other difficult emotions you would add to this list?
- What do you think about Gary's list of "Responses That Heal"?
- When these difficult emotions occur, what does it take to move to a more engaged and proactive place?

4. Share-Out and Closing   5 Minutes

Facilitators should circulate during the pair-and-share conversations and identify three or four pairs who are willing to share a comment with the larger group. Bring the folks back together and have your selected dyads share their comments. Invite others to contribute as time allows. Close with one or two Facilitators sharing a personal story about your experiences of discomfort and growth as you have dealt with your own journey from Social Dominance to Social Justice.

SJ-22 From Dominance to Diversity

SHIFTING THE EMOTIONAL PARADIGM

ZINGER EMOTIONS		RESPONSES THAT HEAL
Fear	⟶	Humility
Denial	⟶	Honesty
Hostility	⟶	Empathy
Blame	⟶	Advocacy
Shame / Guilt	⟶	Action

Phase Four: Classroom Implications and Applications

Goals for Phase Four:

- Reinforcing adult-student relationships as the key to achievement
- Acknowledging classroom successes, challenges, and roadblocks
- Applying the Seven Principles for Culturally Responsive Teaching
- Implementing action research for inclusion and equity

RATIONALE AND OVERVIEW OF ACTIVITIES

In Phase Four, we engage the central purpose and passion of our work—the transformation of classroom practices for the sake of every student's growth and achievement. The tone and trust you established in Phase One, your deep conversations about personal culture among adults in Phase Two, and your honest consideration of privilege and social dominance issues in Phase Three, all of this previous work comes to bear in Phase Four on the quality and effectiveness of your interactions with students. And very importantly, the work here is approached with deep acknowledgment and respect for the good things your people are already doing. As we discussed in the Introduction to the manual, there is a profound need for healing and affirmation among educators, who have too often felt under siege by the demands and punitive consequences of top-down school reform policies. In Phase Four, we honor the professionalism and the good intentions of your faculty and staff, while at the same time challenging them to critically examine how some of their own behaviors and beliefs may be getting in the way.

Phase Four provides a practical integrative framework for all of the work you are presently doing on school improvement and strengthening instruction. The **Seven Principles for Culturally Responsive Teaching (CRT)** are the core conceptual and pedagogical content for this phase of the work. For educators who may feel overwhelmed or unfocused because of the multiple professional development and instructional initiatives that have accompanied school reform mandates, these Seven Principles can help unify their efforts. The Principles are an effective teacher-friendly tool for assessing classroom practice, and they are a powerful set of guidelines for directing and inspiring professional growth.

Your Phase Four work with the Principles will lay a solid foundation for collegial collaboration, wherein faculty and staff can willingly share their strengths and skills with each other, as well as courageously acknowledge their struggles and their fears. This approach to Culturally Responsive Teaching has been welcomed and utilized by thousands of teachers throughout the country. It recharges our pedagogical batteries, makes sense of our work, provides direction for our professional improvement, and validates the many good things we are already doing. Our hope and intention in Phase Four is to engender for ourselves and our teachers that state of self-generated neuroplasticity that leads us to say, "I know I am a good educator, and for that reason I want to push back against any of the barriers I may be putting in the way of my students' success, especially for those students who are most different from me."

After you have viewed the **Phase Four Introductory Video,** begin with the **School Outcomes Assessment** activity. This is a rich and informative open-ended conversation that calls forth varying perceptions of how well you are doing as a school in engaging all of your students. The activity begins with each person reflecting on the question: "For what percent of our students are we doing a good or great job?" They share their answers in small groups, and the overall range of responses across all groups is charted. The follow-up question is then posed: "What percent of our students are we missing or not engaging?" Once again, the range of answers from the lowest perception to the highest perception are charted for everyone to see. What often emerges from the ensuing conversation is a profound realization that our perceptions of our effectiveness with students vary greatly, and our notions of "good-great" and "missing or not engaged" are equally diverse. The activity continues with small groups brainstorming the characteristics of the students they see as fitting into either group. This usually leads to the recognition that most of the students for whom we are doing a good-great job come to us already front-loaded to succeed, and those whom we are missing or not engaging come with the greatest challenges or from cultures that are most different from the dominant norms of "doing school." The School Outcomes Assessment activity lays the groundwork for productive follow-up conversations about what constitutes "quality education" and about the broad diversity of faculty opinions regarding your school's effectiveness in reaching your most challenged populations.

The next activity focuses directly on those students who are most marginalized in your school culture, those who are most likely to be seen as members of the missing or not engaged group. **Equity Environments That Work** provides a vehicle for you and your staff to share some of the successes you are having with even these most challenged students. All participants think of a student in this group with whom they have made significant progress in moving toward greater engagement and school success. In groups of four, they share their stories of success and identify the key adult behaviors that made a difference for students in each of their stories. These behaviors are then charted in the large group as the "Keys to Equity." In this way, you acknowledge the good work people are already doing with some of your most disengaged students, and you begin to define and share the actual practices that have proven effective in your own school.

Sharing stories of success, and the resulting list of Keys to Equity, set the stage for providing your faculty with a **Definition of Culturally Responsive Teaching,** which is *teaching in such a way that more of our students, across more of their differences, are achieving at a higher level and engaging at a deeper level, more of the time, without giving up who they are.* This definition draws on the work you did earlier in Phase One, recognizing the broad range of differences that students bring to us and acknowledging that those differences make a difference in our classrooms. It also highlights the lessons your faculty gleaned from the Culture Toss activity in Phase Two, the importance of creating cultures of inclusion that do not put pressure on students to give up essential aspects of their identity.

After providing this definition, you are ready to introduce your faculty to the **Seven Principles for Culturally Responsive Teaching.** In this Video Segment, Gary Howard provides a 3- to 4-minute explanation of each of the Principles, along with classroom examples and stories to make the conceptual framework real for your teachers. The first three of these Principles form the "front porch" for student learning, creating the physical, personal, and cultural tone that invites even our most challenged students to feel respected, seen, and welcomed in the school environment. The first three Principles are as follows:

1. *Students are affirmed in their cultural connections.*

2. *The teacher is personally inviting.*

3. *Learning environments are physically and culturally inviting.*

In the context of this safe and affirming space, the next two Principles relate to academic engagement:

4. *Students are reinforced for academic development.*

5. *Instructional changes are made to accommodate differences in learners.*

These two Principles are particularly important for those students who do not come to us front-loaded for success and who, by third grade or beyond, have decided that school is not their thing. These two Principles require us to embrace an unrelenting belief in the capacity and intelligence of our students, and a courageous commitment to examine and shift our own practices. The next Principle relates to discipline and classroom management:

6. *The classroom is managed with firm, consistent, caring control.*

The key to this Principle is what Gary Howard refers to as "the art of preemptive respect." Many of our nonengaged students do not come to us with dominant culture values that would lead them to respect us just because we are adults. To the contrary, many children and young people have justifiably learned to distrust adults as a matter of survival. Given this reality, respect must flow first from the adult to the student. This may be discomforting and difficult for many white middle-class teachers, but it is a necessary paradigm shift if we are to be effective. The final Principle relates to the creative use of grouping and community building in the classroom:

7. *Interactions stress collectivity as well as individuality.*

School culture, for the most part, is based on Western notions of individualism. Students are assessed, rewarded, or punished as individuals. In contrast to this, many of our students come to us from cultures that are much more collaborative and collective than the dominant mode. Principle Seven is based on the assumption that the *me* must be balanced with the *we* in all classroom interactions. This Principle highlights the creative ways teachers can incorporate collaborative strategies that reinforce both the sense of community among learners as well as the importance of individual effort and achievement. Taken together, the Seven Principles for Culturally Responsive Teaching provide a dynamic framework for assessing classroom practice and a practical foundation for guiding professional growth.

Once you have introduced the Seven Principles, it is important to make them real in the context of your own school. The **Culturally Responsive Teaching Study Groups** activity creates a jigsaw process in which your faculty and staff identify specific ways they are already implementing the Seven Principles in their interactions with students. They also identify areas where they may be missing opportunities or creating barriers related to each of the Principles. These doorways and barriers are charted and shared with everyone, and in this way you begin to form your own building-specific application of Culturally Responsive Teaching.

The next step in the Phase Four process engages each member of your staff in assessing their own interactions with students related to the Seven Principles. All participants select a "Proficient Principle," which is that area of practice where they feel most comfortable and effective, and a "Growth Principle," which is that area they would like to strengthen. From this, all members create a **CRT Action Research** project aimed at improving their practice related to their Growth Principle. Since all members of your staff self-select the focus of their Action Research, these projects are not seen as teacher evaluation but, once again, are an outgrowth of that self-generated neuro-plasticity you have established by this point in the process. For those members of your staff who still may be resistant to this kind of self-reflection and action, the broad and willing engagement of their peers will hopefully nudge them forward.

The Action Research process creates an excellent foundation for peer sharing, either in Professional Learning Communities or in other settings and formats. The fact that each member of your staff has publically acknowledged his or her own arenas of strength and challenge related to the Seven Principles sets up a natural "each-one-teach-one" opportunity. The **Learning From and With Colleagues** activity creates an excellent venue for this kind of peer support. This activity generates an all-faculty interaction where people meet together in small groups around a Growth Principle, sharing some of the questions and challenges they would like to have addressed by their peers who feel more proficient related to that Principle. Staff members then meet in Proficient Groups and respond to these questions and challenges. Finally, the Growth Groups come back together to consider the responses and suggestions that were generated by their peers. By thus setting the tone and context for collegial sharing of strengths and challenges, it is possible for the Seven Principles of Culturally Responsive Teaching to become part of the "new normal" in your school, a naturally embedded tool for ongoing professional reflection and growth.

The next activity provides a **CRT Classroom Peer Observation** process that further inculcates the Seven Principles into your school culture and can guide your work with CRT over the course of a full school year and beyond. This process invites your faculty and staff to observe their peers in the classroom and identify the teacher behaviors that support each of the Seven Principles, as well as noting any barriers that may be getting in the way. The Peer Observation process reinforces and extends the "learning from and with colleagues" dynamics that were practiced in the previous activity.

Phase Four culminates with the **Achievement Triangle.** This is a short talk and visual organizer that pulls together all of the work you have done so far. This presentation emphasizes the fact that Culturally Responsive Teaching is more than just "good teaching." It is good teaching in the context of a highly diverse and variously challenged student population. It is good teaching that acknowledges the personhood and culture of the student, as well as the personhood and culture of the teacher. It is good teaching wherein relationships drive the process of instruction, even more than content or curriculum. It is good teaching with cultural competence as its core, with the uniqueness of each student as its heart, and with our passion for social justice as its professional soul.

Phase Four: Classroom Implications and Applications **School Video Clips (SVC)**		
Suggested School Video Clips for Phase Four include those listed here.		
SVC #	Title	Video Length
19	**Helping Students Find Their Voice** Julie Davis, 5th Grade Teacher Monroe Elementary School, reflects on her classroom practices and the ways in which she tries to be a culturally responsive teacher.	2:54
20	**A Model Lesson: A Blend of CRT Principles** Holly Clark, 7th Grade English Language Arts Teacher, describes how her lesson integrates and reflects four different culturally responsive teaching principles.	3:58
21	**Little Details Make a Big Difference** Alicia Moore, Social Studies Teacher Blaine High School, describes how she blends and integrates the principles of culturally responsive teaching.	2:11
22	**Bringing in Students' Lives** Megan Hendrix, 10th Grade English Teacher Crossroads Alternative High School, describes how she attends to the principles of culturally responsive teaching in her lessons related to reading *The Crucible*.	3:02

Phase Four: Classroom Implications and Applications School Video Clips (SVC)		
Suggested School Video Clips for Phase Four include those listed here.		
SVC #	Title	Video Length
23	**Student Voices: Changing the Way You Look at School** Gary Howard leads a discussion with high school boys who describe what teachers do that help and support their learning.	6:56
24	**Student Voices: Middle School Boys Talk About What Gets in the Way of Their Learning** Gary Howard leads a discussion with middle school boys who describe the ways in which teachers hinder their learning.	5:21
25	**Student Voices: Middle School Boys Talk About How Teachers Help Their Learning** Gary Howard leads a discussion with middle school boys who describe the ways in which teachers help and support their learning.	3:18
26	**Student Voices: Middle School Girls Talk About What Helps and What Hinders Their Learning** Gary Howard leads a discussion with middle school girls who describe the ways in which teachers help and hinder their learning.	6:46
27	**The Achievement Triangle: Incorporating Relationships and Rigor** Nancy Chave, Principal Crossroads Alternative High School, describes how using the Achievement Triangle helps her teachers increase the rigor throughout the curriculum in all classes and at all grade levels.	2:10
28	**The CRT Principles Breakfast** Jenni Jones, Intern Assistant Principal at Northdale Middle School, describes how her school instituted a Principles Breakfast, which is a way to focus on each of the 7 principles of culturally responsive teaching one at a time, and provides ongoing professional learning for the teaching staff.	3:03

Facilitator Note: *Before implementing any of the activities in this section of the manual, show your faculty and staff the Phase Four Introductory Video.*

Suggested Group Readings for Phase Four

- **White Teachers and School Reform: Toward a Transformationist Pedagogy,** Chapter 7 in Gary Howard's book, *We Can't Teach What We Don't Know: White Teachers, Multiracial Schools.* New York: Teachers College Press, 2006.
- **School Improvement for All: Reflections on the Achievement Gap.** See Gary Howard's articles in the back of the manual.
- **Bright Ribbons: Weaving Culturally Responsive Teaching Into the Elementary Classroom,** by Lotus Linton Howard (2004). Order from Megaperspectives Press at soulspring@earthlink.net.
- *Culturally Responsive Standards-Based Teaching: Classroom to Community and Back,* by S. Saifer, K. Edwards, D. Ellis, L. Ko, & A. Stuczynski. Thousand Oaks, CA: Corwin, 2011.
- *Finding Joy in Teaching Students of Diverse Backgrounds: Culturally Responsive and Socially Just Teaching Practices in U.S. Classrooms,* by S. Nieto. New York: Heinemann, 2013.
- *Creating Culturally Responsive Classrooms.* B. Shade, C. Kelly, and M. Oberg. Washington, DC: American Psychological Association. 1997.

PHASE FOUR ACTIVITIES, FACILITATOR DIRECTIONS, AND VIDEO SEGMENTS

Activity: School Outcomes Assessment	
Phase Four: Classroom Implications and Applications	
Purpose:	• Stimulate a critical reflective conversation about the effectiveness of your classroom and school practices • Recognize the range of perceptions faculty and staff have regarding their effectiveness • Identify the characteristics of students for whom you are doing a good or great job • Compare these characteristics to those of the students you are missing or not engaging • Emphasize that school reform in the 21st century is primarily about engaging those students who do not come to us front-loaded to succeed in school
Suggested Time:	65 minutes
Materials Needed:	Phase Four Introductory Video Video Segment 4:1 Handout CA-1: School Outcomes Assessment Two flipcharts and easels or other recording device
Advanced Preparation:	• View the Introductory Video and Video Segment 4:1 • Review the Facilitator Directions • Discuss how to structure the small groups

Facilitator Note: *This activity launches you into the classroom application part of the work. It engages your whole faculty in thinking about your effectiveness in reaching the broad range of students in your school. Together you will identify where you are doing a great job with some of your students and where you are missing or not engaging others. It is suggested that you carry out this conversation in max-mix small groups, but you may want to organize people into more work-alike groups, by grade level or department. This is something to decide before you do the activity.*

1. Set the Stage   7 Minutes

After you have viewed the **Phase Four Introductory Video** together with your faculty, announce that you have now reached the part of the work that will engage them directly in their practice with students. Whether they are classroom teachers, specialists, counselors, coaches, instruction guides, administrators, or support staff, everyone will be thinking about the ways that cultural competence and culturally responsive practice impact your work. Have people seated in small groups as designated by your Facilitation Team, and distribute copies of Handout CA-1.

2. Start Video Segment 4:1   5 Minutes

Gary Howard makes a few introductory comments about the focus and purpose of Phase Four. He then sets up the first activity by asking a reflective question: "For what percent of our students are we doing a good or great job?" Gary sets some parameters for answering that question and provides personal think time before people begin talking to their colleagues. You will be prompted to **pause the video** while people consider their answers.

Some people may want clarification of the question during this think time, so Facilitators should be ready to go to different groups and/or individuals and encourage them to come up with their answers. Gary will have explained that we are not merely looking at the percentage of students who are passing your state assessments. This question is focusing more broadly on what it means to do a good job of educating our students for life and how effective you have been in addressing issues of inclusion, equity, and excellence in your school. You want everyone to have their number ready, without thinking too much about the complexity of the question at this point. The deeper reflective conversation will come later in the activity. **Restart the video** after a minute or so of personal think time, and Gary will prepare people for their first round of small-group conversation.

3. Small-Group Sharing of Perceptions: Question 1   3 Minutes

You will be prompted to **pause the video** again to allow time for small groups to share their answers. Video prompts will direct them to select someone to record the range of their answers. The sharing of numbers should be done without debate or judgments about which number is right or wrong. This conversation is about sharing perceptions, and everyone should expect to hear a broad range of answers.

4. Large-Group Recording of the Range of Responses   5 Minutes

After the small groups have shared and recorded their answers, pull the large group back together. Don't allow too much time for the small-group discussions; the main thing at this point is to get the numbers recorded. Ask the recorders in each group to look at their range of answers and identify the highest and lowest numbers that were mentioned in their small group. Begin with the highest number, and go quickly around the groups asking them to shout out their high number. After you have heard from all of the groups, ask: What was the highest of the highs? Record this number on a flipchart set up like this:

Good to Great

From _____ % to _____ %

Put the high number on the right-hand blank. Then go around again and ask each group in turn to shout out their lowest number. Record the lowest of the lows in the left-hand blank. You will now have a chart that looks something like this:

Good to Great

From 25 % to 85 %

Gary Howard has done this activity with hundreds of schools around the country, and the range of answers is usually very broad. The reflective question begs many other questions about the meaning of "good-great" and "missing or not engaging." As you are sharing and recording the numbers from the small groups, simply acknowledge that many more conversations need to happen and that you will be engaging those soon.

5. Restart the Video: Question 2   3 Minutes

After you have recorded the range of responses for the Good-Great chart, **restart the video** and Gary will ask the second question: "What percent of our students are we missing or not engaging?" He will make a few comments to clarify the meaning and intent of the question. Once again, you will be prompted to **pause the video** for a minute of think time, with Facilitators circulating to make sure everyone is getting their own answer together before sharing with their colleagues.

After this brief think time, invite everyone to share and record answers in the small groups.

6. Small-Group Sharing of Perceptions: Question 2   3 Minutes

As the groups are sharing and recording their answers, Facilitators should circulate and make sure the participants are not getting distracted by other conversations. You will notice that groups want to talk more about the meaning of the question and the range of answers they are hearing from their colleagues. This is a good thing, and one of the main purposes of the activity is to stimulate just such a conversation, but at this point, you merely want them to get their answers out and recorded.

7. Large-Group Recording of the Range of Responses   5 Minutes

One Facilitator will elicit high and low responses from the groups while another records the highest-of-the-high and the lowest-of-the-low on the second flipchart set up similar to that for Question 1. Once the numbers are recorded, comment on the range of different responses that came out for both of the questions. Suggested comment: "It's interesting that we had such a broad range of responses for both the 'good-to-great' and the 'missing-not-engaging' questions. Obviously, this difference in our perceptions begs all kinds of other questions. Let's explore some of those now."

8. Restart the Video: Characteristics of Students   2 Minutes

Gary will set up the next level of conversation, which is on everyone's minds at this point: "Who are the students we were thinking about as we answered the two questions?" He will get the small groups into a brainstorming process, listing at least seven characteristics of students for each of the groups, the ones with whom you are doing a good-great job and the ones you are missing or not engaging. In the spirit of brainstorming, the small groups are not looking for agreement or consensus while listing these characteristics of students. They are merely recording the various descriptors of the students that were in people's minds as they answered the two questions.

9. Small-Group Brainstorming: Characteristics of Students 7 Minutes

Pause the video and allow time for the small groups to make their lists of student characteristics. Facilitators can check in with the groups about halfway through the brainstorming time to make sure they are focusing on both groups and that they have at least seven characteristics for each one.

10. Large-Group Recording of Characteristics 7 Minutes

Bring the large group back together, and have one Facilitator gather answers from the small groups, while another does the recording on the flipchart (or whatever recording device you may be using). Record the characteristics for each group on the same page as you put the range of responses earlier. Start with the Good-to-Great set of characteristics and ask each small group to share just one of the characteristics from their list for that group. After all groups have shared, then open it up for anyone to add different characteristics that have not been mentioned. You should end up with a list of 10 to 15 characteristics. Your recorded list will now look like this:

	Good to Great	
	From 25 % to 85 %	
	Characteristics of Students	
Good attendance	Parent support	Care about school
Motivated	Sense of a future	Basic needs met
Involved in activities	Self-disciplined	Special needs

Create a similar list for the missing-not-engaged students. Don't be concerned if some of the answers seem contradictory. For example, one small group may say you are doing great work with special needs students, while another had special needs students listed on their missing-not-engaged list. Each of the lists will be diverse, and once again, the perceptions will vary.

11. Small-Group Reflective Conversation 10 minutes

After you have completed the recording of characteristics for both groups, ask one of the participants to come up and read all of the items included on each list. The lead Facilitator for this activity then asks everyone to focus on the final two questions on Handout CA-1:

- How do the characteristics of the students in the first group differ from those in the second?
- What did you learn from this discussion?

By focusing on these two questions, you are asking the small groups to make meaning from this activity. Toward the end of the small-group reflective conversation, ask four or five groups to select a spokesperson and be ready to share one of their insights with the larger group.

12. Large-Group Reflective
Conversation   5 Minutes

Ask each of your selected small groups to share their comments. Invite others to share as time allows.

13. Restart the Video: Gary's
Summary Comments   3 Minutes

Gary brings together some of the intended lessons from this activity and makes connections to your earlier work in other phases. His points include the following:

- As educators working in the same school, we often have very different perceptions of our effectiveness in reaching all of our students.
- It is helpful and instructive for us to share these diverse perceptions and explore the different lenses that we each bring to our work.
- Some of our students come to us front-loaded to be successful, just like the members of Group 1 in the Guessing Game we played earlier.
- For these students, the culture of school often looks much like their home culture, and they do not have to play "give it up" like we did in the Culture Toss activity.
- Students who are front-loaded for success are often benefitting from a system of privilege and preference reinforced by power favoring them—the same structure of social dominance we explored in Phase Three.
- These students allow us to feel comfortable with our classroom practices because they thrive and are successful in our work with them.

- When we look at the list of student characteristics on the Good-to-Great list, it could be said that we are doing a great job with kids who don't need us that much.
- Other students, like the members of Group 4 in the Guessing Game, come with challenges and life experiences that make school success a difficult fit for them.
- These students often feel that school is not designed for them, and they experience daily pressure to not be who they are, similar to the pressure we simulated in the Culture Toss activity.
- Working with these students challenges us to rethink our practices, because what we are presently doing often doesn't seem to be working for them.
- Not finding much access to success, these students sometimes resort to behaviors that get them in trouble, similar to the resistance and acting-out behaviors that we saw in Group 4 when we played the Guessing Game.
- Sometimes we can be tempted to blame these students, or their families, for our inability to engage them.
- On the other hand, we also need to acknowledge that every day we are actually doing many things in our school and our classrooms to reach our nonengaged students.
- In this sense, 21st-century school reform is about finding new and creative ways to engage those very students for whom schooling often feels like a foreign culture.
- The work of engaging the nonengaged is the work of Culturally Responsive Teaching, which will be our focus in all of the upcoming activities.

School Outcomes Assessment

▶ *PRE-THINK*

1. In our school we are doing a great/good job with _____% of our students.

   Characteristics of these students

2. We are not engaging or missing the mark with _____% of our students.

   Characteristics of these students

▶ *SMALL-GROUP DISCUSSION*

- Share your answers with your colleagues.
- How similar or different were your perceptions?
- How do the characteristics of students in the first group differ from those in the second?

   What did you learn from this discussion?

Activity: Equity Environments That Work	
Phase Four: Classroom Implications and Applications	
Purpose:	• Acknowledge the good work that is being done in your school to reach your most challenged students • Engage faculty and staff in sharing their stories of success • Identify the key adult behaviors that lead to greater engagement and success for marginalized students • Provide a Definition of Culturally Responsive Teaching • Lay the groundwork for introducing the Seven Principles for Culturally Responsive Teaching
Suggested Time:	35 minutes
Materials Needed:	Video Segment 4:2 Handout CA-2: Equity Environments That Work Handout CA-3: Definition of Culturally Responsive Teaching Flipchart and easels or other recording device The flipchart notes from your School Outcomes Assessment
Advanced Preparation:	• View Video Segment 4:2 • Review the Facilitator Directions

Facilitator Note: *It would be good to do this activity in close proximity to the School Outcomes Assessment. Equity Environments That Work is a positive and affirming activity that gives your faculty and staff the credit they deserve for the good work they are already doing with students who do not come front-loaded for success. It is also a way to share these good practices with each other, creating a sense that everyone can learn from and with each other.*

1. Set the Stage   2 Minutes

Display the flipchart notes from your School Outcomes Assessment activity, and bring people's attention back to the lists of the characteristics of students in the Good-Great group and those in the Missing-Not-Engaging group. Announce that you are now going to focus on the good work that is being done in your school to reach many of your most challenged students, those who do not come front-loaded for school success. Distribute copies of Handouts CA-2 and CA-3 (these can be copied back-to-back).

2. Play Video 4:2   5 Minutes

Gary Howard introduces the activity and describes the process of forming small groups and sharing stories of success. He will ask people to form groups of four with colleagues with whom they normally don't have much opportunity to interact. You will be prompted to **stop the video** while the small groups form and people begin telling their stories.

3. Forming Groups and Sharing Stories   15 Minutes

Facilitators can support people in forming their groups of four. You may have to form a couple of groups with five people, or a group of three, to make things come out evenly, but be careful not to let groups get too big, since that will not allow time for everyone to share. Members of your Facilitation Team can also join some of the groups and participate in the activity.

4. Restart the Video: The Keys to Equity   2 Minutes

When you sense that most of the small groups have completed their stories, bring their attention back to the video, where Gary will set up the next step in the process. He will ask the small groups to identify the key adult behaviors that made a difference in each of their stories. What were the things they did that turned things around and led to greater engagement and success for their students? These behaviors are called the "Keys to Equity." **Pause the video.**

5. Small Groups Identify
Their Keys to Equity   3 Minutes

While most of the groups are working on their Keys to Equity, any groups who have not finished sharing their stories can do so at this time. One of the Facilitators sets up a flipchart with the title: "Keys to Equity."

6. Large-Group Recording of
Keys to Equity   5 Minutes

Bring everyone's attention back to the large group. One Facilitator calls on each of the discussion groups and asks them to share one of their Keys to Equity. Another Facilitator does the recording. After all groups have spoken, read over the list and ask if anyone has anything else to add to the list.

7. Restart the Video:
Summary Comments   3 Minutes

Gary emphasizes the importance of educators sharing stories of success. Too often we are reminded of the failures of public education and too infrequently do we receive recognition for the good work we are doing. Sharing stories of success is also a good way to strengthen everyone's classroom practice because we have an opportunity to hear what is working for other teachers.

Gary concludes by introducing the **Definition of Culturally Responsive Teaching** (Handout CA-3) and relates that definition directly to the activity your faculty has just completed. Culturally Responsive Teaching is teaching and leading in such a way that more of our students, across more of their differences, are achieving at a higher level and engaging at a deeper level, more of the time, without giving up who they are. This definition sets the stage for sharing the Seven Principles for Culturally Responsive Teaching in the next Video Segment.

Facilitator Note: *Word process the list of Keys to Equity and distribute it to everyone the day after you have completed your Equity Environments That Work activity.*

Equity Environments That Work

▶ SMALL-GROUP DISCUSSION

Think of a situation this past year when the environment you created made a positive difference in the life and success of a student or colleague who faced particular challenges related to equity and/or diversity. This is a time when things came together — when the effort you put into your classroom, school, work, or community environment had a real and positive impact. Give yourself the gift of appreciating what you do. Share your story with the other people in your small group.

▶ REFLECTION

After you have all shared your stories, think about what you learned from this discussion. What did we learn about the important aspects of our work? What were the key behaviors that made a real difference in each of your stories?

Be ready to share the key adult behaviors that made a difference in each of your stories.

Definition of Culturally Responsive Teaching

Teaching and leading in such a way that:

- **More of our students**

- **Across more of their differences**

- **Achieve at a higher level**

- **And engage at a deeper level**

- **More of the time**

- **Without giving up who they are**

Activity: Seven Principles for Culturally Responsive Teaching	
Phase Four: Classroom Implications and Applications	
(Adapted from the work of Barbara Shade, Cynthia Kelly, and Mary Oberg. Used here with their permission.)	
Purpose:	• Describe the Seven Principles for Culturally Responsive Teaching (CRT) • Provide practical classroom examples that illustrate doorways and barriers related to each of the Seven Principles • Engage faculty and staff in conversation that connects their own practice to the Seven Principles of CRT • Establish the conceptual framework for further work with CRT
Suggested Time:	50 minutes
Materials Needed:	Video Segment 4:3 Handout CA-4: Seven Principles of Culturally Responsive Teaching Handout CA-5: The Purpose of Our Work Your Keys to Equity notes
Advanced Preparation:	• View Video Segment 4:3 • Review the Facilitator Directions • Make copies of your "Keys to Equity" notes

Facilitator Note: *This Video Segment presents the central conceptual framework for Phase Four of the work, the Seven Principles for Culturally Responsive Teaching (CRT). It would be good to show this video soon after you have completed the Equity Environments That Work activity. At the end of that activity, Gary Howard presented the Definition of CRT (Handout CA-3), so it would be good to refer back to that definition as you introduce the Seven Principles. It is also helpful to refer back to the list of Keys to Equity that your faculty generated after sharing their stories of success. Most of the items on that list can be directly related to one or more of the Seven Principles.*

1. Set the Stage   2 Minutes

Distribute copies of Handout CA-3 and your Keys to Equity notes copied back-to-back. Remind people of the Equity Environments That Work activity you did earlier, where they shared their stories of success and generated this list of the effective practices they are already using with some of your most challenged students. Announce that the Video

Segment you are going to view will provide a conceptual framework for understanding what Culturally Responsive Teaching actually looks like in our interactions with students. Also distribute copies of Handouts CA-4 and CA-5, copied back-to-back.

2. Play Video Segment 4:3—Principles 1–3   10 Minutes

Gary sets the context for the Seven Principles of CRT by drawing connections to your previous work with the School Outcomes Assessment and the Equity Environments That Work activities. He then introduces the first three Principles, sharing stories that illustrate both the doorways and the barriers that adults create related to each of these Principles. You will be prompted to **stop the video** while your faculty and staff engage in reflective conversations.

3. Pair-and-Share Conversations   3 Minutes

Video prompts will guide your faculty to form dyads and share their thoughts about the first three Principles:

- What do these three Principles have in common?
- What is one way you are using one of these Principles in your work with students?

4. Restart the Video: The Front Porch and Principles 4 and 5   8 Minutes

Gary introduces the concept of the "front porch" as a way of emphasizing the importance of Principles 1 to 3. These are the Principles that create a safe and welcoming environment, particularly for your most marginalized students, the ones who do not come easily or comfortably into the culture of schooling. He then describes some of the doorways and barriers related to Principles 4 and 5. These are the academic Principles that focus on the ways teachers reinforce academic development, connect with the diverse intelligences of their students, and shift their instructional practices to match how their students are smart. You will be prompted to **stop the video** while people reflect on these two Principles.

5. Pair-and-Share Conversations: Principles 4 and 5   3 Minutes

Gary will ask participants to choose a different partner for this conversation, and video prompts will focus their discussion:

- Give one example of an approach you are using to support Principles 4 and 5.
- What is your biggest challenge implementing these two Principles?

6. Restart the Video: Principles 6 and 7   9 Minutes

These two Principles relate to classroom management, both in terms of discipline and the creative use of grouping to support student engagement and learning. Gary shares stories that illustrate how teachers can bring these two Principles into their practice, as well as some of the teacher behaviors that can get in the way. Once again, you will be prompted to **stop the video** and allow for reflective conversation.

7. Groups of Three: Principles 6 and 7   6 Minutes

Gary invites people to form small groups of three to discuss the final two Principles. Video prompts guide the conversation:

- Give one example of a best practice you are using for Principles 6 and 7.
- Look over your Keys to Equity list, and relate one or two of those items to any of the Seven Principles.
- Are the Seven Principles for CRT a helpful model for supporting your work with students? Why or why not?

During the final 2 minutes of this small-group time, Facilitators should select four or five groups and ask them to be ready to share their responses to the final question above.

8. Large-Group Closing Conversation   5 Minutes

Bring the large group back together and ask your selected groups to share their responses to the Seven Principles for CRT. In what ways is this a helpful model for supporting your work? In what ways is it not helpful? What would you like to add to make it more supportive? After your selected groups have spoken, ask if anyone else would like to share their perspective.

9. Restart the Video:
Summary Comments   3 Minutes

In this final section of the video, Gary links your discussion of Culturally Responsive Teaching back to your earlier Phase Two work with Cultural Competence. In this presentation, called "The Purpose of

Our Work" (Handout CA-5), he emphasizes the interrelationship between these two central concepts for dealing effectively with issues of diversity: the power of relationships across differences (Cultural Competence) and the power of effective instructional practices across differences (CRT). When these two dynamics are effectively operating in your school culture and classroom practices, the resulting outcomes are more engaged and successful students and more engaged and reflective citizens.

When the video ends, close the session by asking people to continue thinking about their own practice in light of these Seven Principles of CRT. At your next session, you will be looking at the ways you are already bringing these practices into your work, as well as identifying any barriers you may be creating.

Seven Principles for Culturally Responsive Teaching

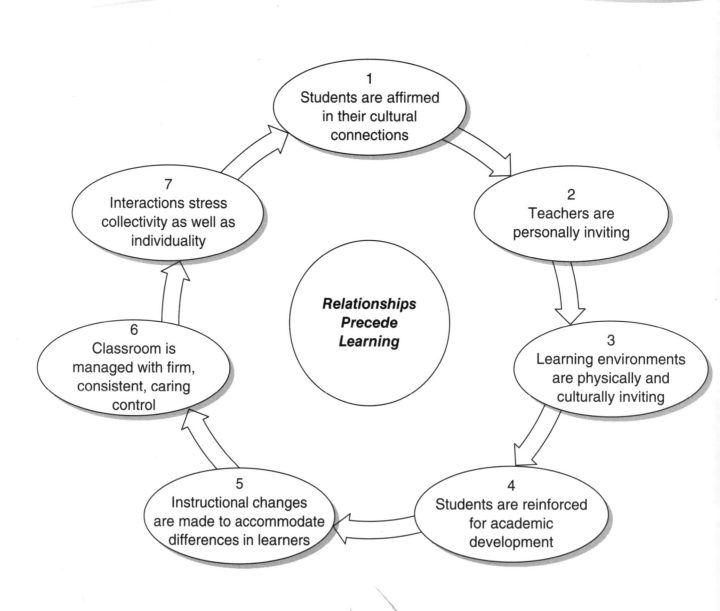

Adapted from: Shade, B.J., Kelly, C., & Oberg, M. (1997). *Creating culturally responsive classrooms.* Washington, DC: American Psychological Association. Used with Permission.

The Purpose of Our Work

CULTURAL COMPETENCE

AUTHENTIC RELATIONSHIPS ACROSS DIFFERENCES

PLUS

CULTURALLY RESPONSIVE TEACHING

POWERFUL INSTRUCTION ACROSS DIFFERENCES

LEADS TO

ACADEMIC ACHIEVEMENT

AND

ENGAGED CITIZENSHIP

Activity: Culturally Responsive Teaching Study Groups	
Phase Four: Classroom Implications and Applications	
Purpose:	• Personalize the concept of Culturally Responsive Teaching • Recognize the good work teachers and other adults are already doing to implement CRT in your school • Identify specific practices and adult actions that support each of the Seven Principles for CRT • Identify possible barriers or missed opportunities that may be getting in the way of CRT • Increase your faculty's interest and motivation to learn more about CRT
Suggested Time:	45–50 minutes
Materials Needed:	Video Segment 4:4 Handout CA-6: Culturally Responsive Teaching Study Groups Handout CA-7: CRT Study Groups Worksheet Handout CA-8: Sample Elementary Classroom Observations Handout CA-9: Sample Secondary Classroom Observations Handout CA-10: CRT Study Groups Recording Sheet
Handout:	• View Video Segment 4:4 • Review the Facilitator Directions • Create the handout packet of CA-6, CA-7, and CA-8 or CA-9 • Organize your faculty into groups of seven

Facilitator Note: *This is a jigsaw activity in which your faculty examines their own practices through the lens of the Seven Principles for CRT. They identify the doorways they are creating for each of the Principles, as well as any barriers or missed opportunities that may be getting in the way. Set up the room with tables of seven chairs each, and have your faculty know which group they are in. It is recommended that you do the Study Groups activity in a max-mix format. The takeaway from this activity will be a list of doorways and barriers for each of the Seven Principles, a list you can build on as you continue to create your school's version of CRT.*

Before implementing the Study Groups, create a stapled packet including Handouts CA-6, CA-7, and either CA-8 or CA-9, depending on whether you are in an elementary or secondary school. Also, make one copy of Handout CA-10 for each table group, all copied on the same colored paper.

1. Set the Stage   2 Minutes

Have the tables of seven preset and ask people to take a seat in their designated groups. Have seven copies of the stapled packet at each table. Let everyone know that this will be a jigsaw activity, focusing on the Seven Principles for CRT.

2. Play Video Segment 4:4   5 Minutes

Gary introduces the activity and walks people through the process outlined on Handout CA-6. First, each person in the groups of seven will select one of the Seven Principles as a focus for the activity. **Pause the video** briefly while these assignments are made. When this is completed, **restart the video.** Gary will now bring their attention to the Sample Classroom Observations (CA-8 or CA-9), which will serve as a resource for them as they prepare a presentation on their assigned Principle. He will invite them into 10 minutes of study time to prepare their presentation, either working alone or with other people who have their same Principle. You will be prompted to **stop the video** as people move into their study time.

There will be a lot of moving around at this point as people find their Principle mates. Facilitators can help people locate folks who have the same Principle. In large faculties, it is better to have several small groups working on the same Principle, rather than having everyone with that Principle together in a single large work group.

3. Study Time Alone or With Others   12 Minutes

Using Handout CA-7 as their worksheet, everyone will prepare for their presentations. Facilitators can circulate at this point to support individuals or study groups who may need some clarification of the task. People will be restating their Principle in their own words, identifying three ways that teachers in your school are bringing that Principle into their work, and suggesting two possible barriers or missed opportunities that could be getting in the way of students' success.

Gary will have mentioned this in his description of the task, but Facilitators should also emphasize that these barriers ought to be things that are within educators' sphere of influence, things you have some chance to change. For example, "large class size" or "lack of parent support" can certainly be barriers to implementing any of the Seven Principles, but they are not things that teachers can easily change on their own. Failure to pay attention to the different learning styles of our students is also a barrier, but one that teachers can get their hands on and work to improve.

After 10–12 minutes of work time, ask everyone to return to their groups of seven. While people are moving back to their groups, Facilitators should place one copy of Handout CA-10 in the middle of each table.

4. Restart the Video: Presentations in Groups of Seven   22 Minutes

When people are back in their original groups, restart the video and Gary will describe the process for reporting out on each of the Seven Principles. Each person will have 2 to 3 minutes to report on their Principle, sharing the information they produced during the work time. After each person reports, they will record one doorway and one barrier on Handout CA-10, the CRT Study Groups Recording Sheet. In this way, you are capturing information in each of the groups that can be transcribed and shared with all participants after the activity. You will be prompted to **stop the video** and allow time for the reporting out in the Groups of Seven.

5. "Culturally Responsive Teaching Is . . ." Statements   3 Minutes

At the end of 20 minutes, or when all groups have completed their reports, assign one more task to the Groups of Seven. On the back of Handout CA-10, ask a recorder at each table to write "Culturally Responsive Teaching is. . . ." Then, ask each group to work together to create an ending for that statement. How would they describe, in a short phrase or sentence, what CRT is all about? Give them a couple of minutes to record their statements.

6. Community Reading of the CRT Statements/Closing   5 Minutes

Invite one member from each Group of Seven to come to the front of the room with the statement their group has just written. Form one line of presenters across the front of the room and ask them to share their statements as one continuous reading. Have each person start with the phrase "Culturally Responsive Teaching is . . ." and then read their group's ending.

After the community reading, thank the presenters for sharing their statements, and collect all of the Handout CA-10 forms. Announce that your Facilitation Team will have these transcribed and distributed to everyone within a week. What you have now created together as a faculty is your own definition of CRT, and your own beginning set of the doorways and possible barriers you are creating related to each of the Principles.

In the next activity, each of you will have an opportunity to look at your own professional practice related to the Seven Principles for CRT, identifying those Principles that are your particular areas of strength, as well as those that are your arena of desired growth.

7. Extension Activity

This might be a good time to show your faculty SVC-28. This video segment demonstrates how a middle school created a monthly theme related to one of the Seven Principles for CRT and held a morning meeting over coffee and bagels to share their ideas and experiences with that Principle. They called this activity their "Principles Breakfast."

Culturally Responsive Teaching Study Groups

Each person in your group selects a different Principle. For your Principle, do the following:

1. Work alone or with a few people from neighboring tables who have the same Principle as you.

2. Look over the Sample Classroom Observations for your Principle: Elementary (Handout CA-8) or Secondary (Handout CA-9).

On your worksheet (Handout CA-7), complete each of the following:

3. Restate your Principle in your own words.

4. Describe three doorways for this Principle that are being created by you or other people in your building.

5. Suggest two possible barriers or missed opportunities that you or others may be creating (things that are in your sphere of influence, not external to your school).

When you get back in your Group of Seven, you will have 2 to 3 minutes to share your responses to Items 3 to 5 above.

CRT Study Groups Worksheet

Restate your Principle in your own words:

Doorways for this Principle that are being created by you or other people in your building:

·

·

·

Possible barriers or missed opportunities that you or others may be creating:

·

·

Be ready to share a 2- to 3-minute summary of your work with your colleagues back in your small group.

ELEMENTARY LEVEL
COMPOSITE NOTES TAKEN FROM OBSERVING 16 DIFFERENT CLASSROOMS
OBSERVER: GARY HOWARD

Summary Comments

Principle 1: Students are affirmed in their cultural connections.

Doorways:

- "I Am From" poems in the hall are connected by yarn to a world map showing where everyone is from. Beautiful display of diversity.
- Color names in Spanish.
- Poem in Russian on the wall.
- Children who speak a second language are honored: One child came up to me and introduced me to her friend who is teaching her Spanish, and then we had a great conversation in Spanish!
- Students writing journal letters home to parents every two weeks, letting parents know what is happening in the classroom
- Several versions of the Gingerbread Man story from different perspectives, not all explicitly cultural, but showing how the same story can be seen through many different lenses.
- Coat of Arms activity: "I am a(n) _____ American." Students can choose what, if anything, to put in the blank.
- Number lines in Spanish.
- Greeting cards in many languages.
- Role models (teachers modeling communication, solving problems, etc.).
- Include parents in classroom.

Possible Barriers or Missed Opportunities:

- A teacher mentioned the need for Asian language translation, and her frustration in not being able to communicate with some language diverse parents — sending printed material home and knowing it cannot by understood.
- How to deal sensitively with the issue of children not knowing or not wanting to identify with their ethnic heritage.
- Teachers are not creative or flexible.
- Not enough time.

CA-8 Culturally Responsive Classroom

Principle 2: Teacher is personally inviting.

Doorways:

- Building is bright and colorful with lots of student work prominently displayed.
- Obvious spirit of love for the children.
- "Come and see what we are going to do, honey."
- Making an ice pack for a child who was overly dramatic about the pain from his bumped head.
- "I have old eyes so I need to see good things — let's see if we can work on this together."
- Gentle voice, modulated, melodic.
- Warm smile and "We missed you this morning." — to a child who arrived late.
  Lots of physical affection and comforting of children.
- Including everyone — visually scanning the room to see who isn't with you.
- Modeling how to acknowledge your own mistakes.
- Greeting in native language.
- Bring something from home to share.

Possible Barriers or Missed Opportunities:

- "The stress we feel from the district, state, and federal mandates makes it difficult to stay positive with the kids."
- Whom to touch and how to touch them — child pulling arm away when gently touched by teacher.
- Tone of voice is a key factor and our styles differ — important to pay attention.
- Not thinking ahead — preventative action.
- Belittling.

CA-8 Culturally Responsive Classroom

Principle 3: Learning environments are physically and culturally inviting.

Doorways:

- Evidence of Integrated Arts is obvious and rich.
- Peaceful, wonderful music to start the day.
- Alphabet line that highlights kids' names.
- Daily schedule prominently displayed outside the door — visitors can get a sense of what is happening.
- Hallway displays tell us what is being learned in the classroom.
- "Be Prepared to Learn" sign outside the room.
- Poster recognizing the many moods of children — all expressed by variety of multicultural faces. "How do you feel today?"
- Many creative strategies for organizing huge numbers of items in ways that can be easily accessed.
- Spaces laid out for easy movement from individual to small-group to large-group activities.
- Child-created art on the walls.
- Child-friendly layout of classroom and supplies.

Possible Barriers or Missed Opportunities:

- Some rooms could do more with colorful display of student work.
- Range of organizational efficiency and ease of movement in the room.
- Wire on the windows.
- Flickering lights.

Principle 4: Students are reinforced for academic development.

Doorways:

- "You get the Guinness Book of Records award for small writing — let's try to write a little bigger today."
- Tutors, educational assistants, and student teachers greatly increase the contact time and attention to each child.
- That's perfect, what beautiful writing!"
- "What book did you get? — Very cool."
- "Our thinking caps are working overtime today."
- A look that clearly says, "You are so smart."
- Stickers, awards, "dimes" to spend, and other creative methods to give recognition.
- Recognizing and honoring different paths to the right answer — "If you are following my pattern, do that; if you have your own pattern, do that."
- "Give yourself a pat on the back." — And everyone in the room does it!
- Writing process is reinforced throughout the school.
- "I'd like to talk about that, but not right now." — teacher response to a child's off-the-wall comment.
- Effective use of "each-one-teach-one".
- Students responding enthusiastically to my question: "What are you doing and what are you learning?" They light up with the knowledge they have to share.
- "This one is harder — wow, did you do that in your head?"
- In response to student "catching" teacher making a mistake, the teacher response is, "Thank you, I don't know what I could have been thinking."
- System for student self-management of goals — earning rewards based on meeting self-determined goals.
- Builds sense of my own control and responsibility for both the learning and the reward.
- Re-visit how we share our data.
- Multiple intelligence driven activities so all strengths can shine.
- Child-friendly layout of classroom and supplies.

Culturally Responsive Classroom

Possible Barriers or Missed Opportunities:

- Some students languish in non-engagement.
- During individual deskwork, some students stay disengaged the whole period.
- "There are so many needs, and it is hard to get to all of them."
- "It's an issue of motivation."
- "A child who comes to 4th grade with no experience writing in English."
- Is there a down side to reward systems? The kids who didn't finish a task sit there while those who did receive a prize. What is the educational benefit/cost of this?
- Segregation of data about ethnic scores.
- How to honor but not compare academic achievement.

Principle 5: Instructional changes are made to accommodate differences in learners.

Doorways:

- Obvious valuing of the differences that kids bring: Teacher introduces me to a Special Education student and tells me what a good job he has been doing.
- Wait time: " I'm going to let you think for a minute, and then I'll come back to you."
- Open-ended assignments that allow students to take their own approach: "What would you say to the gingerbread man?"
- Variety of strategies to teach the same skill: cognitive, kinesthetic, visual, and auditory, and then giving multiple paths to demonstrate mastery.
- Parent receiving advice on dental care for daughter while a third person translates into Spanish.
- Several adults present in the room to accommodate special needs.
- Kinesthetic and breathing exercises late in the day to revive and refocus the kids before they do the last learning activity.
- Offering choices for students in their research projects — whether or not to study a country where they have roots.
- Differentiated instruction where multiple activities, different disciplines, and skill levels are being engaged at the same time, from beginning level to extra credit.
- Recognizing/normalizing diverse family structures/experiences. Divorce, single parent, same sex parents.
- Diverse approaches (stories, poetry, art, literature, celebrations, and music) from a variety of cultures, plus teacher integrates into curriculum diverse perspectives on human issues/history.
- Cooperative learning groups with diverse learning styles, cultures, gender, and abilities.

CA-8 — Culturally Responsive Classroom

Possible Barriers or Missed Opportunities:

- Difficult for one teacher in a room to adjust and connect with the many different learning needs.
- It takes time, clear goals, and a watchful eye to actualize this.
- Traditional textbooks represent dominant viewpoint.
- All teacher-directed learning.

Principle 6: Classroom is managed with firm, consistent, caring control.

Doorways:

- The students can explain the classroom management system.
- Teacher whispers to get attention — the opposite of yelling.
- "I like how Gregory shows me he is ready."
- "How do you get my attention?"
- Classroom rituals in place to allow for full engagement during large group instruction.
- "Everybody likes to be called by their real name." — response to a student who had been teased about his name.
- Facial expressions, hand signals, and rituals that tell students they are on the edge of losing it.
- Polite and respectful requests and guidance: "Get out your calendars, please." "Let's hold it together group."
- Gentle touch to move a wandering student to the appropriate center.
- Giving choices where possible and appropriate.
- Student-made poster on "Using Self-Control":
    1. Stop and count to 10.
    2. Think about how your body feels.
    3. Think about choices.
- Teaching consideration for others and the reasons behind our discipline: "The other students are having trouble concentrating."
- Class meetings (giving class ownership of problems and solutions).
- School-wide policies concerning behavior expectations clearly communicated to parents, staff, and students.

Culturally Responsive Classroom

Possible Barriers or Missed Opportunities:

- "This is increasingly a high needs area, and it's not only the children of color who have high needs."
- Tolerating a "culture of disruption" in the room.
- Unclear expectations/boundaries or inconsistent treatment responses to different students.
- Reinforcing negative behavior.

Principle 7: Interactions stress collectivity as well as individuality.

Doorways:

- Taking care to include everyone — "Let's make room for the people who aren't here yet."
- Taking time to teach students how to work with a partner — not taking it for granted that they know these cooperative skills.
- Teacher teaming: "I have really liked our grade level teaming, and now it helps to be doing vertical teaming."
- "People really like working with you." — comment to a child who didn't want to partner.
- Many ways that teachers design their rooms for easy movement between individual and small-group work.
- Teachers handling large-group instruction very well: all at once, everybody doing the same thing, everybody engaged, clearly defined steps, checking for success.
- "We did this one together, now you do one by yourself."
- Groups that are non-threatening, using a variety of teaching styles, hit on a concept in several ways.
- Peer teaching/cooperative learning.

Possible Barriers or Missed Opportunities:

- Not preparing kids to work together.
- Not clearly working out the reasons for grouping and the combination of students put in each group.
- Difficulty of pacing large-group tasks to meet needs of all students.
- Lot of down time for students who finish large-group tasks quickly.
- It takes time to see students individually and to recognize their different abilities.
- It is easier to teach to the large group.

CA-8 Culturally Responsive Classroom

Other Comments:

- Great examples of teachers breaking learning down into discreet and carefully sequenced steps.
- "Take out your think pads" — as a class ritual when students were being asked to work out a problem on their own.
- Teachers and the school district suffering from MIS: Multiple Initiative Syndrome. I see our school taking some steps to address this by creating focus on certain initiatives. Much needed.
- The challenge of doing large-group instruction with all of the kids on a single activity/lesson. I saw several examples of teachers doing this with great skill (and it takes great skill!), but other situations where kids on the margins of different learning styles and ability levels are disengaged.
- The testing pressure: "Last year I was sick over all the pressure to get every student to standard."
- "This staff is extremely conscientious, and we want to be able to do it all."
- "If we push too much I think we are going to stress out the kids."
- "Let the Feds come in an see if they can do this better."
- "Our principal is good at helping us with this."

Suggestion: Read together some of the articles in the November 2003 issue of *Educational Leadership*, especially the article by Richard Elmore, "The Plea for Strong Practice".

SECONDARY LEVEL SAMPLE OBSERVATIONS
COMPOSITE NOTES TAKEN FROM 2 DAYS OF OBSERVING 11 DIFFERENT TEACHERS
OBSERVER: GARY HOWARD

Summary Comments

Principle 1 : Students are affirmed in their cultural connections.

Doorways:

- Using examples from the students' lives.
- Redlining, Driving While Black, Profiling
- Making personal connections across cultures.
- Multicultural images in the artwork, décor, career options.
- Multicultural content integrated into regular lessons.
- Inclusion of diverse authors/experts/contributors to the field.
- Encouraging students to explore their own interests in project assignments.
- Lot of emphasis on culture in the classroom.
- Teachers sponsor trips to different cultural settings.
- Photos of past students showing the diversity of the school.
- School-wide opportunities for students to learn about their own and other cultures.

Possible Barriers or Missed Opportunities:

- Disciplines where it feels like a stretch to make diverse cultural.
- Bare, sparse classroom environment that looks like kids don't live here.
- Students looking at the racial make-up of a class to determine whether it will be easy or difficult.
- Stereotypes, insensitive comments, hurtful language ignored or tolerated.
- "That's so gay."

Culturally Responsive Classroom

Principle 2 : Teacher is personally inviting.

Doorways:

- Welcoming students at the door.
- Friendly informal demeanor.
- Sharing examples from your own experience.
- Relaxed environment.
- Begin class right away — engaged in activity.
- Gentle approach to high-energy or possibly disruptive students.
- Clearly communicating your enjoyment of the students.
- Having high expectations of everyone.

Possible Barriers or Missed Opportunities:

- Staying only in front of the room.
- Engaging only small number of students in discussion.
- Slowing the class start-up while taking roll at the beginning.
- Non-verbal messages that communicate low expectations.
- Using sarcasm and put-downs with students.
- Management by intimidation.

CA-9 Culturally Responsive Classroom

Principle 3: Learning environments are culturally and physically inviting.

Doorways:

- Décor in room reflects content of the course.
- Visuals of career options related to the course.
- Student work/projects displayed prominently.
- Music played during small-group work time.
- Multicultural images.
- Soft lighting initially as students enter.
- Interesting things to look at and read on the walls.
- Personal interests of the teacher are evident in the room décor.

Possible Barriers or Missed Opportunities:

- Room is bare and sterile.
- Structure of room makes interaction difficult.
- Teacher space and student space are rigidly defined.

CA-9 *Culturally Responsive Classroom*

Principle 4: Students are reinforced for academic development.

Doorways:

- Lot of student work on display.
- Key concepts are explained clearly on posters.
- "Thank you for correcting my mistake."
- "José, didn't you say something earlier about this case?"
- Individualized pacing of lessons.
- Asking students to think — discover the scientific process.
- Review and reinforcement of past learning.
- "Great question."
- Students encouraged to submit work for local and regional contests.
- Step-by-step clear sequencing of learning.
- Holding to high expectations — "Everyone is writing now."
- "I know it's hard, but if you get in this habit now it will be a lot easier."
- Complementing student for positive feedback heard from another teacher.
- Going to study skills class to work with students you have in your class.
- Encouraging students to apply for higher level courses and other special focus programs.
- Catching students being smart.

Possible Barriers or Missed Opportunities:

- Large class size makes it difficult to get to the disengaged student.
- How do we reinforce abilities that we don't see?
- Different abilities all paced the same.
- Allowing some students to languish in non-engagement.
- Not reinforcing student for trying even when response was wrong.
- "Sometimes I forget that for every assignment I give, there are some students who can't do the work. How do I deal with this?"
- Lack of ethnic/racial/economic diversity in higher level classes.
- Accepting mediocrity.
- "How do I accommodate to differences when the district-driven focus on test results is so narrowly scripted?

Principle 5: Instructional changes are made to accommodate differences in learners.

Doorways:

- Allowing students to switch roles when one feels uncomfortable in an assigned classroom interaction.
- Creating an environment where students can concentrate in a way that fits their learning style.
- Valuing diverse learning styles — ways of paying attention.
- Calling on a wide variety of ethnic and style-different students.
- Proactive strategies for getting access to technology for students who don't have that access at home.
- Paying attention to cultural and religious nuances and social interactions.
- Awareness and responsiveness to the tensions in the home country and the way these can impact immigrant students.
- Valuing, learning from, and incorporating into instruction the different languages the students bring.

Possible Barriers or Missed Opportunities:

- Difficulty of "accommodation" in some disciplines.
- Recruitment and retention of Black and Hispanic students to some programs they do not see as their "turf".
- "How do I accommodate if they aren't here?"
- "Failure due to non-attendance."
- Language diverse students — can they access the content in different languages?
- Teaching from only one modality of intelligence or learning style.

Culturally Responsive Classroom

Principle 6: Classroom is managed with firm, consistent, loving control.

Doorways:

- Seating arrangement used as preventative strategy.
- Small groups used as preventative strategy.
- Potentially volatile students handled gently.
- Allowed space within the structure.
- "Can we re-focus?"
- Strong messages of caring and respect.
- Teachers teaming to create consistent strategies for disruptive students.
- High expectations for a learning-centered environment.
- "You know what the routine is."
- "Thank you. Now I know you are listening."
- Teachers of different racial and cultural groups cover each other's backs and approach the students in a consistent way.
- School-wide expectations clearly communicated to everyone.
- Teachers and administrators are mutually supportive in their behavioral interventions.

Possible Barriers or Missed Opportunities:

- "Difficult pairs" allowed to sit or work together.
- Combination of several high maintenance students in the same class.
- Disproportionate energy given to the one student who drives you up the wall.
- Interactive classes with high energy and high maintenance students can be "the longest 50 minutes in your day."
- Unclear or mixed messages from faculty and administrators.
- Playing favorites or playing students against each other.

Culturally Responsive Classroom

Principle 7: Interactions stress collectivity as well as individuality.

Doorways:

- Small-group discussion regularly built into lessons.
- Large-group discussion regularly built into instruction.
- Individual work on problem solving.
- Team work on problem solving.
- Thoughtful formulation of small groups to get maximum diversity of gender, ethnicity, and ability in each team.
- Checking for individual understanding among members of a team.
- Direct teaching of skills for working effectively in teams.
- Personal journaling.
- Allowing students to pick their own small groups initially, then gradually moving them toward more diverse groups.
- Excellent examples of Socratic dialogue.
- Diversity leadership and cultural awareness workshops for students that focus on cultural competence skills.

Possible Barriers or Missed Opportunities:

- Loose or unclear guidelines/expectations for team work.
- Some students need to learn how to work in a team.
- Lack of forethought about team membership.
- Missed opportunities to use peer tutoring.
- Some kids share naturally, for others it needs to be encouraged/taught.
- Structure of the room prevents/discourages small-group work.

CRT Study Groups Recording Sheet

From your discussion of the Seven Principles for Culturally Responsive Teaching, have all participants record one of the doorways and one of the barriers that they presented for their Principle. Leave these notes on your table.

Principle

1. Students are affirmed in their cultural connections.
   Doorway:

   Barrier:

2. Teacher is personally inviting.
   Doorway:

   Barrier:

3. Learning environments are physically and culturally inviting.
   Doorway:

   Barrier:

4. Students are reinforced for academic development.
   Doorway:

   Barrier:

5. Instructional changes are made to accommodate differences in learners.
   Doorway:

   Barrier:

6. Classroom is managed with firm, consistent, and caring control.
   Doorway:

   Barrier:

7. Interactions stress collectivity as well as individuality.
   Doorway:

   Barrier:

Activity: CRT Action Research	
Phase Four: Classroom Implications and Applications	
Purpose:	• Assess your professional practice related to each of the Seven Principles for CRT
	• Select a Proficient Principle and a Growth Principle
	• Create a faculty/staff chart of Proficient and Growth Principles
	• Design an Action Research Project to improve your practice related to your Growth Principle
	• Stimulate a mutually supportive climate of shared growth among adults in your school
Suggested Time:	45 minutes
Materials Needed:	Video Segment 4:5
	Handout CA-11: CRT Personal Reflection and Assessment
	Handout CA-12: Sample Faculty CRT Chart
	Handout CA-13: CRT Action Research
	Handout CA-14: CRT Student-Based Action Research
	Compiled notes from your CRT Study Groups activity
	Blank 3 × 5–inch note cards
Advanced Preparation:	• View Video Segment 4:5
	• Review the Facilitator Directions
	• Make a stapled packet of the notes from CRT Study Groups
	• Plan the timing and process for periodic follow-up conversations, where faculty will share their experiences and progress with their Action Research Projects

Facilitator Note: *CRT Action Research is where the Phase Four work becomes real for every member of your staff. This activity engages all adults in your building in assessing their own professional practice related to the Seven Principles of Culturally Responsive Teaching. All participants select a Proficient Principle, which represents one of their arenas of professional strength, and they select a Growth Principle, which is an area of their practice they would like to improve. With this information, your Facilitation Team will create a chart showing the overall profile of Proficient and Growth Principles across the whole faculty, a profile that can guide you in designing future professional development activities (see Handout CA-12). Finally, faculty members design an Action Research Project to improve their practice related to their Growth Principle. In this way, you engage everyone on your staff in stretching their* *professional muscle, moving the body of their practice in new ways, and exercising that "self-generated neuro-plasticity" discussed in the Introduction to this manual. This action research process can also be incorporated into your annual Professional Growth Plans and can continue to impact your school improvement activities for multiple years.*

1. Set the Stage   5 Minutes

Have people seated in work-alike groups by grade level or department. Distribute copies of the CRT Personal Reflection and Assessment (Handout CA-11) and the compiled notes from your CRT Study Groups activity, showing all of the doorways and barriers for each of the Seven Principles that were generated by your faculty in that earlier activity. Also, have a stack of 3 × 5 cards on each table, one per person, and copies of the CRT Action Research planning form (Handout CA-13). Ask everyone to review the doorways and barriers notes and talk with their colleagues for a couple of minutes. After they have had some time to renew their familiarity with this information, announce that the next step in the process will engage everyone in reflecting on your own practice related to each of the Seven Principles.

2. Start Video Segment 4:5
Personal Assessment   5 Minutes

Gary Howard reviews some of the steps that have led to this point in the process and introduces the Personal Reflection and Assessment activity. He asks people to think about their own professional practice and give themselves a rating from 1 to 10 related to each of the Seven Principles, the upper range of the scale being their areas of greatest comfort and proficiency, and the lower end being the areas in which they would most like to grow. You will be prompted to **stop the video** while people do this. Facilitators should circulate during this time to support people who may need clarification of the task.

3. Restart the Video: 3 × 5 Cards   5 Minutes

After everyone has completed the Personal Assessment on Handout CA-11, restart the video. Gary leads the group in a process of recording their Proficient and Growth Principles on 3 × 5 cards. He informs them that these cards will be used to generate a faculty chart showing the overall distribution of Proficient and Growth Principles (he shows a visual of Handout CA-12). Once you have generated your own version of this chart, you will have a clear picture of the areas of greatest proficiency across the whole faculty, as well as the areas where people most want to grow. Gary emphasizes that his process is not about evaluation—it is about shared strength and growth.

Once people have completed their 3 × 5 cards, Gary will invite them into pair-and-share conversations with another colleague, talking with each other about which Principles they selected for their Proficient and Growth arenas. You will be prompted to **stop the video** and allow a couple of minutes for these conversations in dyads.

Facilitator Note: *This is a critical point in the entire professional development process. If you have established a solid foundation of tone and trust, people will be willing to complete and turn in their 3 × 5 cards. If the tone and trust is problematic, you may experience some resistance and pushback. Gary's words will help minimize any concerns that this information will be used in an evaluative way, but your Facilitation Team may have to reinforce that point and respond to any concerns that surface.*

You don't have to distribute copies of the Sample Faculty CRT Chart (Handout CA-12). Gary will show a visual of that chart during his comments. You can use the sample as a template for creating your own version after you have compiled the 3 × 5 cards.

4. Restart the Video: Initiating Action Research Projects   5 Minutes

After people have completed their pair-and-share conversations, restart the video. Gary leads them in planning their Action Research Projects, using Handout CA-13. He walks through the planning form, giving examples of his and other people's Action Research Projects, and asking your faculty to make some notes about their projects. After this presentation, you will be prompted to **stop the video** while people complete the planning process.

5. Planning Time for Action Research Projects   10 Minutes

While people are writing their Action Research plans on Handout CA-13, Facilitators can circulate and support anyone who may have questions or needs some support in the planning process. Make sure everyone is working on a project, reminding them that you will be checking in with them from time to time to compare experiences and progress with the projects. If people want to work as teams with two or three colleagues collaborating on the same project, encourage them to do so.

Toward the end of the planning time, recruit four or five people who would be willing to share a brief description of their project with the whole faculty. You will ask them to share which Principle they are working on, why they selected that Principle, and one or two ideas for how they will approach their growth process. Recruit people from different grade levels, teams, departments, and role groups to show the diversity of approaches across all of the adults in your school.

6. Large-Group Sharing and Closure   5 Minutes

Pull the large group back together. Ask each of your selected individuals to share some highlights of their Action Research Projects. If time allows, invite others to talk about their projects. After these people have shared, announce the timing and process for follow-up conversations about the action research. It would be good to have one check-in point a month or so after you have initiated the projects and at least one more toward the end of the school year.

Possible Follow-up Activities

1. Distribute the CRT Faculty Chart

Shortly after collecting the 3 × 5 cards, create and distribute your faculty charting of Growth and Proficient Principles modeled after Handout CA-12. Take a few minutes at a subsequent faculty meeting to show the chart, and ask people what impressions they have about the overall profile of Proficient and Growth Principles. The chart will give people an opportunity to see who may be resources or allies for them in carrying out their Action Research Projects—people who are proficient in their arena of desired growth or those who share the same Growth Principle.

2. Periodic Check-in Conversations

At your first check-in session, have people organized in sharing groups. You could do this by grade level or department, or by people who have the same Growth Principle. These conversations could also take place in Professional Learning Communities if you are using that process in your school. At the first check-in, ask people to share their progress with their projects, both in terms of the growth they are experiencing, as well as the struggles.

3. Year-End Reports

Toward the end of the first year that you have initiated the CRT Action Research process, create a time and place for faculty and staff to share their overall lessons and outcomes from the projects. Do this is small-group discussions, and ask each small group to report out to the larger faculty one of the insights or takeaways that has surfaced in their conversation.

4. Student-Based Action Research

As an extension, or second year follow-up, to the Action Research process, you can introduce Handout CA-14: CRT Student-Based Action Research. This is similar to the activity described above, but the focus is different. Instead of selecting a Growth Principle to work on, faculty members choose a struggling student as the focus of their project. They identify the student's strengths, challenges, and the possible access points for connecting more effectively with that student. They then choose which of the Seven Principles for CRT would be most helpful in reaching this student. If everyone in your school is focused on a different student who is in need of more attention and support, you can have significant impact across your student population over the course of a school year. This process also allows for valuable mutually supportive conversations as faculty members share their experiences with the Student-Based Action Research.

CRT Personal Reflection and Assessment

For each of the Seven Principles for Culturally Responsive Teaching, give yourself a 1–10 rating indicating how well you feel you are doing in implementing the intent of that Principle.

Principle	Your Rating 1–10
Students are affirmed in their cultural connections.	_____
Teacher is personally inviting.	_____
Learning environments are physically and culturally inviting.	_____
Students are reinforced for academic development.	_____
Instructional changes are made to accommodate differences in learners.	_____
Classroom is managed with firm, consistent, and caring control.	_____
Interactions stress collectivity as well as individuality.	_____

If you were going to select one of these Principles to work on improving in your practice over the course of the school year, which one would it be?

What are some of the doorways you think you could open related to this Principle?

Who among your colleagues is particularly good at this Principle and could perhaps support you?

Sample Faculty Charting of Proficient and Growth Principle.

Principle 1 Students are affirmed in their cultural connections.	Principle 2 Teachers are personally inviting.	Principle 3 Learning environments are physically & culturally inviting.	Principle 4 Students are reinforced for academic development.	Principle 5 Instructional changes are made to accommodate differences in learners.	Principle 6 Classroom is managed with firm, consistent, caring control.	Principle 7 Interactions stress collectivity as well as individuality.
Hepner K.	Hepner	Fameni	Dehaven-Dawson	Hines	McKenzie	Baker-Luttrell
Harbaugh	Stevens	Dowdy	McKay	White	Caslin	Sheys
Cassutto	Seebeck	DeMark	McCarthy	Taffe	Cona	Johnston
Harris	Lemp	Menard	Fameni	Hartmetz	Simpson	Brosh
	Rovang	O'Neil	Rimmell	Cucinell	Haugh	
	Price	Hall	Woodland	Kitka	Blackshire	
	Ritz	Jones	Purvis	Richard	Kramer	
	Dick		Beglau	Cottner	Dowling	
	O'Neil			Flannery	VanTassell	
	Lenz			Gladden	Mumpower	
	Grooms			Sweeney	Lewandowski	
	Duffy			Rumer	Igoe	
	Thompson			Hoppert	Brian	
	Todd				Martel	
	VanGilder				Barton	
	Shores				Thompson	
	Thomas				Yacoub	
	Pizana				Staneart	
	Murphy					
	Whetsel					

Proficient

Sample Faculty Charting of Proficient and Growth Principles

Principle 1	Principle 2	Principle 3	Principle 4	Principle 5	Principle 6	Principle 7
Students are affirmed in their cultural connections.	Teachers are personally inviting.	Learning environments are physically & culturally inviting.	Students are reinforced for academic development.	Instructional changes are made to accommodate differences in learners.	Classroom is managed with firm, consistent, caring control.	Interactions stress collectivity as well as individuality.
Whetsel	Purvis	Lewandowski	Thomas	Pizana	Rumer	Murphy
Staneart	Cassutto	Kramer	Yacoub	Shores	Grooms	Jones
VanGilder	Johnston	Rovang	Brian	Todd	Beglau	Hoppert
Thompson	Kittka	Lemp	Harbaugh	Duffy	Igoe	Sweeney
Gladden	Blackshire	Cucinell	White	Barton	Stevens	Martel
Flannery		Taffe		Hall	McKay	O'Neil
Dick		McKenzie		Lenz		Cottner
Brosh				Ritz		Richard
Dowling				Menard		VanTassell
DeMark				Mumpower		Fameni
Dowdy				Woodland		Cucinell
Seebeck				Rimmell		McCarthy
Sheys				Price		Cona
Simpson				Haugh		Hepner
Hartmetz				Harris		Hines
Caslin				Hepner K.		
				Baker-Luttrell		
				Dehaven-Dawson		

Growth

CA-13 Personal Action Research Projects

Step 1: Set Your Goal

Select one of the Seven Principles for CRT that you want to work on strengthening in your own practice this year.

My Principle to work on:

Possible Barriers or Missed Opportunities I may have created:

Step 2: Plan Your Actions

What will you do to grow your own skills related to this Principle and what behaviors/actions will you be adding or changing in your practice?

My Actions and Doorways I will open:

Step 3: Evaluate Your Results

How will you know that you have achieved your desired goal or improvement? What will be the evidence that it is working?

My Evaluation Criteria:

Step 4: Choose a Critical Friend

With whom among your colleagues will you discuss your project and ask for support along the way?

My Critical Friend:

Keep some notes and be ready to give periodic progress reports to your critical friend and to other colleagues at our future meetings.

CRT Student-Based Action Research

CRT Student-Based Action Research

Step 1: Select a Student

- Someone from a group who is most challenged related to achievement and school success

Step 2: Describe the Present State

- What are the strengths, challenges, and access points for this student?

Step 3: Describe the Desired State

- What is the observable outcome you are looking for?

Step 4: Doorways You Will Create

- What are the ways you will change your behavior and approach with this student?

- Which of the Seven CRT Principles will be most helpful?

Step 5: Assessment

- How will you know that you have reached your goal?

- What are the metrics of success for this student?

Be ready to share your observations and outcomes in future discussions with your colleagues.

Activity: Learning From and With Colleagues	
Phase Four: Classroom Implications and Applications	
Purpose:	• Deepen your work with the Seven Principles for CRT • Create a climate of mutual growth and support • Stimulate conversation about Growth and Proficient Principles • Engage faculty in reflective conversation about their practice • Identify issues and struggles faculty are encountering in implementing the Seven Principles • Generate action strategies for addressing these issues and struggles
Suggested Time:	50 minutes
Materials Needed:	Video Segment 4:6 Handout CA-15: Worksheet Packet (3 pages)
Advanced Preparation:	• View Video Segment 4:6 • Review the Facilitator Directions • Discuss your method for organizing the discussion groups • Create stapled packets of the three CA-15 worksheets • Create Seven Principle tent cards for each table

Facilitator Note: *This activity creates a conversation about the Seven Principles for CRT, a conversation that is deeply grounded in the real work your faculty and staff are doing with students every day. This activity provides a mutually supportive opportunity for your faculty to share their struggles and issues and to help each other design possible strategies for improving their practice. As the process unfolds, everyone will be gaining a deeper understanding of the Seven Principles and a better grasp of the power of CRT in reaching more of your students.*

It works best to have people seated in max-mix groups of five to seven at the beginning of this activity. Each group will be focusing on a different Principle, so you will have a minimum of seven groups, with tent cards indicating the Principle focus for each group. For larger faculties, you may want to have two groups for each Principle, or simply double up on some of the Principles that have generated more interest or concern among your faculty.

Set up your numbered tables in such a way that each group can easily shift to an adjacent table that has a different Principle number than the one they started with. Have tent cards placed on each table with the Principle for that table written out.

Gary will be prompting people to change tables during the second round of the process, so your Facilitation Team needs to have that shift organized ahead of time.

Either before or after this activity may be an excellent time to show your faculty selected pieces from SVC-19 through SVC-22. Each of these video segments shows a teacher interacting with students and reflecting on their classroom practice related to the Seven Principles for CRT. Your Facilitator Team can preview theses clips and decide which ones would be most appropriate for your faculty.

1. Set the Stage   2 Minutes

Have people seated at seven tables (or more for larger faculties), with tent cards identifying the Principle focus for each table. Place one copy of the stapled CR-15 packet on each table. Announce that today's activity will take you into a deeper conversation about the Seven Principles for CRT, and allow everyone to share some of the challenges and issues that are emerging in your work with the Principles.

2. Start Video Segment 4:6   4 Minutes

Gary describes the process for this activity and launches people into the first level of conversation. Each small group will consider themselves to be a Growth Group related to the Principle that has been assigned to their table. After selecting a recorder, their task is to identify two issues, challenges, or questions that could emerge for someone who is not feeling proficient with this Principle. Gary asks them to make these issues as real as possible, hopefully emerging from struggles they are having in their own work. As clearly and specifically as possible, they will describe these two issues on the first page of their packet. During the next step in the process, a different set of people will be coming to your table to respond to the issues, so you want them to have something solid to work with. Facilitators will be prompted to **stop the video** while groups identify and record their issues.

3. Growth Group Recording of Issues   8 Minutes

While Growth Groups are working, Facilitators should circulate and make themselves available for support. Watch the time and tell people at the halfway point they should be moving on to their second issue or question. Remind them to state their issues as clearly as possible. Also, make sure they have recorded their Principle number at the top of all three pages in their worksheet packet.

4. Restart the Video: Shifting to Proficient Groups   5 Minutes

Bring the group's attention back to the video where Gary sets up the second step in the process. Every small group is now going to move to an adjacent table (clockwise around the room, or however the Facilitators have decided). As the groups move, make sure they are each moving to a table with a different Principle than the one they worked on in their Growth Groups. The worksheet packets will be left at the original table. The people move, but the packets don't. Also, each recorder will stay behind for a couple of minutes while the rest of their group moves to the adjacent table. Gary will direct this process, and while the groups are moving and settling in, you will be prompted to **stop the video.**

5. Brief Clarification of Issues With the Original Recorder   2 Minutes

When all of the people, except for recorders, have settled into their new tables, allow a couple of minutes for the new group to read over the notes left by the Growth Group. They can ask the recorder for clarification or more details if needed. Don't allow this process to go on too long. At the end of 2 minutes or so, tell the recorders they can now rejoin their teammates at the new table.

6. Restart the Video: Proficient Group Directions   3 Minutes

When all recorders have rejoined their groups, start the video. Gary asks everyone to imagine they are now a Proficient Group related to this new Principle. They will be responding to the issues listed by the Growth Group, giving their best advice and counsel, suggesting strategies for addressing the first group's concerns. Gary will have each Proficient Group select a new recorder and begin their work. With these directions in place, you will be prompted to **stop the video.**

7. Proficient Group Responses   8 Minutes

Everyone will now be working on the second page of the packet. They will discuss the issues and challenges identified by the Growth

Group and record their suggestions and strategies for how to approach each of those concerns. Once again, it will be helpful for Facilitators to circulate and support the Proficient Groups as they do their work. Remind them to make their responses as specific and relevant as possible, suggesting interventions and resources that would be helpful to any teacher or support person who is dealing with the issues that have been raised by the Growth Group. Watch the time, and at the halfway point, remind the groups to be moving on to their second issue.

8. Shifting Back to Growth Groups   2 Minutes

At the end of the Proficient Group discussion time, thank everyone for their work, and let them know you are now going to initiate the third step in the process. Ask each small group to now move back to their original table, where they will have an opportunity to see how the Proficient Group responded to the issues they recorded on page 1 of their original packet. All worksheets will be left on the tables as the groups move. Once again, ask the Proficient Group recorders to stay behind for a couple of minutes while the rest of their group moves back to their original table.

9. Brief Clarification With
Proficient Group Recorders   2 Minutes

As soon as the groups (minus their recorders) have settled in at their original tables, announce that they will now have a couple of minutes to read over the Proficient Groups' responses and ask for clarification from the Proficient Group recorders. Don't let this process go on too long. Then invite the recorders to rejoin their teammates at their original table.

10. Restart the Video: Directions
for the Final Step   2 Minutes

Gary describes the process for completing page 3 of the packet, where Growth Groups review the Proficient Group responses and design action strategies for addressing each of the issues they originally stated. After Gary gives the directions, you will be prompted to **stop the video** while the Growth Groups work.

11. Designing Action Strategies   8 Minutes

Growth Groups will reflect on the suggestions given by the Proficient Groups and consider more deeply how they would address the two issues they stated on page 1 of their packet. Combining the Proficient Group's ideas with their own further thinking, they will now write the action strategies they would actually take to address each of the challenges. Facilitators can move around the room supporting the groups as needed and reminding them to move on to their second issue when half of the work time has passed.

12. Large-Group Reflection and Debrief   5 Minutes

At the end of the final work time, call the large group back together. Ask two or three groups to read one of the issues as they originally stated it on page 1, then the Proficient Group's suggestions for that issue on page 2, and finally the action strategy they wrote on page 3 of their packet. After a few groups have shared in this way, ask the large group for responses to these questions:

- How was this process helpful?
- How could it have been more helpful?
- What did you learn?

Announce that your Facilitation Team will be collecting the worksheet packets and transcribing them so everyone can see the outcomes for all Seven Principles.

It would be valuable at this point to acknowledge that together as a school, you have now moved to a point where the CRT work can become "business as usual" for your faculty. It is not an add-on or "one more thing we have to do," but rather a conceptual framework and tool for discussing and improving what you do every day. You created your own lists of doorways and barriers for each Principle when you did the CRT Study Groups activity. Then, during the CRT Action Research activity, each member of your faculty, staff, and administration created an Action Research Project to improve your practice with one of the Principles. And now today, you have identified issues and challenges and designed action strategies for strengthening your work with each of the Seven Principles. You can now say, "Culturally Responsive Teaching is what we do."

Follow-up Activity

Shortly after completing the Learning From and With Colleagues process, transcribe and distribute the notes from each of the Principle groups. Organize these notes in the following way:

Principle 1: Students are affirmed in their cultural connections.

    Issue 1: As stated by the Growth Group (page 1)
    Issue 1: Suggestions as given by the Proficient Group (page 2)
    Issue 1: Action strategies as designed by the Growth Groups (page 3)

    Issue 2: As stated by the Growth Group
    Issue 2: Suggestions as given by the Proficient Group
    Issue 2: Action strategies as designed by the Growth Groups

Principle 2: Teachers are personally inviting.

    Etc.
    Etc.
    Etc.

Create a time and place for people to review and discuss these notes, either in faculty meetings, grade-level teams, department meetings, Professional Learning Communities, or some other venue.

CA-15
Learning From and With Colleagues

Culturally Responsive Teaching

Learning from and with Colleagues

<u>Growth Group</u> Notes for Principle #: _____

8-Minute Discussion and Recording: Imagine you are a group of educators who have selected this as your Growth Principle, ar area in which you would like to improve your practice. What might be some of the struggles you would be having? Record below two issues, questions, and challenges for which you would like to hear responses from the Proficient Group. State your issues as clearly and specifically as possible, so the Proficient Group will have something solid to work with.

Issue 1:

Issue 2:

Learning From and With Colleagues

Culturally Responsive Teaching

Learning from and with Colleagues

Proficient Group Responses for Principle #: _____

8-Minute Discussion and Recording: Imagine you are a group of educators who have selected this as your Proficient Principle, an area of practice where you feel strong and confident in your work. Discuss each of the issues and questions raised by the Growth Group for this Principle and record below your responses, suggestions, and advice. Be as practical and real as you can, giving the Growth Group ideas they can directly apply in their work.

Issue 1 Possible Responses:

Issue 2 Possible Responses:

CA-15 Learning From and With Colleagues

Culturally Responsive Teaching

Learning from and with Colleagues

<u>Growth Group</u> Closing Discussion for Principle #: _____

8-Minute Discussion and Recording: Read over each of the responses from the Proficient Group, and record two or three possible action steps or strategies you could use to grow your own practice related to each of the issues you raised. Make these action ideas as real and doable as possible.

Issue 1 Action Strategies:

Issue 2 Action Strategies:

Activity: CRT Classroom Peer Observation	
Phase Four: Classroom Implications and Applications	
Purpose:	• Provide a structure and rubric for CRT classroom observations • Create opportunities for teachers and other adults to observe their peers as they work with students • Deepen teachers' understanding of the Seven Principles • Identify additional doorways, missed opportunities, and possible barriers for each of the Seven Principles
Suggested Time	15-minute Introduction Implementation Over the Course of Multiple School Years
Materials Needed:	Video Segment 4:7 Handout CA-16: CRT Classroom Observation Rubric
Advanced Preparation:	• View Video Segment 4:7 • Review the Facilitator Directions • Design a process for implementing classroom observations

Facilitator Note: *This is a process that can take place over the course of a full school year and possibly be ongoing for multiple years. It involves all members of your faculty and staff having an opportunity to observe their peers in the classroom, recording behaviors and practices that demonstrate how the Seven Principles for CRT are being implemented on a daily basis. Your faculty should have a fairly good grounding in the Seven Principles before you initiate the observation process, and that process in itself will be a powerful way to deepen their understanding of CRT. In Video Segment 4:7, Gary Howard provides a brief orientation to the CRT Classroom Observation Rubric. Based on his recommendations, it will be up to your Facilitation Team to design the timing and process that would allow each adult in your building to have this opportunity to observe the professional practice of their peers.*

In addition to your faculty being familiar with the Seven Principles for CRT before you invite them into the observation process, you also want them to have established sufficient trust to not feel overly threatened by the idea of peers observing them in their work. Much of this tone and trust is dependent on how you introduce the process. Gary Howard's comments in the Video Segment are intended to support you in establishing that tone. Also, following *the Facilitator Directions below, you will find a list of **Planning Ideas and Suggestions** and a set of **Guidelines for Peer Observers** to further support your implementation of this activity.*

1. Set the Tone   2 Minutes

Announce that you are now going to take the next step in your work with the Seven Principles for CRT. Remind people of the activities you have completed so far, and let them know that your Facilitation Team is excited about what is coming next.

Distribute copies of Handout CA-16, and start the video.

2. Start Video Segment 4:7—Introduction to the Process   5 Minutes

In this short video, Gary introduces the idea of peer observation and walks people through the Classroom Observation Rubric. He emphasizes that this process is not about teacher evaluation; it is about collaboration and learning from and with each other. And it's fun! He will also suggest that the first round of peer observations take place on a voluntary basis, with other people joining in later as they feel comfortable with the process. You will be prompted to **stop the video.**

3. Pair-and-Share Conversations   3 Minutes

At the end of Gary's comments, invite people to choose a partner and talk with each other about the Observation Rubric and their feelings about the idea of peer observations. Facilitators can circulate during these conversations and respond to questions.

4. Practice Observations With the School Video Clips   Timing Is Variable

This is an excellent time to use SVC-23 through SVC-26 as an opportunity to practice using the Observation Rubric. Facilitators should preview these video segments and decide which ones would be most useful for your faculty. Each segment shows Gary Howard interviewing a group of students, asking them to describe those teacher behaviors that make them feel smart and want to learn, as well as those behaviors that get in the way of their learning. Your teachers can watch these clips and record on the Observation Rubric which Principles relate most directly to the student comments. Following these observations, they can talk together in small groups and compare their notes. Gary provides a brief introduction to each of the video segments.

5. Invitation to Round 1 of Classroom Observations   5 Minutes

Following the pair-and-share conversations, your Facilitation Team will describe your plans for the Classroom Observation process. Gary suggests that you start with volunteers, both people who are willing to be observed as well as those who want to do the observations. Create a process for signing up for this first round. Ask if there are any questions or concerns at this point, and announce that an email will soon go out inviting volunteers to take part in the first round.

Planning Ideas and Suggestions

- Before you announce the Peer Observation activity to your faculty, you might have some informal conversations with teachers who would be most likely to want to participate in the first round of the process. Members of your Facilitation Team can be some of the first teachers to volunteer.

- Don't worry if the initial group of volunteers is small. Once you share the results from the observations, and people see that this activity is not threatening or punitive, others will want to join.

- Work out a way to free up the time for teachers and other staff members to do their observations. It is usually sufficient to have 15 minutes in a classroom, and it would be optimal if each observer could be in at least two or three different classrooms.

- Create an opportunity for observers to gather after they have completed their round of observations. One of the most positive outcomes from this process is the learning that happens for the observers as they watch their peers in action. They are excited to share what they have learned, and it is helpful to provide them this opportunity.

- After the first round, compile the notes from all of the observers in a format similar to Handouts CA-8 and CA-9. Notes should include doorways, possible barriers, and missed opportunities.

- Distribute and discuss these notes at a subsequent faculty meeting, where you will invite more people to participate in Round 2.

- You can continue to implement multiple rounds of peer observation over the course of a year or more, always compiling and distributing the notes, and hopefully engaging most of your faculty over time.

- Teacher names are never included on the compiled notes—these are teacher behaviors that everyone can learn without feeling singled out.

- If teachers who have been observed do want to see the notes taken in their classroom, provide an opportunity for this to happen.

Guidelines for Peer Observers

1. Go over these Guidelines with observers before each round of observations.

2. Observers should have multiple copies of the Observation Rubric on a clipboard. List the teacher's name at the top of each form, doing one form for each classroom you observe.

3. Teachers' names will not be connected to the compiled notes that will be shared with the faculty, but some of the teachers you observe may want to talk with you about your notes from their classroom.

4. Observers' task is to find examples/doorways for each of the Seven Principles—things teachers are doing that support each of the Principles.

5. You are also watching for any possible barriers or missed opportunities—things that may be getting in the way of the Principles or simply not happening.

6. Don't limit your observations to only those indicators that are listed on the Observation Rubric—those are intended merely as suggestions. Use the back of the form for your additional comments.

7. Bring your notes back to the debrief session with your colleagues after you have completed your round of observations.

8. Talk about your observation experiences with other colleagues who have not yet participated in the Peer Observation process. Encourage them to volunteer for the next round.

Facilitator Note: Integrating CRT Into Your School Improvement Process

Once your faculty has become familiar with the Seven Principles and the Peer Observation process, you can move toward systemic integration of CRT into your school change efforts. This is best achieved by building CRT language and the Seven Principles into any Look-For or Walkthrough instruments your school district is currently using. You can also build CRT outcomes into your teacher evaluation process. This is where the work becomes real, when it becomes part of business-as-usual for your school and part of the DNA of your school district.

CRT Classroom Peer Observation Rubric

CA-16

_____ _____ _____
Teacher   Grade Level/Subject   Date/Time/Period

Place a checkmark next to each of the doorways you observe:

1. Students' cultural connections are affirmed.

_____ Concepts and activities are relevant to students' interests and experiences.

_____ Multiple perspectives are included in curriculum, content, and materials.

_____ Teacher shows appreciation for students' knowledge and their cultures.

2. Teacher is personally inviting.

_____ Teacher demonstrates open and trusting relationships with students.

_____ Teacher values student input and perspectives.

_____ Teacher's tone of voice demonstrates caring and respect.

3. Learning environments are physically and culturally inviting.

_____ Student work is showcased both in and out of the classroom.

_____ Multicultural images, photographs, decor, and artwork are displayed.

_____ Classroom ambience exudes a recognition and appreciation of culture.

4. Students are reinforced for academic development.

_____ Learning expectations are clearly communicated using a variety of approaches.

_____ Teacher expresses a belief in students' capacity and intelligence.

_____ Teacher frequently interacts with individual students to check for understanding.

5. Instructional changes are made to accommodate differences.

_____ Students are provided choices in demonstrating their understanding of concepts.

_____ Teacher addresses a variety of learning styles in lesson delivery.

_____ Teacher uses interventions and extensions to address individual needs.

6. Classroom is managed with firm, consistent, and caring control.

_____ Students are actively engaged in learning most of the time.

_____ Teacher effectively redirects potentially disruptive behavior.

_____ Discipline issues are handled in an instructive and respectful manner.

7. Interactions stress collectivity as well as individuality.

_____ Classroom setup facilitates both small-group and individual work.

_____ Teacher effectively employs a variety of grouping strategies.

_____ Students are able to function effectively both as individuals and as group members.

Use the back of the page to record specific teacher behaviors that represent the following:

Additional Doorways:

Possible Barriers of Missed Opportunities:

Other Comments/Questions:

Developed in collaboration with the Granite School District, Office of Educational Equity, Salt Lake City, UT Charlene Lui, Director. Used here with permission.

Activity: Achievement Triangle	
Phase Four: Classroom Implications and Applications	
Purpose:	• Provide a unified model that brings together Phases One through Four of the professional development process • Summarize the key concepts that have been presented so far • Support faculty and staff in making meaning from their experiences with all of the previous activities
Suggested Time:	15 Minutes
Materials Needed:	Video Segment 4:8 Handout CA-17: Achievement Triangle (3 pages)
Advanced Preparation:	• View Video Segment 4:8 • Review the Facilitator Directions • Decide the best time to use this Video

Facilitator Note: *The Achievement Triangle is a summative presentation, bringing together the lessons and key conceptual framework from all of your work in Phases One through Four. It can be used anytime during Phase Four but works best after your faculty has become conversant in the Seven Principles for CRT. This is primarily a talk piece, with a short time built in for people to talk about their responses to the presentation.*

1. Set the Tone   1 Minute

Distribute copies of Handout CA-17, which consists of three pages stapled together. Announce that this Video Segment will provide a summary and integrative model for pulling together much of the professional development work you have been doing together.

2. Show Video Segment 4:8   9 Minutes

Gary walks your faculty and staff through the three levels of analysis and the nine key concepts that are included in the Achievement Triangle. In the course of his comments, he links together many of the activities you have completed in Phases One through Four. At the end of his presentation, Gary invites people to form small groups of three to discuss their responses to the Achievement Triangle. You will be prompted to **stop the video** at this point.

3. Conversations in Triads   4 Minutes

Video prompts will guide the small groups of three in sharing their reactions and thoughts related to the Achievement Triangle. Video prompts will ask them to address the following questions:

- Which part of the Triangle is most important for you?
- Which part presents the greatest challenge to you in your work?
- Is there anything missing in this model you would like to add?

4. Closing Comments   1 Minute

One of the members of your Facilitation Team can close the session by sharing his or her personal responses to the three questions above. If you have more time, you can also invite other people to share their thoughts with the larger group. This would also be a good time to show SVC-27, a brief video segment with a high school principal sharing her reflections on the Achievement Triangle.

The Achievement Triangle 1

For a complete discussion and graphics of the Achievement Triangle, see Chapter 7, pp. 126–134 in *We Can't Teach What We Don't Know*, Second Edition (2006), by Gary Howard.

The Achievement Triangle 2

For a complete discussion and graphics of the Achievement Triangle, see Chapter 7, pp. 126–134 in *We Can't Teach What We Don't Know*, Second Edition (2006), by Gary Howard.

The Achievement Triangle 3

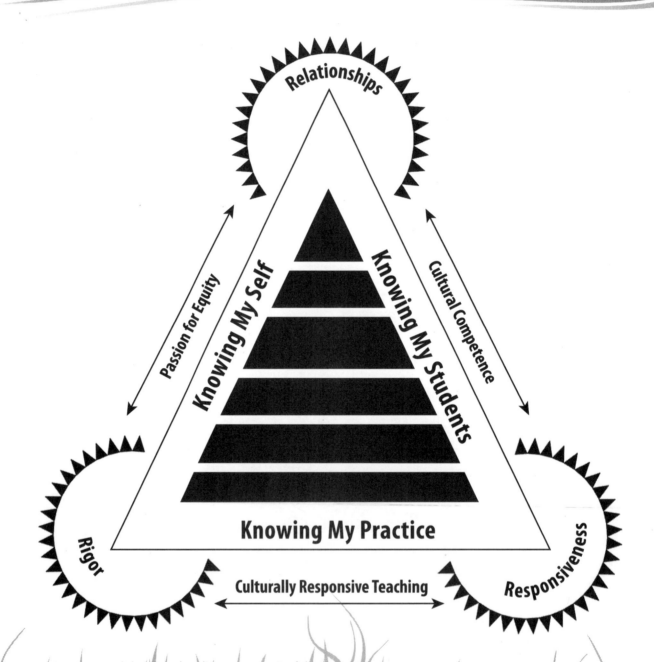

Achievement Triangle: Transformationist Pedagogy, ©2005 Gary Howard

Phase Five: Systemic Transformation/ Planning for Change

Goals for Phase Five:

- Identifying organizational barriers to equity and inclusion
- Applying a three-stage model for organizational transformation
- Action planning for staff development and systemic change
- Creating a holistic integrated approach to school improvement

---

RATIONALE AND OVERVIEW OF ACTIVITIES

Phase Five focuses on the organizational dimension of the work (see Figure 1 in the manual Introduction). The activities and tools provided in this section are divided into two categories. The first four pieces are designed to engage your faculty and staff in looking at your school culture as a whole. These all-faculty activities will help you summarize the work done in the previous four phases, highlighting the dynamic interplay and mutuality of outcomes that can occur across the personal, professional, and organizational dimensions of growth. Staff members will work with a three-phase model for assessing your school's culture of inclusion and equity, and they will examine the various catalysts that can energize that work. They will identify the successes you have achieved to date in improving your school culture, acknowledge the challenges that still await your attention, and design strategies for addressing those challenges.

The final five pieces in this section of the manual are designed specifically for your leadership team. You will initially study these activities as a team and then decide how, when, and where to share them with your faculty and staff. These activities will support you in planning for and assessing your progress with the entire professional development process. The first of these pieces focuses on issues of resistance, guiding your facilitation team in a reflective examination of the types of difficult and challenging behaviors, attitudes, and beliefs that may show up in your work with faculty and staff. As we have mentioned earlier, not everyone is going to be open and willing to engage in the deep reflection and personal growth that is being encouraged by this professional development process. Materials in this section of the manual will help you deal proactively with these resistance issues. This section of the manual also provides your team with planning tools for scheduling, designing, and assessing your overall multiyear implementation of the professional development process. You will be given ideas and resources for integrating the cultural competence and culturally responsive teaching work with everything else you are doing for school improvement, strategically establishing a seamless connection between and among your many efforts toward positive growth.

And finally, you will be able to observe a model program for engaging and empowering Youth Voices as an essential tool in your overall approach to inclusion, equity, and excellence.

Begin your all-faculty activities by showing the **Phase Five Introductory Video,** which will demonstrate how faculty, staff, and administrators have engaged in the planning and systemic change work in actual school settings. Then, introduce the **Dimensions of Growth** conversation. In this Video Segment, Gary Howard provides a brief overview and summary of your work in the previous four phases and introduces the organizational component as your next arena of focus. His presentation revisits the Levels of the Work design (Figure 1) that was presented in the very first video segment and connects each of those Levels of Work with a corresponding dimension of personal, professional, or organizational growth. In this context, Cultural Awareness is about growing our *personal knowledge and experience,* Cultural Competence is about deepening our *personal will and skill* to connect across differences, Culturally Responsive Teaching is about transforming our *professional practice,* and creating a culture of Inclusion, Equity, and Excellence is about *systemic change and improving organizational outcomes.*

The next piece, **Stages of Organizational Growth,** provides your faculty and staff with a conceptual model for understanding and assessing the culture of your school. The same developmental approach that informed your Phase Two work related to the personal and professional dimensions of growth is now brought to bear on your organizational climate and schoolwide practices. This model brings attention to five arenas of organizational life: Level of Self-Awareness, Emotional Responses to Differences, Mode of Cultural Interaction, Approach to Education and Curriculum, and Approach to Leadership. Related to these arenas, three stages of organizational culture and climate are described in the Video Segment: the *Monocultural Stage*, which is characterized by conformity and avoidance of diversity issues; the *Compliance Stage*, which is characterized by impressive rhetoric but only a surface-level commitment to equity; and the *Inclusive/Equitable Stage*, which is characterized by a deep institutional commitment to social justice and the transformation of educational practices. Following the Video Segment, your faculty will be engaged in assessing the climate and culture of your school through the lens of these three stages. They will also have an opportunity to identify **Catalysts for Organizational Transformation,** which are those policies, actions, and beliefs that can help move your school toward a Stage 3 culture.

Organizational Kudos and Challenges provides a natural follow-up to your work with the Stages of Organizational Growth, or, as a time-saving device, it could be used in place of the Stages activity. In this activity, your staff members work together in small groups to identify the successes you have had to date as a school in moving toward the Inclusive/Equitable Stage. They list the programs, practices, and initiatives that have helped you grow your culture of inclusion and improve your educational outcomes across all groups of students. They also acknowledge some of the challenges and roadblocks that still hinder your journey as a school, identifying any "elephants in the room" that have yet to be addressed.

Using the list of issues and struggles that was produced in your Kudos and Challenges conversations, the **Co-Responsibility Work Groups** activity moves you into the action planning phase of the work. The "co-responsibility" concept acknowledges that none of us alone has created the problems we face, and none of us alone can solve them. In this collaborative and blame-free spirit, your faculty and staff will create action strategies to address the challenges you have identified and prioritized. These suggested strategies will include actions that could be taken at both the personal and the organizational levels. Some issues require us as individuals to make the necessary changes in our own beliefs and behaviors, and other challenges require us to work together. The action ideas that flow from these Co-Responsibility Work Groups can then be fed directly into your school improvement process.

The next five activities in Phase Five relate specifically to work you will do together with your leadership and facilitative team. **Dealing With Resistance** is a conversation you will inevitably need to have and probably revisit several times in the course of the overall professional development process. Even though most of the activities and discussions in Phases One through Four are specifically structured to prevent or minimize the impact of resistant behaviors, resistance will inevitably occur. Complex personal, professional, and political dynamics underlie such resistance and nonengagement, and it will be important for your leadership team to approach these issues sensitively and strategically, always focusing on the positive growth of the critical mass of your people, while not being derailed by the cynics, resistors, or naysayers.

Phase Five also provides you and your leadership team with tools for planning, managing, and assessing your progress with the entire professional development process. The **Implementation Planning Guide** gives you the big picture, listing all of the activities across the Five Phases of the work. The Guide provides space for you to project the dates for pieces to be implemented in the future and check off activities as they are completed. In this way, the Implementation Guide is your primary planning tool for the entire professional development process. The **Implementation Self-Assessment Form** works hand-in-hand with the Planning Guide. This form divides the work into seven stages of implementation that will help you track and sequence the order in which you implement the various activities.

This section of the manual also provides you with **Ideas for Integrating and Sustaining the Work,** a set of strategies and materials that other schools and districts have used to connect the dots and make sense of the work. Cultural Competence and Culturally Responsive Teaching are intimately connected to school improvement, to powerful instruction, and to eliminating educational disparities, but these connections are not always obvious to teachers. Ideas and activities in this section will help you integrate your efforts in ways that are meaningful, clear, and explicit.

Phase Five also offers you a model for empowering and engaging **Youth Voices and Student Equity Leadership**. This is an essential and often neglected resource for guiding your school improvement efforts. The approach to Youth Voices presented here grows out of Gary Howard's partnering with his son, Benjie Howard; son-in-law, Maketa Wilborn; and their colleague, Wade Colwell-Sandoval. Their New Wilderness Project (www.newwildernessproject.com) approach to youth empowerment has proven effective in school districts throughout the country. Gary often brings them in to support his long-term systemic professional development efforts. A powerful video series documents how the New Wilderness Project helped the Anoka-Hennepin Public Schools, the largest school system in Minnesota, tap the wisdom, passion, and real-life experiences of their high school youth to inform and inspire their teachers and administrators. These students vividly demonstrate how issues of racism, classism, sexism, homophobia, and other inequities impact their lives in school and in their communities on a daily basis. Through the Youth Voices process, they become champions for the movement from Social Dominance to Social Justice both with their peers and with adults. The language these students learn in their New Wilderness Project experience is aligned with the same five-phase conceptual framework you are sharing with your faculty throughout this professional development process. This alignment of language and analysis creates an opportunity for intergenerational collaboration in improving the culture and climate of your school.

The final section in Phase Five provides a **Sample Research and Assessment Design** that grew out of Gary's systemic work in the Jefferson County Public Schools (JCPS) in Louisville, Kentucky. Over a 5-year period, JCPS implemented the professional development design outlined in this manual in many of their schools, while other schools, with similar student demographics, were not involved in the Cultural Competence and Culturally Responsive Teaching work. This offered them the opportunity to compare student outcome and climate data across schools that were involved in the work with those that weren't. The results are strikingly positive, with significantly greater achievement gains and significantly lowered discipline referrals across race and poverty in those schools where the adults had participated in the professional development process outlined here. It is strongly suggested that you share the PowerPoint presentation in this section of the manual with the assessment people in your district and work with them to implement an evaluation design that can effectively and efficiently monitor the impact of this professional development process in your school and district.

A Final Word

This entire manual is intended to serve as a flexible guide to a multiyear professional development process. It is the role of your Facilitation Team to customize that process to fit the culture and needs of your school. The planning, program, and assessment tools provided in Phase Five will support you in tailoring and timing the work to be most compatible with your people, your challenges, and your opportunities.

This customization process requires that you integrate the cultural competence and culturally responsive teaching work with all other initiatives you have in place. As was stated in the Introduction to the manual, it is critically important that this work *not* be seen by your faculty and staff as "one more thing" to aggravate their already acute case of Multiple Initiatives Syndrome.

The integrated approach presented in Phase Five of the manual is intended not only for the purpose of efficiency and focus. It is, first and foremost, designed to ensure that all of your work is flowing from a deep, consistent, and authentic commitment to social justice, a commitment to resist and reverse the pernicious forces of dominance that are killing the Dream for far too many of our kids.

Phase Five: Systemic Transformation/Planning for Change **School Video Clips (SVC)**		
The following school video clips are provided for Phase Five.		
SVC #	*Title*	*Video Length*
29	**A Superintendent Makes the Case for Systemic Change** Dennis Carlson, Superintendent Anoka-Hennepin School District, describes how the Gary Howard work that his district initiated over a five-year period was the key to finding common ground for all stakeholders and allowed the district to make unprecedented progress in boosting student achievement and closing the achievement gap.	5:09
30	**Walking a Political Tightrope** Dennis Carlson, Superintendent Anoka-Hennepin School District, describes the political tensions he needed to navigate within the district's community and with his staff as he instituted the systemic work with Gary Howard.	3:15
31	**A Superintendent Talks About the Power of Student Voices** Dennis Carlson, Superintendent Anoka-Hennepin School District, explains the importance of training students to be leaders now so that they can help create safe environments in all the places that adults cannot access, such as social media sites, so that what happens after school does not spill over and infect the school climate for the most vulnerable students.	3:52

	Phase Five: Systemic Transformation/Planning for Change School Video Clips (SVC)	
	The following school video clips are provided for Phase Five.	
SVC #	*Title*	*Video Length*
32	**Empowering Students: New Wilderness Project** Cassidy Pohl, Student Achievement Advisor Blaine High School, describes the parallel process her school went through teaching the five phases of Gary Howard's word with students and the impact this learning has had on the culture of the school.	2:43
33	**Assessing Student Outcomes in a Large Urban System** Aukram Burton, Multicultural Education Specialist, describes the way in which a large urban school district measured the effectiveness of the systemic work it did with Gary Howard.	3:28

Facilitator Note: *Before initiating these activities with your staff, show them the Phase Five Introductory Video.*

Suggested Group Readings for Phase Five

- **Our Unfinished Work: La Tierra Transformativa.** Chapter 8 in Gary Howard's book, *We Can't Teach What We Don't Know: White Teachers, Multiracial Schools.* New York: Teachers College Press, 2006.
- **Dispositions for Good Teaching.** See Gary Howard's articles in the back of the manual.

PHASE FIVE ACTIVITIES, FACILITATOR DIRECTIONS, AND VIDEO SEGMENTS

Activity: Dimensions of Growth	
Phase Five: Systemic Transformation and Planning for Change	
Purpose:	• Identify key areas of personal and professional growth • Link these arenas of growth to Phases One through Four • Introduce Phase Five and the need for systemic transformation and growth • Connect the Cultural Competence and CRT work to your overall approach to school improvement
Suggested Time:	30 minutes
Materials Needed:	Phase Five Introductory Video Video Segment 5:1 Handout ST-1: Dimensions of Growth Figure 1: Levels of Engagement (From the Introduction)
Advanced Preparation:	• View the Introductory Video and Video Segment 5:1 • Review the Facilitator Directions • Talk with your Facilitation Team about your overall approach and timing for the Phase Five activities

Facilitator Note: *The Phase Five Introductory Video will help you transition into the Planning and Systemic Transformation aspects of the work. Share this with your faculty and staff before you start the other Phase Five activities. In Video Segment 5:1, Gary Howard's comments place all of your previous Phase One through Four activities in the context of three dimensions of personal and professional growth. He then makes a case for the fourth dimension of change, which calls for transformation at the organizational and systemic levels. In this phase of the work, you will be connecting and aligning the CRT professional development process with your overall approach to school improvement and growing your school culture. This presentation can be implemented whenever you think it will be most helpful in communicating the "Big Picture" of why you are doing this work.*

1. Set the Stage   5 Minutes

Make a few comments about your transition into Phase Five, and show the Introductory Video. State your intention to connect the Cultural Competence and Culturally Responsive Teaching work to all of your other school improvement efforts. Distribute copies of Handout ST-1 and Figure 1, copied back-to-back.

2. Start Video Segment 5:1   10 Minutes

Gary provides an overview of the four dimensions of growth, sharing stories from his own experience, and making connections to several of the Phase One through Four activities you have implemented with your faculty. He brings attention back to the Levels of Engagement model (Figure 1) that was presented in the Introduction to the manual. Similar to the intent of the Achievement Triangle, this presentation is designed to provide a holistic view of the work you have been doing. It also helps launch you into the Phase Five activities and conversations. Gary will set up the small-group conversations, and you will be prompted to **stop the video.**

3. Groups of Four: Making Personal Connections   8 Minutes

People will move into small groups of four, and video prompts will ask each person to respond to the following two questions:

- What is one way you have noticed your own thinking or practice changing as a result of the work you have been doing together?
- How has this work influenced the overall tone or feel or focus of your faculty and staff as a whole?

During the small-group discussion time, Facilitators can recruit four groups to select a spokesperson and be ready to share some of their responses to each of the questions, two groups for the first question and two for the second.

4. Large-Group Sharing and Closing Comments   7 Minutes

Pull the large group back together, and ask each of your selected small groups to share examples of their responses to the two questions. If time allows, ask for other groups or individuals to share as well. Take the last 2 minutes for your Facilitation Team to talk about some of the next steps you have planned for the Phase Five activities.

Dimensions of Growth

▶ *Cultural Sensitivity...*

is about **Personal Awareness.**

▶ *Cultural Competence...*

is about **Personal Will and Skill.**

▶ *Culturally Responsive Teaching and Leadership...*

are about **Professional Practice.**

▶ *A Culture of Inclusion, Equity, and Excellence...*

is about **Systemic Outcomes.**

Figure 1 Levels of Engagement

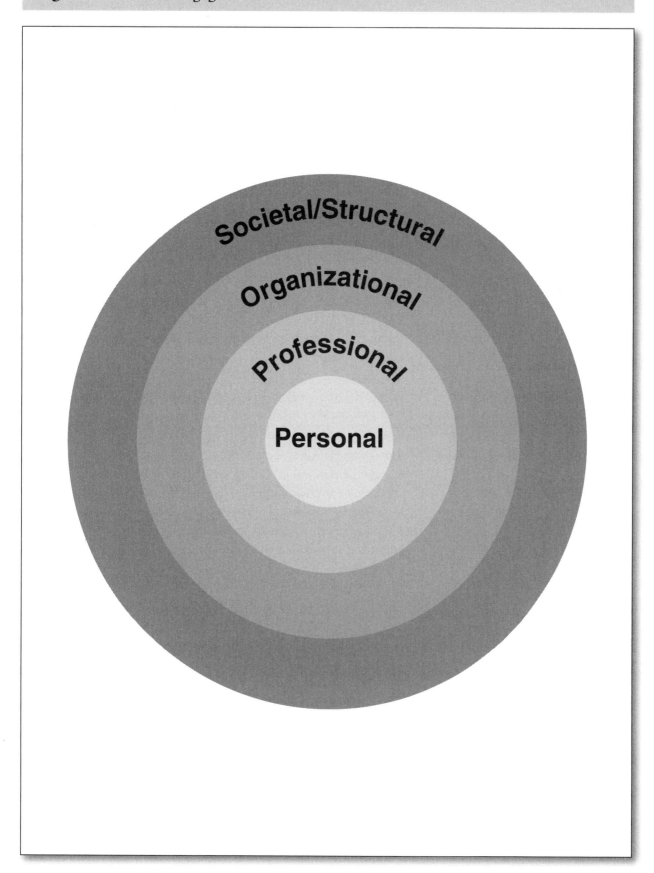

Activity: Stages of Organizational Growth	
Phase Five: Systemic Transformation and Planning for Change	
Purpose:	• Provide a conceptual model for understanding and discussing organizational growth • Approach school change as a developmental process that proceeds in recognizable stages • Create a reflective conversation about the culture of your school • Assess the equity culture of your school related to the Three Stages of Organizational Growth • Identify the key catalysts for progressive change • Suggest catalysts and actions for future growth
Suggested Time:	35 minutes for the Stages and Assessment Activity 20 minutes for the Catalysts Activity
Materials Needed:	Video Segment 5:2 Handout ST-2: Stages of Organizational Growth Handout ST-3: Assessing Your Equity Culture Handout ST-4: Catalysts for Organizational Transformation Handout ST-5: Catalysts Conversation Discussion Handout ST-6: Catalysts Conversation Recording Sheet Three flipcharts or other recording device
Advanced Preparation:	• View Video Segment 5:2 • Review the Facilitator Directions • Decide the optimal grouping arrangement for the Assessment Activity • Discuss whether and when to use the Catalysts Activity • Look at the next two activities in the manual, Organizational Kudos and Challenges and Co-Responsibility Work Groups, and decide whether these would be more helpful than the Catalysts Discussion extension provided here

Facilitator Note: *This presentation is a logical next step from the Dimensions of Growth framework you discussed in the previous activity. Here the focus is placed directly on the fourth dimension of change, the organizational culture of your school. Similar to individuals, institutions also pass through developmental stages on their way to becoming more inclusive, equitable, and excellent in serving the needs of their constituents and employees. The model presented here provides you with a practical and user-friendly framework for discussing and assessing your school culture.*

Talk together with your Facilitation Team and decide the best way to organize the small groups for the assessment activity. This is where faculty and staff will identify evidence for your school being in any of the three stages of growth. It is probably most productive to do this in max-mix groupings, where people are talking across diverse perspectives. However, you now have enough experience with this professional development process to know what would work best for your school.

As a possible extension activity, the Catalysts Discussion gives you a way to identify those actions, policies, beliefs, and practices that have supported your school improvement efforts so far, as well as those that could be implemented in the future to strengthen your work for inclusion, equity, and excellence. Your Facilitation Team should review this extension option and compare it to the next two activities in the manual to see which approach would be more relevant and helpful for your school.

1. Set the Stage   2 Minutes

Have people organized in small groups of five to seven, and distribute copies of Handout ST-2. Also, have one copy of Handout ST-3 on each table, copied on colored paper. Announce that this discussion will focus on the organizational culture of your school.

2. Play Part 1 of Video Segment 5:2   10 Minutes

Gary connects the present conversation with the developmental approach that was used earlier in Phase Two to map the Stages of Personal Development Toward Cultural Competence (Handout PC-13) and in Phase Three to discuss White Identity Orientations (Handout SJ-19). He walks people through each of the three Stages of Organizational Growth as related to five arenas of organizational life: Level of Self-Awareness, Emotional Response to Differences, Mode of Cultural Interaction, Approach to Education and Curriculum, and Approach to Leadership and Governance.

After this description of the Stages model, Gary invites the small groups to engage in the assessment activity. You will be prompted to **stop the video** to allow time for these conversations.

3. Small-Groups Assessment
Conversations   10 Minutes

Using the single copy of Handout ST-3 that is on their table, small groups will appoint a recorder and work together to identify evidence within your school culture for each of the three Stages of Organizational

Growth. Most organizations are in all three Stages at once, and this will become obvious for your school as groups gather their evidence.

Toward the end of the small-group work time, interrupt the conversation briefly to announce that you will be asking each small group to share some of their evidence, so make sure they have at least two items of evidence recorded under each of the three Stages. Allow groups to complete their evidence gathering while one of the Facilitators sets up three flipcharts or other recording device with separate headings for Stage 1, Stage 2, and Stage 3 evidence.

4. Large-Group Sharing and Recording of Evidence   10 Minutes

Bring the large group back together. Focusing on one Stage at a time, the lead Facilitator asks small groups to share one example of their evidence, while another Facilitator records that evidence under the corresponding Stage of Growth. Include evidence from all of the small groups as you proceed through the three Stages of evidence. It is sufficient to elicit four or five examples of evidence for each of the three Stages. Some groups may list the same item of evidence under a different Stage of Growth. If this occurs, acknowledge the difference, but don't spend time debating which listing is "right." People have different perceptions of both the evidence and the Stages of Growth.

5. Lessons From This Discussion   2 Minutes

After the evidence for all three Stages has been recorded, give the small groups a couple of minutes to talk together and share their thoughts about the overall impressions of your school culture that emerge from the charts. Ask them to prepare a statement to share out with the large group: "Something we learned from this discussion about our school culture is. . . ." They should record their completed statement on the back of Handout ST-3, and be ready to read it to the large group.

6. Large-Group Sharing of Statements   3 Minutes

Ask each small group to share their statement. After they have done so, you can close the session here by announcing that your Facilitation Team will collect the Handout ST-3 recording sheets from each table, and have all of the evidence, along with the closing statements, transcribed and distributed via email over the next few days.

If time permits, or at a future session, you can proceed to the extension activity below, which focuses on Catalysts for Change.

Extension Activity: Catalysts for Change

7. Set the Stage   2 Minutes

Distribute Handouts ST-4 and ST-5 copied back-to-back. Place one copy of Handout ST-6 on each table, copied on colored paper. Let people know that this discussion is going to continue your work with the Stages of Organizational Growth.

8. Play Part 2 of Video Segment 5:2   4 Minutes

Here Gary takes the Stages of Organizational Growth discussion to a deeper level by focusing on the dynamics that move organizations from one stage to another. Those interventions that support movement from Stage 1 to Stage 2 are very different from those that stimulate movement from Stage 2 to Stage 3. Gary will invite your faculty and staff into a conversation about the Catalysts for Change as they perceive them in your school. You will be prompted to **stop the video** for this conversation.

9. Small-Group Catalysts Conversation   10 Minutes

Participants will take a minute of personal time to think about the Catalysts for Change as they have observed them operating in the culture of your school. They will then share these perceptions in their small groups. Finally, they will complete one copy of Handout ST-6, recording their suggestions for the kind of Catalysts and Actions that are needed to move your school closer to being a Stage 3 organization.

10. Large-Group Sharing of
Ideas for Growth   4 Minutes

Bring the large group back together. Ask each small group to share out one of their ideas for a Catalyst that could move your school forward on your journey to greater inclusion, equity, and excellence. Also, ask them to share one of the Action ideas they recorded. You don't need to chart this information at this time. As you close the session, thank everyone for their work and collect the Handout ST-6 Recording Sheets. Announce that your Facilitation Team will compile these ideas and distribute them to everyone. These data will also be given to your school improvement and leadership teams to help in planning the next steps in your school's journey.

Stages of Organizational Growth

	STAGE 1 MONOCULTURAL	STAGE 2 COMPLIANCE	STAGE 3 INCLUSIVE
Level of Self-Awareness	My perspective is right (the only one)	My perspective is **one** of many	My perspective is changing and being enhanced
Emotional Response to Differences	Fear Rejection Denial We're all alike	Interest Awareness Beginning Openness	Appreciation Respect Joy Enthusiasm Active curiosity
Mode of Cultural Interaction	Isolation Avoidance Hostility	Integration Interaction Beginning Acceptance	Transforming Internalizing Rewarding Challenging Allies

Approach to Education and Curriculum	Assimilation
	Conformity
	"Be Like Us"
		Learning **about** those who are different
		Voyeuristic
			Learning
			   from and **with**
			   all of us
			Reflective
			Engaging

Approach to Leadership and Governance	Monocultural
	Autocratic
	Directive
	Controlling
		Compliance
		"Image" over
		   Substance
		"Managing"
		   Diversity
			Collaborative
			Inclusive
			Empowering
			Leading for Equity

Risk Taking • Personal/Organizational Growth • Ongoing Process

Stages of Organizational Growth

ASSESSING THE DIVERSITY/EQUITY ENVIRONMENT OF YOUR ORGANIZATION

What evidence is there that your organization is in Stage 1?	What evidence is there that your organization is in Stage 2?	What evidence is there that your organization is in Stage 3?
Stage 1 Evidence:	Stage 2 Evidence:	Stage 3 Evidence:

your overall opinion, is your organization primarily in Stage 1, 2, or 3?

ST-4 **Stages of Institutional Growth**

CATALYSTS FOR ORGANIZATIONAL TRANSFORMATION

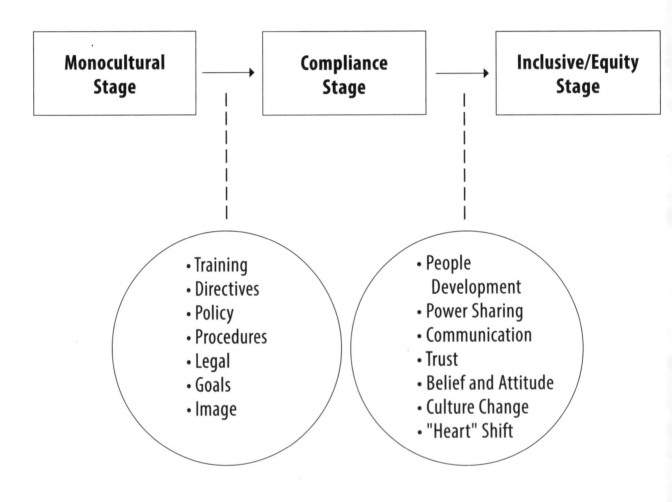

Catalysts Conversation

Definition

Catalysts are those elements of behavior, belief, leadership, policy, and organizational activity that have proven effective in producing desired changes toward greater inclusion, equity, excellence, and social justice.

Personal Think

In your school, what have been the most powerful Catalysts for inclusion and equity—those things that have helped move you, your colleagues, and your organization toward Stage 3 beliefs, behaviors, and outcomes?

Small-Group Conversation

In your small group, describe and discuss the Catalysts you have observed/experienced/created in your school. Look for the connections and the differences in your stories.

Suggestions for Next Steps

What Catalysts are needed now to move you and your school to the next level of change?

Record your ideas on Handout ST-6, the Catalysts Recording Sheet.

Be ready to share at least one of your ideas with the large group.

Catalysts Conversation Recording Sheet

From your small-group conversation about Catalysts, list below 3 of the Catalysts that are needed for further organizational growth, and two or three specific actions related to that Catalyst.

▶ **Catalyst:**

    Action:

▶ **Catalyst:**

    Action:

▶ **Catalyst:**

    Action:

Activity: Organizational Kudos and Challenges	
Phase Five: Systemic Transformation and Planning for Change	
Purpose:	• Acknowledge the strategies and organizational practices that have been most successful in moving your school forward on its journey to inclusion, equity, and excellence • Identify those roadblocks and challenges that have yet to be adequately addressed
Suggested Time:	25 minutes
Materials Needed:	Video Segment 5:3 Handout ST-7: Organizational Kudos and Challenges
Advanced Preparation:	• View Video Segment 5:3 • Review the Facilitator Directions • Talk with your Facilitation Team about the best grouping arrangement for this activity

Facilitator Note: *This activity can be used in conjunction with, or as a substitute for, the Stages of Organizational Growth and Catalysts Conversation outlined earlier. As a time-saving device, Organizational Kudos and Challenges, used in combination with the next activity, Co-Responsibility Work Groups, may be the most efficient way to assess the progress of your school to date, as well as gather ideas for next steps in your journey.*

Discuss with your Facilitation Team the best way to set up small groups for this activity. You want people to talk freely about both the gains and the struggles they are experiencing in your school improvement process. Decide what grouping strategy would best facilitate this openness and freedom of expression.

1. Set the Stage   2 Minutes

Have people seated in your designated groupings. Distribute Handout ST-7, and have one copy on colored paper placed on each table for recording purposes. Let people know that you are going to spend some time looking at your overall efforts at creating a productive school climate of inclusion, equity, and excellence.

2. Start Video Segment 5:3   2 Minutes

Gary provides a brief context and introduction for the activity. He asks everyone to think about the progress they have made as a school in their efforts to be inclusive and effective in serving all of their diverse students and families. What specific programs, policies, and actions have led to positive change? He will also ask them to think about any challenges, roadblocks, or struggles that are still unresolved or in the way. You will be prompted to **stop the video** while everyone has some personal think time to record their ideas on Handout ST-7.

3. Personal Think Time and Notes   2 Minutes

Provide quiet time for people to think and record their ideas. Facilitators should remind everyone this is not a time for conversation; that will happen next.

4. Restart the Video: Directions
for Small-Group Sharing   2 Minutes

Gary gives a brief setup for the small-group conversations, emphasizing the need to be open-minded and nonjudgmental as the Kudos and Challenges are shared. People may have very different ideas about the successes and struggles your school is having; the important thing here is to listen and learn, not debate. When he provides the video prompts for the conversations, you can **stop the video.**

5. Conversation in Small Groups:
Kudos and Challenges   12 Minutes

Invite the small groups to begin their conversations. They will do one round of everyone sharing at least a Kudo, and then a round of sharing Challenges. After these two rounds, they will appoint a recorder and list two of their Kudos and two of their Challenges on the colored copy of Handout ST-7 to be turned in at the end of the activity. Toward the end of the recording time, Facilitators can recruit three to five groups who would be willing to share one of their Kudos and one of their Challenges with the large group.

6. Large-Group Sharing and Closure   5 Minutes

Invite your selected groups to share their Kudos and Challenges with the large group. Invite more groups to share as time allows. Collect the colored note sheets and announce that you will have these transcribed and distributed to everyone. This input will be important data for your school leadership team and your school improvement team, both in terms of acknowledging what is working, as well as recognizing and addressing what isn't.

Organizational Kudos and Challenges

▶ *In what ways has your school/school district/organization made positive steps toward creating inclusive, welcoming, and equitable learning and working environments for all students, parents, and employees?*

1.

2.

▶ *What are one or two of the major equity challenges, unresolved issues, or roadblocks that still need to be addressed?*

1.

2.

Activity: Co-Responsibility Work Groups	
Phase Five: Systemic Transformation and Planning for Change	
Purpose:	• Address organizational issues, challenges, and roadblocks • Identify individual actions that will support positive change • Suggest organizational actions to address specific issues and challenges • Contribute action strategies that can be incorporated into your school improvement planning processes
Suggested Time:	30–35 minutes
Materials Needed:	Video Segment 5:4 Handout ST-8: Co-Responsibility Work Groups
Advanced Preparation:	• View Video Segment 5:4 • Review the Facilitator Directions • Talk with your Facilitation Team about the best grouping arrangement for this activity • Look over your compiled notes from previous Phase Five activities and identify several specific issues and challenges to be addressed by the Co-Responsibility Work Groups • Prepare copies of Handout ST-8 with these issues and challenges described in the space at the top

Facilitator Note: *This activity is an excellent follow-up to your work with either the Stages of Organizational Growth assessment process or your Organizational Kudos and Challenges conversation. Here your faculty and staff will identify some of the ways that individual teachers, administrators, specialists, and support staff can become catalysts for positive change. They will also be suggesting actions that could be taken at the organizational level to address the issues and challenges that you and your staff have identified in earlier conversations. The action ideas that are generated at both the individual and organizational levels can be incorporated into your school improvement planning process.*

Before you implement this activity with your faculty, review the compiled notes from any of the Phase Five discussions that have taken place with your faculty, including Assessing Your Equity Culture, Catalysts for Change Conversation, and Organizational Kudos and Challenges. Select several recurring themes and issues from these conversations that you would like to address at a deeper level. These should be challenges that are on the cutting edge of your school's organizational journey, things that need to be dealt with to move your school culture toward greater inclusion, equity, and excellence. You will be assigning these issues to different Work Groups, so prepare several different versions of Handout ST-8 that have these issues described in the space at the top of the handout. Make multiple copies of each of these different versions, one copy per person for each of the groups that will be working with that issue. For large faculties with many small groups, you can have more than one group working on the same issue. Also, make one copy of each version of Handout ST-8 on colored paper for note-taking purposes at the tables.

1. Set the Stage   2 Minutes

Ask people to sit in their designated groupings as determined by your Facilitation Team. Have your prepared versions of Handout ST-8 on the tables, one copy per person for each issue group. Also give each group one copy of their Handout on colored paper to use for recording purposes. Let people know that this will be an action planning session to address some of the issues, challenges, and roadblocks they have identified in earlier conversations.

2. Start Video Segment 5:4   5 Minutes

Gary introduces the activity and connects it to other Phase Five conversations you have had with your faculty. He talks about organizational change in the context of "co-responsibility," which means that every person on the faculty and staff has a co-equal and necessary part in improving the overall culture and effectiveness of your school. None of us alone can make the changes needed to address the issues and challenges we have identified, yet none of those changes can fully take place without each of us making our unique contribution. He sets up the action planning process outlined on Handout ST-8, and you will be prompted to **stop the video.**

3. Action Planning in Issue-Related Work Groups   15 minutes

Small groups work together to identify the individual and organizational actions that could address the issue or challenge that has been assigned to their group. Members of your Facilitation Team should move around the room and support them in their work, particularly in clarifying any questions about the issues and challenges that have been assigned. Toward the end of the action planning time, announce that you will be asking each group to share out one of the individual actions and one of the organizational actions they have identified.

4. Large-Group Sharing of Action Ideas   9 Minutes

Take some time for each of the work groups to describe the issue they have been working with and examples of one individual and one organizational action they have identified. For larger faculties, time may not allow you to have every group report out, but make sure you hear from at least one group for each of the assigned issues. Thank everyone for their work and collect the colored copies of Handout ST-8. Announce that these action ideas will be compiled and distributed to everyone and become a part of your leadership team and school improvement team planning.

Follow-Up Activity

When the notes from your Co-Responsibility Work Groups session have been compiled, send them out with a note similar to the following:

Faculty and Staff,

Thank you for your hard work and contribution to our Co-Responsibility Work Groups session, where several of our school's issues and challenges were addressed and the attached action ideas were identified. Please read these over and continue to discuss them in your meetings and conversations with colleagues. Some of the Organizational Actions will take planning and approval from our school leadership and/or school improvement teams, but many of the Individual Actions can be taken by each of us in our day-to-day work with students and colleagues. We encourage each of you to keep these ideas in mind over the coming weeks and months.

Co-Responsibility Work Groups

ST-8

Your assigned issue or challenge:

Considering all that we have discussed in our Cultural Competence and Culturally Responsive Teaching professional development sessions, what are some individual and organizational actions we could take to address the issue described above and enhance our work for inclusion, equity, and excellence?

Individual Actions

1.

2.

3.

Organizational Actions

1.

2.

3.

Prepare one copy to be turned in at the end of your conversation.

FACILITATION TEAM RESOURCES FOR PLANNING, INTEGRATING, AND SUSTAINING THE WORK

Facilitator Note: *All of the remaining activities in Phase Five are intended for use by your Facilitation Team in planning and supporting your work. If you have not already done so, take a few minutes with your Facilitation Team to view Gary's Video Introduction for Facilitators, which is an informal conversation meant only for your leadership team, not for the larger faculty and staff. After viewing and discussing this video, you can continue on with the other Facilitation topics presented here in Phase Five.*

Activity: Dealing With Resistance	
Phase Five: Systemic Transformation and Planning for Change	
Purpose:	• Support your Facilitation Team in recognizing and dealing with faculty resistance and negativity • Acknowledge the range of resistance behaviors • Explore sources and reasons for resistance • Identify strategies for preventing resistance and responding to resistance
Suggested Time:	30- to 60-minute initial conversation Ongoing implementation and discussion
Materials Needed:	Video Segment 5:5 Handout ST-9: Resistance Behaviors, Sources, and Responses Handout ST-10: Strategies for Dealing With Resistance
Advanced Preparation:	• View Video Segment 5:5

Facilitator Note: *This discussion and each of the remaining activities in Phase Five are intended for use by your Facilitation Team in planning and supporting your work. Dealing with resistance is a topic you can revisit many times during your implementation of the overall professional development design. There are many reasons that members of your faculty and staff may find it difficult to engage fully in the discussions and activities you are presenting. It is important for your team to acknowledge resistance when it is happening and discuss your possible interventions.*

1. View Video Segment 5:5 and
Follow the Prompts   30–60 Minutes

Gary guides your team through a conversation about resistance. At several points you will be prompted to stop the video and talk with your Facilitation Team. Have copies of Handout ST-9 available to guide the conversation. You can take as much time as you want with these conversations, and you can revisit portions of the video as needed when issues of resistance emerge in your work with the faculty and staff. Topics covered on Video Segment 5:5 include the following:

- **Resistance Behaviors**
  - You will share your observations of resistance behaviors that are occurring in your work with faculty, as well as your anticipation of those that might surface in different Phases of the work.

- **Sources of Resistance**
  - Here you will look below the behaviors to consider the causes or sources of resistance. Gary shares stories and lessons from the many forms of resistance he has observed over 40 years of doing this work.

- **Responses to Resistance**
  - When resistance does occur, it is important for your team to respond, even if that response is to ignore the resistance. Here you will work with actual instances of resistance as they are occurring in your work and plan your strategies for dealing with both the behaviors and the sources of that resistance. Refer to Handout ST-9 for a review of possible responses.

- **Preventing Resistance**
  - The entire professional development process is designed with resistance in mind. Many of the activities are intended as resistance prevention strategies, building a respectful tone and a climate of trust and mutual engagement that will hopefully preempt much of the resistance that could occur. Gary will share his ideas about prevention, and your team will discuss which activities and sequencing of activities might best serve this preventative function for your faculty.

Resistance Behaviors, Sources, and Responses

1. Doing this work with your colleagues, what might be some resistance **BEHAVIORS** you will encounter or have already encountered?

2. What might be some of the different **SOURCES** of this resistance—what might cause people to resist this work?

3. What are some possible **RESPONSES** that you and your team could make to deal with specific resistance behaviors and sources?

4. How might some of the activities in this professional development manual be used to either **PREVENT** resistance or limit its impact? What prevention strategies have you used to date? What might be needed next?

Strategies for Dealing With Resistance

When resistance occurs, possible Facilitator responses include the following:

Recognize the Resistance

Look for signs of resistance in the workshop and acknowledge them to yourself and your Facilitation Team.

Ignore Behaviors

It is sometimes best simply to ignore the behavior for a while. See where it goes. Participants test us just like kids test teachers.

Delay

When you experience any behavior that feels like a direct verbal attack or negative challenge, simply tell the participant you will be dealing with that issue in a future activity or session. "We'll be getting to that, so just hold the thought and we'll deal with it during our next session."

Respond

In the case of a direct verbal challenge, you can also respond directly. Treat the issue not as an attack but as a reasonable question or concern, and give your best response to it. This can help reduce resistance by demonstrating that you can take any reaction seriously without becoming defensive.

Team

If you find yourself feeling angry or thrown off balance by a comment or behavior, turn to your Facilitator teammates and ask if one of them has a response. This has the added advantage of giving you some time to think or count to ten.

Back-Door Approach

In dealing with particularly negative behavior or attitudes, you may want to meet with the person during lunch or a break. Don't confront the resistance; just try to establish rapport and create a sense of inclusion. The realization that you aren't rejecting or avoiding the person because of his or her negative behavior can in itself sometimes reduce the resistance.

Direct Confrontation

Occasionally, a person or group becomes so negative that you need to confront the behavior directly during the session or perhaps privately afterward. This is necessary to demonstrate to the other participants that you value their feelings and commitment and will not allow one or two people to destroy the experience for others.

Regrouping

In the case of negative groups of participants, people who seem to reinforce each other's resistance or negativity, use small-group activities that separate these people. Plan ahead for the next activity, and organize the groups so these clusters of negativity are neutralized.

Evaluation Review

When you are reviewing any Evaluation Comments you have gathered from your participants, use this opportunity to directly or indirectly acknowledge or confront resistance behaviors and issues. Make public the most "damaging" evaluation comments you have heard or read. Once again, this demonstrates that your Facilitation Team is willing to deal directly with any feedback from the group. Also, bring up any comments that suggest other participants are being negatively affected by some of the resistance or distracting behaviors evident in the group. Ask the group to respond, and give your response if it seems appropriate. Be creative with the evaluation review—if you and the other Facilitators have an issue, bring it up. You are part of the group, too.

Activity: Implementation Planning Guide	
Phase Five: Systemic Transformation and Planning for Change	
Purpose:	• Provide an outline of the complete professional development process and manual • Serve as a tool for multiyear planning and scheduling • Create a checklist for assessing your progress over time
Suggested Time:	Ongoing planning, implementation, and assessment
Materials Needed:	Video Segment 5:6 Handout ST-11: Implementation Planning Guide Handout ST-12: Implementation Self-Assessment Checklist
Advanced Preparation:	• View Video Segment 5:6 with your Facilitation Team • Create a schedule for ongoing planning meetings

Facilitator Note: *The two forms presented here will support your Facilitation Team in planning your implementation process and assessing your implementation progress. As noted in the "Guidelines for Using the Leadership Manual and Videos," it would be good for your team to use the Implementation Planning Guide from the very beginning of your work. It will also be helpful to revisit the Implementation Self-Assessment Checklist from time to time to track your progress and plan for next steps.*

1. View Video Segment 5:6 and Follow the Prompts   Variable Time as Needed

Use this video early in your planning process. Gary walks your Facilitation Team through the Implementation Planning Guide and the Self-Assessment Checklist, giving suggestions for ongoing planning and adjustment of the professional development process. You will continue to work with both of these forms over the multiple years of your implementation process.

It would be helpful at this point for your Facilitation Team to view SVC-29, where you can hear a school superintendent talk about his rationale for using the professional development design presented in this manual. You may also consider showing this video segment to your faculty as a way of introducing the work to them.

ST-11

Implementation Planning Guide

Cultural Competence and Culturally Responsive Teaching

Orientation to the Professional Development (PD) Process

Date Planned	Date Completed	Activities, Videos, and Handouts
_____	_____	Video Orientation to the PD Process
_____	_____	IN-1: Inclusion, Equity, and Excellence
_____	_____	IN-2: Phases and Objectives of the Work
_____	_____	IN-3: Levels of Engagement

Phase One: Tone and Trust

Date Planned	Date Completed	Activities, Videos, and Handouts
_____	_____	Phase One Introductory Video
_____	_____	**Video 1:1 Working Agreements**
_____	_____	TT-1: Working Agreements
_____	_____	**Video 1:2 Questions to Consider**
_____	_____	TT-2: Questions to Consider
_____	_____	**Video 1:3 Cultural Bingo**
_____	_____	TT-3: Cultural Bingo Activity
_____	_____	TT-4: Cultural Bingo Answer Sheet
_____	_____	TT-5: Blank Cultural Bingo Template
_____	_____	**Video 1:4 ¿Quiénes Somos?**
_____	_____	TT-6: ¿Quiénes Somos?
_____	_____	**Video 1:5 Tone and Trust Assessment**
_____	_____	TT-7: Tone and Trust Assessment

Implementation Planning Guide

Phase Two: Personal Journey and Personal Culture

Date Planned	Date Completed	Activities, Videos, and Handouts
————	————	Phase Two Introductory Video
————	————	**Video 2:1 Sharing Personal Culture**
————	————	PC-1: Personal Culture Preparation Memo
————	————	PC-2: Personal Culture Discussion Guide
————	————	PC-3: Reflective Conversation
————	————	**Video 2:2 Culture Toss**
————	————	PC-4: Culture Toss Activity Sheet
————	————	PC-5: Culture Toss Discussion Guide
————	————	**Video 2:3 Definition of Cultural Competence**
————	————	PC-6: Lenses of Difference
————	————	PC-7: Definition of Cultural Competence
————	————	PC-8: Stereotype Threat Research Summary
————	————	**Video 2:4 I Am From Poems**
————	————	PC-9: I Am From Writing Prompts
————	————	PC-10: Sample I Am From Poem
————	————	PC-11: I Am From Writing Page
————	————	PC-12: I Am From Reflective Conversation
————	————	**Video 2:5 Stages of Personal Growth**
————	————	PC-13: Cultural Competence Growth Stages
————	————	PC-14: Growth Stages Reflective Conversation
————	————	**Video 2:6 Personal Growth Project**
————	————	PC-15: Personal Growth Project Planning

Implementation Planning Guide

ST-11

Phase Three: From Social Dominance to Social Justice

Date Planned	Date Completed	Activities, Videos, and Handouts
_____	_____	Phase Three Introductory Video
_____	_____	**Video 3:1 We, the People**
_____	_____	SJ-1: We, the People Activity Sheet
_____	_____	SJ-2: We, the People Reflective Conversation
_____	_____	**Video 3:2 The Guessing Game**
_____	_____	SJ-3 to SJ-6: Round 1 Clues
_____	_____	SJ-7 to SJ-10: Round 2 Clues
_____	_____	SJ-11: Guessing Game Answer Sheet
_____	_____	**Video 3:3 Definition/Dynamics of Dominance**
_____	_____	SJ-12: Definition of Social Dominance
_____	_____	SJ-13: Dynamics of Social Dominance
_____	_____	**Video 3:4 From Dominance to Social Justice**
_____	_____	SJ-14: Definition of Social Justice
_____	_____	SJ-15: Dynamics of Social Justice
_____	_____	SJ-16: From Social Dominance to Social Justice
_____	_____	SJ-17: Qualities of Social Justice Allies
_____	_____	**Video 3:5 Privilege and Power Assessment**
_____	_____	SJ-18: Privilege and Power School Discussion
_____	_____	**Video 3:6 Focus on Race Conversation**
_____	_____	SJ-19: White Identity Orientations
_____	_____	SJ-20: Race and Whiteness Conversation
_____	_____	SJ-21: *Mirrors of Privilege* Discussion Guide
_____	_____	**Video 3:7 Shifting the Emotional Paradigm**
_____	_____	SJ-22: Shifting the Emotional Paradigm

ST-11

Implementation Planning Guide

Phase Four: Classroom Implications and Applications

Date Planned	Date Completed	Activities, Videos, and Handouts
_____	_____	Phase Four Introductory Video
_____	_____	**Video 4:1 School Outcomes Assessment**
_____	_____	CA-1: School Outcomes Assessment
_____	_____	**Video 4:2 Equity Environments That Work**
_____	_____	CA-2: Equity Environments That Work
_____	_____	CA-3: Culturally Responsive Teaching Defined
_____	_____	**Video 4:3 Seven Principles for CRT**
_____	_____	CA-4: The Seven Principles for CRT
_____	_____	CA-5: The Purpose of Our Work
_____	_____	**Video 4:4 CRT Study Groups**
_____	_____	CA-6: CRT Study Groups
_____	_____	CA-7: CRT Study Groups Work Sheet
_____	_____	CA-8: Sample Elementary Observations
_____	_____	CA-9: Sample Secondary Observations
_____	_____	CA-10: CRT Study Groups Recording
_____	_____	**Video 4:5 CRT Action Research**
_____	_____	CA-11: Personal Assessment and Reflection
_____	_____	CA-12: Sample Faculty CRT Chart
_____	_____	CA-13: CRT Action Research
_____	_____	CA-14: CRT Student-Based Action Research
_____	_____	**Video 4:6 Learning From/With Colleagues**
_____	_____	CA-15: Worksheet Packet
_____	_____	**Video 4:7 CRT Peer Observation Process**
_____	_____	CA-16: CRT Classroom Observation Rubric
_____	_____	**Video 4:8 Achievement Triangle**
_____	_____	CA-17: Achievement Triangle

Implementation Planning Guide

Phase Five: Systemic Transformation and Planning for Change

Date Planned	Date Completed	Activities, Videos, and Handouts
_____	_____	Phase Five Introductory Video
_____	_____	**Video 5:1 Dimensions of Growth**
_____	_____	ST-1: Dimensions of Growth
_____	_____	**Video 5:2 Stages of Organizational Growth**
_____	_____	ST-2: Stages of Organizational Growth
_____	_____	ST-3: Assessing Your Equity Culture
_____	_____	ST-4: Catalysts for Transformation
_____	_____	ST-5: Catalysts Discussion
_____	_____	ST-6: Catalysts Recording Sheet
_____	_____	**Video 5:3 Kudos and Challenges**
_____	_____	ST-7: Organizational Kudos and Challenges
_____	_____	**Video 5:4 Co-Responsibility Work Groups**
_____	_____	ST-8: Co-Responsibility Work Groups

Implementation Planning Guide

Facilitation Team Resources for Planning, Integrating, and Sustaining the Work

Date Assigned	Date Completed	Activities, Videos, and Handouts
‾‾‾‾‾	‾‾‾‾‾	**Video 5:5 Dealing With Resistance**
‾‾‾‾‾	‾‾‾‾‾	ST-9: Resistance Behaviors, Sources, and Responses
‾‾‾‾‾	‾‾‾‾‾	ST-10: Strategies for Dealing With Resistance
‾‾‾‾‾	‾‾‾‾‾	**Video 5:6 Implementation Planning**
‾‾‾‾‾	‾‾‾‾‾	ST-11: Implementation Planning Form
‾‾‾‾‾	‾‾‾‾‾	ST-12: Implementation Self-Assessment
‾‾‾‾‾	‾‾‾‾‾	**Video 5:7 Ideas for Integrating and Sustaining the Work**
‾‾‾‾‾	‾‾‾‾‾	ST-13a–c: Sample Evaluation/Reflection Forms
‾‾‾‾‾	‾‾‾‾‾	ST-14: Sample Compiled Evaluation Comments
‾‾‾‾‾	‾‾‾‾‾	ST-15: Ideas for Sustaining the Work
‾‾‾‾‾	‾‾‾‾‾	ST-16: CRT and Safe, Respectful Learning Environments
‾‾‾‾‾	‾‾‾‾‾	**Video 5:8 Student Voices and Youth Equity Leadership**
‾‾‾‾‾	‾‾‾‾‾	Link to purchase New Wilderness Project Youth Voices Video Series
‾‾‾‾‾	‾‾‾‾‾	**Video 5:10 Sample Research and Assessment Design**
‾‾‾‾‾	‾‾‾‾‾	Jefferson County Public Schools Assessment Design PowerPoint

Implementation Planning Guide

Suggested Readings From Gary Howard

Date Assigned	Date Completed	Article
_____	_____	*As Diversity Grows, So Must We*
_____	_____	*Speaking of Difference: Reflections on the Possibility of Culturally Competent Conversations*
_____	_____	*Whites in Multicultural Education: Rethinking Our Role*
_____	_____	*How We Are White*
_____	_____	*School Improvement for All: Reflections on the Achievement Gap*
_____	_____	*Dispositions for Good Teaching*

Implementation Self-Assessment Checklist

Cultural Competence and Culturally Responsive Teaching

Implementation Self-Assessment

Pre-Implementation
____ Facilitation Team has been formed
____ Team has read through and discussed the Manual
____ Team has done initial implementation planning using Handout ST-11

Level One Implementation
____ Faculty/staff have viewed the Video Introduction to the PD Process
____ Faculty/staff have engaged in at least three Phase One activities
____ Faculty/staff members have completed the Tone and Trust Assessment

Level Two Implementation
____ Faculty/staff have engaged in at least three Phase Two activities
____ Faculty/staff members have designed their Personal Growth Projects
____ Faculty/staff are familiar with the definition of Cultural Competence

Level Three Implementation
____ Faculty/staff have done the School Outcomes Assessment Activity
____ Faculty/staff have been introduced to the Seven Principles for CRT
____ Faculty/staff have been engaged in the CRT Study Groups Activity
____ Faculty/staff have completed the CRT Personal Reflection and Assessment

Level Four Implementation
____ Teachers have identified their Proficient and Growth CRT Principles
____ Teachers are working on CRT Personal Action Research Projects
____ Faculty/Staff have participated in Learning From and With Colleagues

Level Five Implementation
____ Faculty/Staff have participated in CRT peer observations
____ Faculty Staff have participated in the We, the People activity from Phase Three
____ Faculty/Staff know the Definition and Dynamics of Social Dominance
____ Faculty/Staff have engaged in the Guessing Game activity
____ Faculty/Staff have participated in at least one of the following: Privilege and Power School Assessment, Race and Whiteness Conversation, Shakti Butler video and discussion

Level Six Implementation
____ Student Voices and Youth Equity Leadership work have been initiated
____ New-teacher orientation using Gary's online course is in place
____ The Seven Principles for CRT have been incorporated into Look-For and Walkthrough rubrics
____ CRT outcomes have been included in Teacher Evaluation and Principal Evaluation formats

Overall assessment of your school: Our school is at Level _____ Implementation.

Activity: Ideas for Integrating and Sustaining the Work	
Phase Five: Systemic Transformation and Planning for Change	
Purpose:	• Provide sample Evaluation/Reflection forms for gathering participant feedback • Suggest activities for sustaining and deepening the work • Integrate CRT work with other school improvement initiatives
Suggested Time:	For use at any time during the PD process
Materials Needed:	Video Segment 5:7 Handout ST-13a–c: Sample Evaluation/Reflection Forms Handout ST-14: Sample Compiled Evaluation Comments Handout ST-15: Ideas for Sustaining and Deepening the Work Handout ST-16: CRT and Safe, Respectful Learning Environments
Advanced Preparation:	• View Video Segment 5:7 with your Facilitation Team • Plan where and when to use these resources • Revisit this section of the manual from time to time • Create your versions of the Evaluation/Reflection Forms

Facilitator Note: *Materials in this section are intended to support your Facilitation Team in your multiyear rollout of the Professional Development program. It is critically important that you find ways to integrate the Cultural Competence and Culturally Responsive Teaching work with all other instructional and school improvement initiatives you may have in place. Your faculty and staff need to see this focus as an integral part of the "real work," not as "one more thing." Familiarize yourself with these resources early in your planning process, and come back to this section occasionally to see how you might continually adapt these materials to fit your needs.*

This would also be a good time for your Facilitation Team to view SVC-30, where a superintendent talks about the often complex politics of doing equity work in communities that have competing perspectives coming from both ends of the political spectrum. He also provides some helpful insights into why he chose to partner with Gary Howard in doing this systemic work.

1. View Video Segment 5:7   Variable Time as Needed

Gary describes the tools and resources included in this section of the manual and suggests ways that you might use and adapt these materials to support your work. Your Facilitation Team should watch the video segment together and pause where needed to discuss how and whether each of the resources could be helpful in your setting. The pieces include the following:

- **Sample Evaluation/Reflection Forms: Handouts ST-13a–c and ST-14**
  - Provided here are several participant feedback forms Gary has used in his work with school districts and faculties throughout the country. The questions included on these forms are offered here as templates for your use and adaptation in gathering data from your faculty and staff. Also included here is a sample compilation of feedback comments generated by the Evaluation/Reflection forms. The compilation summarizes participant feedback from one of Gary's sessions and demonstrates how you can share evaluation data with your faculty. It is not necessary to gather and compile this kind of written feedback after each activity or event, but it is helpful to do so from time to time and use the data to inform your next steps and future planning.

- **Ideas for Deepening and Sustaining the Work: Handout ST-14**
  - This is a list of suggested activities that can be used to strengthen, support, and sustain your work. You can revisit this list occasionally to inform your planning and stimulate additional ideas.

- **CRT and Safe, Respectful Learning Environments: Handout ST-15**
  - This piece comes from Gary's work with a school district whose central vision for positive climate and anti-bullying was built around the theme of "Safe, Respectful Learning Environments." Gary's overlay of that concept with the Seven Principles of CRT can serve as a model for your integration of CRT with other initiatives you already have in place.

- **Integration and Alignment Discussion   Time as Needed**

After viewing and discussing Video Segment 5:7, take some time to list all of the programs and initiatives you presently have in place to address issues of school improvement, strengthen instruction strategies, promote equity, and develop a positive school climate. Some of these might include Response to Intervention (RTI), Positive Behavior Interventions and Supports (PBIS), Advancement through Individual Determination (AVID), Charlotte Danielson's work, Robert Marzano's work, Professional Learning Communities (PLCs), Seeking Educational Equity and Diversity (SEED), Courageous Conversations about Race, or other initiatives. Brainstorm all of the possible connections you see between these initiatives and your work with Cultural Competence and Culturally Responsive Teaching. How can you make the case to your faculty and staff that this work is directly and necessarily connected to all other school improvement and instructional work you are doing? Challenge yourselves to create a visual organizer that will demonstrate these connections and make them explicit.

EVALUATION / REFLECTION

▶ **Session 1**

1. What were the most helpful/positive aspects of today's session?

2. What is one idea or lesson for your own journey and/or work that you connected with today?

3. What challenge or concern has not been addressed here that you would like to explore further at a future session?

4. To date, how successful has your school/district been in creating a courageous and real conversation about issues of equity, cultural competence, social justice, and closing the achievement gaps?

   Low Success   **High Success**

   1   2   3   4   5   6   7   8   9   10

   What, in your opinion, is needed to go further and deeper?

ST-13b

Cultural Competence and Courageous Practice

EVALUATION / REFLECTION

▶ **Session 2**

1. **What were the most helpful/positive aspects of today's session?**

2. **Do the Seven Principles for Culturally Responsive Teaching provide a helpful tool for you? Why or why not?**

3. **How are you feeling at this point about your growth as a culturally competent and culturally responsive educator?**

4. **So far, what has been most helpful/valuable for you in this series of workshops? How could these sessions be more helpful for you?**

EVALUATION / REFLECTION

▶ **Session 3**

1. **What were the most helpful/positive aspects of today's session?**

2. **Considering our 3 days of work together, what has been the most significant outcome, insight, or result for you personally?**

3. **What are you thinking at this point about your (or your team's) progress and potential for doing some positive and courageous work in your school/organization?**

4. **What, if anything, is missing in your readiness/ability/preparation to do this work?**

Cultural Competence and Courageous Practice

SAMPLE COMPILED EVALUATION COMMENTS

▶ **Session 1**
Work with Gary Howard

1. What were the most helpful / positive aspects of today's session?

- Sharing / reflecting
- The framework of the agenda—presenting it at the end was very helpful in answering—what are we going to do with all this?
- Positive—experiences discussed, but no preaching.
- I enjoyed the feedback/discussion in small groups and large groups. Thank you for the time to reflect as part of this process.
- Small-group discussions of issues/values/different perspectives.
- Sharing with the small group.
- Making people aware of issues. Opening eyes.
- Friendly and interesting conversations with colleagues.
- Opening conversations and the opportunity to go deeper into the topics.
- Group facilitated discussion.
- Establishing tone and trust. Opening conversation in comfortable setting.
- The acceptability of the "gob-smac" in your presentation.
- The discussion during the "give-it-up" activity.
- Positive interactions, safe environment to discuss.
- For me, giving thought to what is most important to me and what I would be willing to give up. Extending this to our expectation of students to conform to our beliefs.
- Good trust and comfort to discuss real and difficult issues due to race, ethnicity, etc. was established.
- Getting beyond surface conversations and allowing us to challenge each other.
- Open and real sharing among the group members.
- Very important to get us to begin the process of thinking about these issues in a different light.
- Talking among colleagues about their feelings toward equity.
- Enjoyed people at my table/their ideas and perspectives.
- Discussion of what cultural competence is in the educational setting.

ST-14

Cultural Competence and Courageous Practice

SAMPLE COMPILED EVALUATION COMMENTS (CONTINUED)

2. **What is one idea or lesson for your own journey and / or work that you connected with today?**

- That relationships between faculty and students (tone and trust) must take place before anything can really be accomplished.
- I'm on the right track with several of my initiatives.
- The one idea that really hit me today was about teaching minorities in such a way that they do not have to give up who they are.
- Be willing to acknowledge race and ethnicity as a difference, then work with those differences.
- That you do need to maneuver in different environments to survive.
- I like your term cultural competence rather than diversity.
- That my view of these issues is not going to be the same as those of a Black, Asian, Hispanic student.
- Students need to feel that you truly care about their success.
- I appreciated the definitions and notion of cultural competency.
- The idea of relationships as a primary force in allowing maximum education.
- Reaffirms how important my job is to... just connect, be kind, be inviting and loving to each student. Get them to dream! Visualize what they want their future to be!
- That this is a journey, we are just starting and that is OK (better than not starting).
- Leadership in school to help others join me on this journey.
- The idea that my life values and vocation are connected.
- I will become more aware of creating a non-biased climate in my classroom and with my instruction.
- Eye-opening that folks don't see the challenges that women, for example, still face.
- How hard it was to "give it up" and perhaps I teach children who are in that very vein.
- I need to explore my own intolerance to intolerance.
- We all come with different experiences and they define and influence who we are and how we teach.
- The importance of recognizing what's important and what's not.
- One of the things I learned from the "give it up" activity was that there are many ways of approaching those tough decisions. Interesting discussion.
- Work on collectivity activities. Work out a multicultural "norm" for a work place such as our school system.

Cultural Competence and Courageous Practice

ST-14

SAMPLE COMPILED EVALUATION COMMENTS (CONTINUED)

8. **What challenge or concern has <u>not</u> been addressed here that you would like to explore further at a future session?**

- How to get individual teachers on board with assessing themselves in this area of cultural competence.
- How to talk courageously.
- Perhaps more expectations of sharing this with our staff.
- How to deal with or combat issues such as "race card".
- How to encourage faculty to go beyond their comfort zone and address cultural issues.
- How does the community, especially the parents, get involved in this issue?
- Implementation.
- More interaction between white students and minority students. I believe we have groups that help with the success of minority students, but none to help the different races intermix.
- Listening more to kids—letting them help us know what the roadblocks, hurdles are.
- What concrete ways are used to encourage teachers to use the steps toward cultural competency?
- What other examples (in other schools) programs that are actually working to bridge the achievement gap?
- Skill building for teachers in cultural competence and student engagement.
- Anticipation of negativity from certain faculty members. They will completely shut down on this.
- The attitude of faculty and staff toward student differences. Also, the attitudes and perceptions of the community need to be addressed.
- Practical/real-life scenarios and solutions to deal with education of faculty, students, and parents.
- How to open the eyes of fellow teachers.
- Role-playing difficult situation with students and staff.
- How do we open teachers who feel uncomfortable to this conversation and turn conversation to positive action?
- Addressed here (yes!). Elaboration desired—individual steps to change behavior—how to start the conversations in a positive manner with adults who impact so many on a daily basis.
- More about teachers recognizing/acknowledging/embracing differences in background and experience among individuals.
- The fashioning of a multicultural acceptance—"norm" within a narrowly defined "white dominant cultural" classroom.

SAMPLE COMPILED EVALUATION COMMENTS (CONTINUED)

4. **Over the past 2–3 years, how successful has your school been in creating a courageous and real conversation about issues of diversity, equity, social justice, and cultural responsiveness?**

1)
2)
3) 4
4) 2
5) 4
6) 4
7) 4
8) 2
9)
10) 1
Average: 5.6

What, in your opinion, is needed to go further and deeper?

- We are beginning to address it in all sorts of ways.
- More time to meet and discuss these issues.
- Staff willingness to self-assess.
- To follow up on the direction that we are pursuing.
- Deciding if this is a priority and working to achieve it.
- Have the discussion with others, implement ideas. Measure where we are now.
- Time—more interaction with students and honest sharing—asking questions about beliefs—and even hopes—how do students see things and want them to change.
- More time for reflection and discussion.
- Strategies/programs.
- Increased awareness. Skill building. Collaboration among all faculty.

ST-14

Cultural Competence and Courageous Practice

SAMPLE COMPILED EVALUATION COMMENTS (CONTINUED)

- Discussion about how we can more easily talk to one another.
- Absolutely
- Needs to go further now. This process has only just begun.
- Addressing needs of minority students other than African-American.
- Addressing / embracing the uniqueness of all students, rich, poor, gay, blue collar vs. academic, etc.
- Work with other teachers.
- Perseverance.
- Making changes that matter for kids.
- Leadership pushing more to improve individual changes.
- Inclusion of all groups — we have a growing Asian population that hasn't been addressed.
- Much more conversation and reflection time.

Ideas for Sustaining and Deepening the Work

1. Keep your Facilitation Team together and meet regularly.

2. Meet with your principal regularly if he or she is not a member of your team.

3. Revisit and update your Implementation Planning Guide (Handout ST-11) every quarter.

4. Utilize the Implementation Self-Assessment Checklist (Handout ST-12) to track your progress and plan ahead.

5. Gather faculty and staff feedback using Evaluation/Reflection forms adapted from Handouts ST-13a to ST-13c.

6. Compile the feedback data in a form similar to Handout ST-14, and share with your faculty and staff. Discuss the themes that emerge from these data.

7. Create opportunities for Facilitation Teams from different schools to connect and share successes and struggles.

8. Invite Student Voices into the process.

9. Develop cadres of Youth Equity Leaders modeled after the New Wilderness Project Youth Voices video series (see Video Segment 5:8).

10. Invite Student Equity Leaders to make presentations to your staff.

11. Bring new teachers on board using Gary Howard's e-course, Becoming a Culturally Responsive Teacher. www.ghequityinstitute.com

12. To support and deepen your work with Phase Three, utilize Shakti Butler's films, *Mirrors of Privilege: Making Whiteness Visible* and *Cracking the Codes: The System of Racial Inequity.* www.world-trust.org

13. Read Gary's articles listed in the back of the manual and convene reflective conversations using the discussion guide provided. Do a group reading of his book: *We Can't Teach What We Don't Know: White Teachers, Multiracial Schools.*

14. Integrate the CRT work into your school improvement process and link it to all other building/district initiatives.

15. Integrate Cultural Competence and Culturally Responsive Teaching indicators into all Look-For, Walkthrough, and Teacher Evaluation rubrics.

Safe and Respectful Learning Environment

CONNECTING WITH THE SEVEN PRINCIPLES OF CRT

▶ *SAFE: STUDENTS CAN BE WHO THEY ARE WITHOUT HARASSMENT*

CRT Principle #1: Students are affirmed in their cultural connections.

"Students get it that we get them."

▶ *RESPECTFUL: DIFFERENCES ARE WELCOMED AND APPRECIATED*

CRT Principle #2: Teacher is personally inviting.

"Students get it that we like them."

CRT Principle #6: Classroom is managed with firm, consistent, caring control.

"Teachers show pre-emptive respect."

▶ *LEARNING: EVERYONE IS GROWING SMARTER AND MORE AWARE*

CRT Principle #4: Students are reinforced for academic development.

"Teachers catch kids being smart."

CRT Principle #5: Instructional changes are made to accommodate differences in learners.

"Teachers sing harmony to each student's intelligence."

▶ *ENVIRONMENT: WE HONOR BOTH DIVERSITY AND COMMUNITY*

CRT Principle #3: Learning environments are physically and culturally inviting.

"This classroom/school feels like me."

CRT Principle #7: Activities stress collectivity as well as individuality.

"We can learn together and we can learn alone."

Activity: Youth Voices and Student Equity Leadership	
Phase Five: Systemic Transformation and Planning for Change	
Purpose:	• Include student voices as a key factor in school change • Model an effective approach to empowering youth voices • Provide video documentation of student equity leadership • Suggest activities for student engagement
Suggested Time:	For use at any time during the PD process
Materials Needed:	Video Segment 5:8 New Wilderness Project Youth Voices Video Series (Order from: www.newwildernessproject.com) Youth Voices Video Viewing Guidebook (Comes with the Video Series)
Advanced Preparation:	• View Video Segment 5:8 with your Facilitation Team • Acquire a set of the Youth Voices Video Series and view these films together • Plan when and how to share these resources with your faculty and staff • Connect with people who are doing Youth Voices work in your school district and community

Facilitator Note: *An essential and often missing piece of any effective school improvement strategy is the inclusion of student perspectives, experiences, and voices. The top-down approach to school reform, besides failing to listen to the actual experiences of teachers and school leaders, has also neglected to consult our primary customers, the students. The materials in this section provide you a model for student engagement at the secondary level, a model that has been powerful and productive in school districts throughout the country. The videos have also been used effectively for faculty professional development at both the elementary and secondary levels. Since the students in these films are engaging in the same five Phases and conceptual framework used in this Leadership Manual, the Youth Voices videos are well aligned with the work you are doing with adults in your building.*

1. View Video Segment 5:8   15 Minutes

Gary introduces the Youth Voices Video Series and describes the school district setting in which the filming took place. He also shares information about the process and approach that are used by New

Wilderness Project in their work with youth empowerment and student equity leadership. He makes the case for including student voices as an essential and integral part of your overall approach to school change. Integrated with his comments, you will see clips from the Youth Voices Video Series, which will provide your team with a preview of the films and offer you an opportunity to discuss whether to purchase a set for your school.

2. View and Discuss the Youth Voices Video Series   Variable Time as Needed

Once you have acquired your set of the Video Series, make time as a team to view the five different videos. The series is closely aligned with the same conceptual framework and Phases of the Work that you are using with the adults in your school, so you may want to think about how to use the different films over time to reinforce your work with faculty. Titles of the separate videos are as follows:

- **Personal Journey/Personal Culture**
- **Social Dominance to Social Justice**
- **Creative Expression/Creative Resistance**
- **Leadership in Action**
- **Bridging the Gap Across Differences**

3. Implement a Youth Voices Process in Your School District   Multiyear

After viewing the Youth Voices Video Series and reading through the accompanying Viewing Guidebook, consider how you might initiate a similar program in your school or district. You may already have a youth empowerment process in place. How can you tap into that resource to strengthen your work with adults? If you don't have such a program, the Video Series and Viewing Guidebook can be valuable tools in fashioning your own approach. You can also contact the people at New Wilderness Project (www.newwildernessproject.com) for their assistance in the work.

Facilitator Note: *For additional information about the Student Voices process, view SVC-31 and SVC-32. In these two video segments you will hear a superintendent talk about the power and purpose of student engagement, and you will hear a youth advocate describe how she collaborated with New Wilderness Project to empower students in her high school.*

Activity: Sample Research and Assessment Design	
Phase Five: Systemic Transformation and Planning for Change	
Purpose:	• Demonstrate the effectiveness of the Professional Development process • Provide a model for outcomes research and assessment
Suggested Time:	Implement during the entire PD process
Materials Needed:	Video Segment 5:9 Jefferson County Public Schools (JCPS) PowerPoint (Created by Aukram Burton and Judi Vanderhaar. Used here with their permission.)
Advanced Preparation:	• View Video Segment 5:9 with your Facilitation Team • Study and discuss the JCPS assessment design • Plan your approach to evaluating your overall Professional Development program • Connect with other schools and the evaluation and assessment people in your school district

Facilitator Note: *Jefferson County Public Schools, in Louisville, Kentucky, has conducted the most comprehensive evaluation of the professional development process presented in this manual. In this section, you will learn about the essential pieces of that evaluation design and view a PowerPoint presentation organized by Aukram Burton and Judi Vanderhaar, the two key people responsible for overseeing the Cultural Competence work and assessment in JCPS. Hopefully, their contribution will serve as inspiration and guidance for your team in tracking the results of this work in your school and district.*

1. View Video Segment 5:9   12 Minutes

Gary provides background information about the JCPS evaluation study and walks you through some of the key slides in the PowerPoint presentation. The JCPS study demonstrated significantly positive outcomes in the following arenas:

• Teacher and staff awareness of Cultural Competence issues in the classroom
• Reduction in discipline referrals across race and poverty

- Increase in students' connectedness and engagement across race and poverty
- Achievement gains in reading and math across race and poverty

2. View School Video Clip 33: An Administrator Talks About Assessment Outcomes

In SVC-33, you will have an opportunity to hear Aukram Burton's perspective on the work in Jefferson County Public Schools in Louisville.

3. Review and Discuss the
JCPS PowerPoint   Variable Time as Needed

Once you have listened to Gary's comments on Video Segment 5:9 and watched SVC-33, take some time with your Facilitation Team to review the JCPS slides and talk about what might be helpful or appropriate to adapt to your own setting. The slides are embedded in Video Segment 5:9.

4. Plan and Implement
Your Assessment Design   Multiyear

Work with your Facilitation Team and people from your district assessment office to design your method for evaluating the progress and outcomes of the professional development process. What are the outcomes you want to see? How will you assess the impact of your professional development efforts related to Cultural Competence and Culturally Responsive Teaching?

Selected Articles
From Gary Howard's
Collected Works

- *As Diversity Grows, So Must We*
- *Speaking of Difference: Reflections on the Possibility of Culturally Competent Conversation*
- *Whites in Multicultural Education: Rethinking Our Role*
- *How We Are White*
- *School Improvement for All: Reflections on the Achievement Gap*
- *Dispositions for Good Teaching*
- *Article Discussion Guide*

As Diversity Grows, So Must We

Gary R. Howard
www.ghequityinstitute.com

Schools that experience rapid demographic shifts can meet the challenge by implementing five phases of professional development.

Originally published in: *Educational Leadership,* **March 2007, Volume 64, Number 6, Responding to Changing Demographics, p. 16-22 .**

Many school districts nationwide are experiencing rapid growth in the number of students of color, culturally and linguistically diverse students, and students from low-income families. From my work with education leaders in some of these diversity-enhanced school districts, I know they are places of vibrant opportunity—places that call us to meaningful and exciting work. In these "welcome-to-America" schools, the global community shows up in our classrooms every day, inviting us—even requiring us—to grow as we learn from and with our students and their families.

THE NEED FOR GROWTH

All is not well, however, in these rapidly transitioning schools. Some teachers, administrators, and parents view their schools' increasing diversity as a problem rather than an opportunity. For example, in a school district on the West Coast where the number of Latino students has quadrupled in the past 10 years, a teacher recently asked me, "Why are they sending these kids to our school?" In another district outside New York City—where the student population was once predominantly rich, white, and Jewish but is now about 90 percent low-income kids of color, mostly from the Caribbean and Latin America—a principal remarked in one workshop, "These kids don't value education, and their parents aren't helping either. They don't seem to care about their children's future." In a school district near Minneapolis with a rapidly increasing black population, a white parent remarked, "Students who are coming here now don't have much respect for authority. That's why we have so many discipline problems."

Other educators and parents, although less negative, still feel uneasy about their schools' new demographics. In a high school outside Washington, D.C., where the Latino immigrant population is increasing rapidly, a teacher told me that he was disappointed in himself for not feeling comfortable engaging his students in a discussion on immigration issues, a hot topic in the community in Spring 2006. "I knew the kids needed to talk, but I just couldn't go there." And a black teacher who taught French successfully for many years in predominantly white suburban schools told me recently, "When I first found myself teaching classes of mostly black kids, I went home frustrated every night because I knew I wasn't getting through to them, and they were giving me a hard time. It only started getting better when I finally figured out that I had to reexamine everything I was doing."

This teacher has it right. As educators in rapidly transitioning schools, we need to reexamine everything we're doing. Continuing with business as usual will mean failure or mediocrity for too many of our students, as the data related to racial, cultural, linguistic, and economic achievement gaps demonstrate (National Center for Education Statistics, 2005). Rapidly changing demographics demand that we engage in a vigorous, ongoing, and systemic process of professional development to prepare all educators in the school to function effectively in a highly diverse environment.

Many education leaders in divesity-enhanced schools are moving beyond blame and befuddlement and working to transform themselves and their schools to serve all their students well. From observing and collaborating with them, I have learned that this transformative work proceeds best in five phases: (1) building trust, (2) engaging personal culture, (3) confronting issues of social dominance and social justice, (4) transforming instructional practices, and (5) engaging the entire school community.

PHASE 1: BUILDING TRUST

Ninety percent of U.S. public school teachers are white; most grew up and attended school in middle-class, English-speaking, predominantly white communities and received their teacher preparation in predominantly white colleges and universities (Gay, Dingus, & Jackson, 2003). Thus, many white educators simply have not acquired the experiential and education background that would prepare them for the growing diversity of their students (Ladson-Billings, 2002; Vavrus, 2002).

The first priority in the trust phase is to acknowledge this challenge in a positive, inclusive, and honest way. School leaders should base initial discussions on the following assumptions:

- Inequities in diverse schools are not, for the most part, a function of intentional discrimination.
- Educators of *all* racial and cultural groups need to develop new competencies and pedagogies to successfully engage our changing populations.
- White teachers have their own cultural connections and unique personal narratives that are legitimate aspects of the overall mix of school diversity.

School leaders should also model for their colleagues inclusive and nonjudgmental discussion, reflection, and engagement strategies that teachers can use to establish positive learning communities in their classrooms.

For example, school leaders in the Apple Valley Unified School District in Southern California, where racial, cultural, and linguistic diversity is rapidly increasing, have invested considerable time and resources in creating a climate of openness and trust. They recently implemented four days of intensive work with teams from each school, including principals, teacher leaders, union representatives, parents, clergy, business leaders, and community activists from the NAACP and other organizations.

One essential outcome in this initial phase of the conversation is to establish that racial, cultural, and economic differences are real—and that they make a difference in education outcomes. Said one Apple Valley participant, "I have become aware that the issue of race needs to be dealt with, not minimized." Said another, "I need to move beyond being colorblind." A second key outcome is to establish the need for a personal and professional journey toward greater awareness. As an Apple Valley educator noted, "There were a lot of different stories and viewpoints shared at this inservice, but the one thing we can agree on is that everyone needs to improve in certain areas." A third key outcome in the trust phase is to demonstrate that difficult topics can be discussed in an environment that is honest, safe, and productive. One Apple Valley teacher commented, "We were able to talk about all of the issues and not worry about being politically correct."

Through this work, Apple Valley educators and community leaders established a climate of constructive collaboration that can be directed toward addressing the district's new challenges. From the perspective of the school superintendent, "This is a conversation our community is not used to having, so we had to build a positive climate before moving to the harder questions of action."

PHASE 2: ENGAGING PERSONAL CULTURE

Change has to start with educators before it can realistically begin to take place with students. The central aim of the second phase of the work is building educators' *cultural competence*—their ability to form authentic and effective relationships across differences.

Young people, particularly those from historically marginalized groups, have sensitive antennae for authenticity. I recently asked a group of racially and culturally diverse high school students to name the teachers in their school who really cared about them, respected them, and enjoyed getting to know them as people. Forty students pooling their answers could name only 10 teachers from a faculty of 120, which may be one reason this high school has a 50 percent dropout rate for students of color.

Aronson and Steele's (2005) work on stereotype threat demonstrates that intellectual performance, rather than being a fixed and constant quality, is quite fragile and can vary greatly depending on the social and interpersonal context of learning. In repeated studies, these researchers found that three factors have a major effect on students' motivation and performance: their feelings of belonging, their trust in the people around them, and their belief that teachers value their intellectual competence. This research suggests that the capacity of adults in the school to form trusting relationships with and supportive learning environments for their students can greatly influence achievement outcomes.

Leaders in the Metropolitan school District of Lawrence Township, outside of Indianapolis, have taken this perspective seriously. Clear data showed gaps among ethnic groups in achievement, participation in higher-level courses, discipline referrals, and dropout rates. In response, district teachers and administrators engaged in a vigorous and ongoing process of self-examination and personal growth related to cultural competence.

Central-office and building administrators started with themselves. Along with selected teachers from each school, they engaged in a multi-year program of shared reading, reflective conversations, professional development activities, and joint planning to increase their own and their colleagues' levels of cultural competence.

As this work among leaders began to be applied in various school buildings, one principal observed, "We are talking about things that we were afraid to talk about before—like our own prejudices and the biases in some of our curriculum materials." In another school, educators' discussions led to a decision to move parent-teacher conferences out of the school building and into the apartment complexes where their black and Latino students live.

PHASE 3: CONFRONTING SOCIAL DOMINANCE AND SOCIAL JUSTICE

When we look at school outcome data, the history of racism, classism, and exclusion in the United States stares us in the face. Systems of privilege and preference often create enclaves of exclusivity in schools, in which certain demographic groups are served well while others languish in failure or mediocrity. As diversity grows in rapidly transitioning school districts, demographic gaps become increasingly apparent.

In phase three, educators directly confront the current and historical inequities that affect education. The central purpose of this phase is to construct a compelling narrative of social justice that will inform, inspire, and sustain educators in their work, without falling into the rhetoric of shame and blame. School leaders and teachers engage in a lively conversation about race, class, gender, sexual orientation, immigration, and other dimensions of diversity and social dominance. David Koyama, principal of a diversity-enhanced elementary school outside Seattle, said, "One of my most important functions as a school leader is to transform political jargon like 'no child left behind' into a moral imperative that inspires teachers to work toward justice, not mere compliance."

Unraveling social dominance takes courage—the kind of courage shown by the central office and school leadership team in the Roseville Area School District outside the twin cities of Minneapolis and St. Paul. Roseville is in the midst of a rapid demographic shift. As we approached this phase of the work, I asked Roseville leaders to examine how issues of privilege, power, and dominance might be functioning in their school to shape educators' assumptions and beliefs about students and create inequitable outcomes.

One of the workshop activities engaged participants in a forced-choice simulation requiring them to choose which aspects of their identity they would give up or deny for the sake of personal survival in a hostile environment. Choosing from such identities as race, ethnicity, language, religion, values, and vocation, many white educators were quick to give up race. Among the Roseville administrative team, which is 95 percent white, the one white principal who chose to keep his racial identity during the simulation said during the debriefing discussion, "I seriously challenge my white colleagues who so easily gave up their race. I think if we are honest with ourselves, few would choose to lose the privilege and power that come with being white in the United States."

As an outgrowth of the authentic and sometimes contentious conversations that emerged from this and other activities, several core leaders and the superintendent identified a need to craft a strong Equity Vision statement for the district. The Equity Vision now headlines all opening-of-school events each year and is publicly displayed in district offices and schools. It reads,

> Roseville Area Schools is committed to ensuring an equitable and respectful educational experience for every student, family, and staff member, regardless of race, gender, sexual orientation, socio-economic status, ability, home or first language, religion, national origin, or age.

As a result of the increased consciousness about issues of dominance and social justice, several schools have formed Equity Teams of teachers and students, and an Equity Parent Group has begun to meet. The district is looking seriously at how many students from dominant and subordinate groups are in its gifted and AP classes and is conscientiously working for more balance.

Like Roseville, other diversity-enhanced districts must establish clear public markers that unambiguously state, "This is who we are, this is what we believe, and this is what we will do." Any approach to school reform that does not honestly engage issues of power, privilege, and social dominance is naïve, ungrounded in history, and unlikely to yield the deep changes needed to make schools more inclusive and equitable.

PHASE 4: TRANSFORMING INSTRUCTIONAL PRACTICES

In this phase, schools assess and, where necessary, transform the way they carry out instruction to become more responsive to diversity. For teachers, this means examining pedagogy and curriculum, as well as expectations and interaction patterns with students. It means looking honestly at outcome data and creating new strategies designed to serve the students whom current instruction is not reaching. For school leaders, this often means facing the limits of their own knowledge and skills and becoming co-learners with teachers to find ways to transform classroom practices.

In Loudoun County Public Schools, outside Washington, D.C., teachers and school leaders are taking this work seriously. One of the fastest-growing school systems in the United States, Loudoun County is experiencing rapid increases in racial, cultural, linguistic, and economic diversity on its eastern edge, closer to the city, while remaining more monocultural to the west. Six of Loudoun's most diverse schools have formed leadership teams to promote the following essential elements of culturally responsive teaching (CRT):

- Forming authentic and caring relationships with students.
- Using curriculum that honors each student's culture and life experience.
- Shifting instructional strategies to meet the diverse learning needs of students.
- Communicating respect for each student's intelligence.
- Holding consistent and high expectations for all learners. (Gay, 2000; Ladson-Billings, 1994; McKinley, 2005; Shade, Kelly, & Oberg, 1997)

CRT teams vary in size and membership but usually include principals, assistant principals, counselors, lead teachers, specialists, and, in some cases, parents. In addition to engaging deeply in the phases outlined above, these teams have begun to work with their broader school faculties to transform instruction. At Loudoun County's Sugarland Elementary, teacher members of the CRT team have designed student-based action research projects. They selected individual students from their most academically challenged demographic groups and then used the principles of CRT to plan new interventions to engage these students and track their progress.

In one action research project, a 5th grade teacher focused on a Latino student, an English language learner who "couldn't put two sentences together, let alone write the five-paragraph essay that is required to pass our 5th grade assessment." The teacher's first reaction was to ask, "How was this student allowed to slip by all these years without learning anything beyond 2nd grade writing skills?" When the teacher launched her CRT project, however, her perspective became more proactive. She realized that she couldn't just deliver the 5th grade curriculum—she had to meet this student where he was. She built a personal connection with the student, learned about his family culture and interests (a fascination with monkeys was a major access point), and used this relationship to reinforce his academic development. The student responded to her high expectations and passed his 5th grade writing assessment. And after missing its No Child Left Behind compliance goals in past years. Sugarland recently achieved adequate yearly progress for all subgroups in its highly diverse student population.

This phase required a crucial paradigm shift, in which teachers and other school professionals stop blaming students and their families for gaps in academic achievement. Instead of pointing fingers, educators in Loudoun schools are placing their energies where they will have the most impact—in changing their own attitudes, beliefs, expectations, and practices. I frequently ask teachers and school leaders, "Of all the many factors that determine school success for our students, where can we as educators have the most influence?" After educators participate in the work outlined here, the answer is always, "Changing ourselves."

PHASE 5: ENGAGING THE ENTIRE SCHOOL COMMUNITY

Changing demographics have profound implications for all levels and functions of the school system. To create welcoming and equitable learning environments for diverse students and their families, school leaders must engage the entire school community.

Leaders in the East Ramapo Central School District in New York State have committed themselves to just such a systemwide initiative. The school district, which lies across the Tappan Zee Bridge from New York City, has experienced a dramatic shift in student population in the past 15 years as low-income Haitian, Jamaican, Dominican, Latino, and black families from the city have moved into the community and middle-class white families have, unfortunately but predictably, fled to private schools or other less diverse districts.

In the midst of this demographic revolution, East Ramapo's broad-based diversity initiative has engaged all groups and constituencies in the school district community, not just teachers and administrators. For example, the district has provided workshops to help classified employees acknowledge their powerful role in setting a welcoming tone and creating an inclusive climate for students, parents, and colleagues in school offices, lunchrooms, hallways, and on the playground. For bus drivers, this work has meant gaining cultural competence skills for managing their immense safety responsibilities while communicating clearly and compassionately across many languages and cultures on their buses.

In one session that I led with school secretaries, we worked through their confusion and frustration related to all the diverse languages being spoken in the school offices and, in some cases, their feelings of anger and resentment about the demographic changes that had taken place in "their" schools. Asked what they learned from the session, participants commented, "I saw the frustration people can have, especially if they are from another country." "We all basically have the same feelings about family, pride in our culture, and the importance of getting along." "I learned from white people that they can also sometimes feel like a minority."

In addition to these sessions, East Ramapo has created learning opportunities for school board members, parents, students, counselors, and special education classroom assistants. The district has convened regular community forums focusing on student achievement and creating conversations across many diverse cultures. White parents who have kept their children in the public schools because they see the values of diversity in their education have been significant participants in these conversations.

As a result of East Ramapo's efforts, the achievement gap in test scores along ethnic and economic lines have significantly narrowed. In the six years since the district consciously began implementing the professional development model discussed here, the pass rate for black and Hispanic students combined on the New York State elementary language arts test increased from 43 percent to 54 percent in 2006; on the math test, the pass rate increased from 40 percent to 61 percent. During that same period, the gap between black and Hispanic students (combined) and white and Asian students (combined) decreased by 6 percentage points in language arts and 23 percentage points in math. The achievement gap between low-income elementary students and the general population decreased by 10 points in language arts and 6 points in math—results that are particularly impressive, given that the proportion of economically disadvantaged students grew from 51 percent in 2000 to 72 percent in 2006.

A JOURNEY TOWARD AWARENESS

Professional development for creating inclusive, equitable, and excellent schools is a long-term process. The school districts described here are at various stages in the process. Everyone involved would agree that the work is messier and more complex than can be communicated in this brief overview. However, one central leadership commitment is clear in all of these rapidly transitioning districts: When diversity comes to town, we are all challenged to grow.

REFERENCES

Aronson, J., & Steele, C. M.(2005). Stereotypes and the fragility of human competence, motivation, and self-concept. In C. Dweck & E. Elliot (Eds.), *Handbook of competence and motivation* (pp. 436–456). New York: Guilford.

Gay, G. (2000). *Culturally responsive teaching: Theory, research, and practice.* New York: Teachers College Press.

Gay, G., Dingus, J. E., & Jackson, C. W. (2003, July). *The presence and performance of teachers of color in the profession.* Unpublished report prepared for the National Collaborative on Diversity in the Teaching Force, Washington, D.C.

Howard, G. (2006). *We can't teach what we don't know: White teachers in multiracial schools.* (2nd ed.). New York: Teachers College Press.

Ladson-Billings, G. (1994). *The dreamkeepers: Successful teachers of African American students.* San Francisco: Jossey-Bass.

Ladson-Billings, G. (2002). *Crossing over to Canaan: The journey of new teachers in diverse classrooms.* San Francisco: Jossey-Bass.

McKinley, J. H. (2005, March). *Culturally responsive teaching and learning.* Paper presented at the Annual State Conference of the Washington Alliance of Black School Educators, Bellevue, WA.

National Center for Education Statistics. (2005). *The nation's report card.* Washington, D.C.

Shade, B. J., Kelly, C., & Oberg, M. (1997). *Creating culturally responsive classrooms.* Washington, D.C.: American Psychological Association.

Vavrus, M. (2002). Transforming the multicultural education of teachers: Theory, research and practice. New York: Teachers College Press.

Wheatley, M. (2002). *Turning to one another: Simple conversations to restore hope to the future.* San Francisco: Barrett-Koehler.

REFLECTIONS ON THE POSSIBILITY OF CULTURALLY COMPETENT CONVERSATION

Gary R. Howard
www.ghequityinstitute.com

> But once the realization is accepted that even
> between the closest human beings infinite
> distances continue to exist, a wonderful living side
> by side can grow up, if they succeed in loving the
> distance between them which makes it possible
> for each to see the other whole and against a wide
> sky! ... All companionship can consist only in the
> strengthening of two neighboring solitudes.
>
> — Rainer Maria Rilke

Originally published by New Horizons for Learning, Spring 2003 <www.newhorizons.org>

There seem to be at least two schools of thought, two separate realms of rhetoric whenever well-intentioned discussions of multicultural issues emerge. One school opts for sameness and emphasizes commonalities. "I don't see color." "We're all alike." "Cut the skin and we all bleed red." "There's only one race—the human race." "Why do some people insist on hyphenated identities—can't we all just be Americans?"

The other end of the rhetorical spectrum weighs in on issues of difference and emphasizes the distance between us. "If you don't see color, you don't see me." "As long as there's racism, we have to talk about race." "My race *is* who I am." "I am both Asian *and* American." "Until you acknowledge my difference from you, you can never know me."

Our attempts to have honest and courageous conversations on topics of difference often become polarized by these two worldviews. We seem to be able to talk forever without getting anywhere. If we define cultural competence as the ability to form authentic relationships across our differences, then a beginning point in the journey toward cultural competence would surely require us to find a way to talk productively with one another about issues of race, culture, gender, religion, sexual orientation, and the many other dimensions of difference.

There is shallowness in the rhetoric that divides us, whether from the purveyors of sameness or from the champions of difference. This shallowness is born from our unreflective certainty, each of us steeped in images of our own rightness, blind to the nuance and complexity of our actual lived experience of both difference and connection.

There are no easy answers or magic elixirs for the kind of growth that would allow us greater ease, competence, and effectiveness in the multicultural conversation. Neither are there any quick fixes for transforming our schools to be more user-friendly for the diverse people who inhabit these spaces.

The "river of diversity and healing" that serves as the central metaphor in my book, *We Can't Teach What We Don't Know*, is a long river of learning, whereupon, if we are fortunate and strong, we can encounter one another in the clear reflection of shared honesty, eyes wide open to both our infinite oneness as well as our equally unfathomable difference. Both sides of the rhetorical polarity are true. At times I can know you and connect with you in such a deep commonality that it may seem as though there is no difference between us as we swim together in the flow of our human beingness. Yet, at other times, if I am awake and conscious of you in your full reality, I am pierced by the otherness, which I can never fully know and certainly never be.

Both are true, and herein exists the problem with any simplistic rhetoric of difference. We are forever and inextricably one and united in our humanness, and at the same time unavoidably and irreconcilably other. I am simultaneously you and not-you, as you are both me and not-me. Together we *are* the dance of unity and diversity. With the poet Rainer Maria Rilke, perhaps the best we can do for and with each other is to respectfully stand guard at the door of one another's solitude, defending and honoring the otherness of the other, while always ready to join as one when we emerge from this solitude to meet on the threshold of our separate realities.

This is the appropriate context in which to speak of cultural competence and authentic relationship across our differences. This place of meeting, which I refer to as "la tierra transformativa", is a place of deep respect for differences and equally intentional openness to the possibility of connection. It is a place where neither of us loses anything of value to us. We are only asked to sacrifice our proprietary assumptions of our own rightness and our unreflective grip on our own certainty. It is a place of ambiguity as well as certainty, of solitude as well as community, and a place of knowing as well as never-knowing.

Those of us who would hope to lead others to this place must ourselves have spent some time there, facing our own issues of sameness and difference. We must have made a home for ourselves in the space of our own identity and solitude, and emerged to meet the other (student, parent, colleague) in full honesty, yielding our arrogance in the spirit of humility and real connection.

This dissolution of the rhetorical either-or-dichotomy of sameness and difference is the key to dissolving that other classroom conundrum, the achievement gap. Without clear connection and conversation across differences, we have little hope of building the respectful relationships upon which equitable learning depends.

We earn our way to cultural competence one rapid at a time, feeling the full force of the river, giving ourselves to its power, and discovering our way in its flow. It is a life-long adventure worthy of our full attention. For the sake of the richly diverse children, families, communities, and schools that we serve, it is imperative that some of us in the vocation of education find our way to this place of authentic engagement within and across our differences. High-stakes testing and political rhetoric will surely never take us there, but powerful teaching and courageous leadership might.

Whites in Multicultural Education

RETHINKING OUR ROLE

Gary R. Howard
www.ghequityinstitute.com

Originally published in the September 1993 Edition of the *Phi Delta Kappan*

How does an ethnic group that has historically been dominant in its society adjust to a more modest and balanced role? Put differently, how do white Americans learn to be positive participants in a richly pluralistic nation? These questions have always been a part of the agenda of multicultural education but are now coming more clearly into focus. Most of our work in race relations and multicultural education in the United States has emphasized—and appropriately so—the particular cultural experiences and perspectives of black, Asian, Hispanic, and American Indian groups. These are the people who have been marginalized to varying degrees by the repeated assertion of dominance by Americans of European ancestry. As the population of the United States shifts to embrace everlarger numbers of previously marginalized groups, there is an emerging need to take a closer look at the changing role of white Americans.

Part of this need is generated by the growing evidence that many white Americans may not be comfortable with the transition from their dominant status. As our population becomes more diverse, we have seen an alarming increase in acts of overt racism. The number and size of hate groups in the United States is rising. Groups such as the Aryan Nation, neo-Nazis, and skinheads tend to play on the anger, ignorance, and fears of the more alienated, disenfranchised, and uneducated segments of white society.

Too many segments of our white American population remain committed to their position of dominance; they are willing to defend it and legitimize it, even in the face of overwhelming evidence that our world is rapidly changing.1 Taken as a whole, these realities strongly suggest that a peaceful transition to a new kind of America, in which no ethnic or cultural group is in a dominant position, will require considerable change in education and deep psychological shifts for many white Americans. Attempting to effect these changes is part of the work of multicultural education, and that challenge leads us to a central question; What must take place in the minds and hearts of white Americans to convince them that now is the time to begin their journey from dominance to diversity?

There is much that needs to be said to help us understand our collective past, as well as the present. In a sense we are all victims of our history, some more obviously and painfully than others. It is critical that we white Americans come to terms with our reality and our role. What does it mean for white people to be responsible and aware in a nation where we have been the dominant cultural and political force? What can be our unique contribution, and what are the issues we need to face? How do we help create a nation where all cultures are accorded dignity and the right to survive?

I explore these questions here from the perspective of a white American. Each nation, of course, has its own special history to confront and learn from, but the depth and intensity of our struggle with diversity in the United States has significant lessons to teach both our own people and the rest of the world.

AMERICAN IMMIGRANTS

European Americans share at least one commonality; we all came from somewhere else. In my own family, we loosely trace our roots to England, Holland, France, and perhaps Scotland. However, with five generations separating us from our various "homelands," we have derived little meaning from these tenuous connections with our ancestral people across the water. This is true for many white Americans, who are often repulsed by the appellation "European American" and would never choose such a descriptor for themselves. They simply prefer to be called "American" and to forget the past.

On the other hand, many white Americans have maintained direct and strong ties with their European roots. They continue after many generations to draw meaning and pride from those connections. In the Seattle region there is an Ethnic Heritage Council composed of members of 103 distinct cultural groups, most of them European. These people continue to refer to themselves as Irish American, Croatian American, Italian American, or Russian American—terminology that acknowledges the two sides of their identity.

European Americans are a diverse people. We vary broadly across extremely different cultures or origin, and we continue here in the United States to be diverse in religion, politics, economic status, and lifestyle.[2] We also vary greatly in the degree to which we value the notion of the melting pot. Many of us today are ignorant of our ethnic history because our ancestors worked so hard to dismantle their European identity in favor of what they perceived to be the American ideal. The further our immigrant ancestors' cultural identities diverged from the white Anglo-Saxon Protestant image of the "real" American, the greater was the pressure to assimilate. Jews, Catholics, Eastern Europeans, Southern Europeans, and members of minority religious sects all felt the intense heat of the melting pot. From the moment they arrived on American soil, they received a strong message: forget the home language, make sure your children don't learn to speak it, change your name to sound more American—or, if the immigration officials can't pronounce it, they'll change it for you.

In dealing with the history and culture of European Americans, it is important to acknowledge the pain, suffering, and loss that were often associated with their immigrant experiences. For many of these groups, it was a difficult struggle to carve out a niche in the American political and economic landscape and at the same time to preserve some sense of their own ethnic identity. Some white Americans resist the multicultural movement today because they feel that their own history of suffering from prejudice and discrimination has not been adequately addressed.

FAMILY REALITIES

Like many white Americans, I trace my roots in this country back to the land—the Minnesota farm my mother's great-grandparents began working in the 1880s. My two uncles still farm this land, and I spent many of the summers of my youth with them. It was there that I learned to drive trucks and tractors at the age of 12. I learned the humor and practical wisdom of hard-working people. I learned to love the land—its smell and feel; its changing moods and seasons; its power to nurture the crops, the livestock and the simple folks who give their lives to it. On this land and with these people I have known my roots, my cultural heritage, much more deeply than through any connection with things European. The bond of my Americanness has been forged in my experience with the soil.

Yet, as I have grown to understand more of the history of this country, a conflict has emerged in my feelings about our family tradition of the land. I have a close friend and colleague, Robin Butterfield, whose traditional Ojibwe tribal lands once encompassed the area now occupied by my family's farm. This farm, which is the core experience of my cultural rootedness in America, is for her people a symbol of defeat, loss, and domination. How do I live with this? How can I incorporate into my own sense of being an American the knowledge that my family's survival and eventual success on this continent were built on the removal and near extermination of an entire race of people?

And to bring the issue closer to the present, many of my relatives today hold narrow and prejudicial attitudes about cultural differences. The racist jokes they tell at family gatherings and the ethnic slurs that punctuate their daily chatter have been an integral part of my cultural conditioning. It was not until my college years, when I was immersed in a rich multicultural living situation, that these barriers began to break down for me. Most of my relatives have not had that opportunity. They do not understand my work in multicultural education. "You do what?" The racist jokes diminish in my presence, but the attitudes remain. Yet, I love these people. They are my link with tradition and the past, even though many of their beliefs are diametrically opposed to what I have come to know and value about different cultures.

My family is not atypical among white Americans. Internal contradictions and tensions around issues of culture and race are intrinsic to our collective experience. For most white Americans, racism and prejudice are not theoretical constructs; they are members of the family.

When we open ourselves to learning about the historical perspectives and cultural experiences of other races in America, much of what we discover is incompatible with our image of a free and democratic nation. We find conflicting realities that do not fit together easily in our conscious awareness, clashing truths that cause train wrecks in the mind. In this sense, white Americans are caught in a classic state of cognitive dissonance. Our collective security and position of economic and political dominance have been fueled in large measure by the exploitation of other people. The physical and cultural genocide perpetrated against American Indians, the enslavement of African peoples, the exploitation of Mexicans and Asians as sources of cheap labor—on such acts of inhumanity rests the success of the European enterprise in America.

This cognitive dissonance is not dealt with easily. We can try to be aware. We can try to be sensitive. We can try to deal with racism in our own families, yet the tension remains. We can try to dance to the crazy rhythms of multiculturalism and race relations in the U.S., but the dissonant chords of this painful past and present keep intruding.

LUXURY OF IGNORANCE

Given the difficulty of dealing with such cognitive dissonance, it is no mystery why many white Americans simply choose to remain unaware. In fact, the possibility of remaining ignorant of other cultures is a luxury uniquely available to members of any dominant group. Throughout most of our history, there has been no reason why white Americans, for their own survival or success, have needed to be sensitive to the cultural perspectives of other groups. This is not a luxury available to people of color. If you are black, Indian, Hispanic, or Asian in the United States, daily survival depends on knowledge of white America. You need to know the realities that confront you in the workplace, in dealing with government agencies, in relation to official authorities like the police. To be successful in mainstream institutions, people of color in the U.S. need to be bicultural—able to play by the rules of their own cultural community and able to play the game according to the rules established by the dominant culture. For most white Americans, on the other hand, there is only one game, and they have traditionally been on the winning team.

The privilege that comes with being a member of the dominant group, however, is invisible to most white Americans.[3] Social research has repeatedly demonstrated that if Jessie Myles, an African American friend, and I walk into the same bank on the same day and apply for a loan with the same officer, I will be more likely to receive my money—and with less hassle, less scrutiny, and less delay. This is in spite of the fact that Jessie has more education and is also more intelligent, better looking, and a nicer person. Likewise, if I am turned down for a house purchase, I don't wonder whether it was because of my skin. And if I am offered a new job or promotion, I don't worry that my fellow workers may feel that I'm there not because of my qualifications, but merely to fill an affirmative action quota. Such privileged treatment is so much a part of the fabric of our daily existence that it escapes the conscious awareness of most white Americans. From the luxury of ignorance are born the Simi Valley neighborhoods of our nation, which remain painfully out of touch with our experiences and sensibilities of multicultural America.

EMOTIONS THAT KILL

The most prevalent strategy that white Americans adopt to deal with the grim realities of history is denial. "The past doesn't matter. All the talk about multicultural education and revising history from different cultural perspectives is merely ethnic cheerleading. My people made it, and so can yours. It's an even playing field and everybody has the same opportunities, so let's get on with the game and quit complaining. We've heard enough of your victim's history."

Another response is hostility, a reaction to cultural differences that we have seen resurfacing more blatantly in recent years. The Aryan Nation's organizing in Idaho, the murder of a black man by skinheads in Oregon, the killing of a Jewish talk show host by neo-Nazis in Denver, cross burnings and Klan marches in Dubuque, and the increase in racist incidents on college campuses all point to a revival of hate crimes and overt racism in the U.S. We can conjecture why this is occurring now: the economic down-turn, fear of job competition, the rollback on civil rights initiatives by recent administrations. Whatever the reason, hostility related to racial and cultural differences has always been a part of American life and was only once again brought into bold relief by the first Rodney King decision and its violent aftermath in Los Angeles.

Underlying both the denial and the hostility is a deep fear of diversity. This fear is obvious in the Neanderthal violence and activism of white supremacist groups. Because of their personal and economic insecurities, they seek to destroy that which is not like them.

The same fear is dressed in more sophisticated fashion by Western traditionalists and neoconservatives who campaign against multicultural education. They fear the loss of European and Western cultural supremacy in the school curriculum.[4] With their fraudulent attempt to characterize "political correctness" as a new form of McCarthyism and with their outcries against separatism, particularism, reverse racism, and historical inaccuracy in multicultural texts, they defend cultural turf that is already lost. The United States was never a white European Christian nation and is becoming less so every day. Most public school educators know the curriculum has to reflect this reality, but many guardians of the traditional canon still find it frightening to leave the Old World.

Denial, hostility, and fear are literally emotions that kill. Our country—indeed, the world—has suffered endless violence and bloodshed over issues of racial, cultural, and religious differences. And the killing is not only physical, but emotional and psychological as well. With this hostility toward diversity, we threaten to destroy the precious foundation of our national unity, which is a commitment to equality, freedom, and justice for all people. It is not multiculturalism that threatens to destroy our unity—as some neoconservative academics would have us believe—but rather our inability to embrace our differences and our unwillingness to honor the very ideals we espouse.

Ironically, these negative responses to diversity are destructive not only for those who are the targets of hate but also for the perpetrators themselves. Racism is ultimately a self-destructive and counter-evolutionary strategy. As is true for any species in nature, positive adaptation to change requires a rich pool of diversity and potential in the population. In denying access to the full range of human variety and possibility, racism drains the essential vitality from everyone, victimizing our entire society.

Another emotion that kills is guilt. For well-intentioned white Americans guilt is a major hurdle. As we become aware of the realities of the past and the present—of the heavy weight of oppression and racism that continues to drag our nation down—it is natural for many of us of European background to feel a collective sense of complicity, shame, or guilt. On a rational level, of course, we can say that we didn't contribute to the pain. We weren't there. We would never do such things to anyone. Yet, on an emotional level, there is a sense that we were involved somehow. And our membership in the dominant culture keeps us connected to the wrongs, because we continue to reap the benefits of past oppression.

There is a positive side to guilt, of course. It can be a spur to action, a motivation to contribute, a kick in the collective consciousness. Ultimately, however, guilt must be overcome, along with the other negative responses to diversity—for it, too, drains the lifeblood of our people. If we are finally to become one nation of many cultures, then we need to find a path out of the debilitating cycle of blame and guilt that has occupied so much of our national energy.

RESPONSES THAT HEAL

How do we as white Americans move beyond these negative responses to diversity and find a place of authentic engagement and positive contribution? The first step is to approach the past and the present with a new sense of honesty. Facing reality is the beginning of liberation. As white Americans we can face honestly the fact that we have benefited from racism. The point is simply to face the reality of our own privilege. We can also become supportive of new historical research aimed at providing a more inclusive and multidimensional view of our nation's past. Scholars and educators are searching for the literature, the experiences, the contributions, and the historical perspectives that have been ignored in our Eurocentric schooling. It is important that white Americans become involved in and supportive of this endeavor, which is, of course, highly controversial.

Many white Americans feel threatened by the changes that are coming. One of our responsibilities, therefore, is to help them understand that our nation is in a time of necessary transition. This is part of the honesty we are trying to address. It took 500 years to evolve our present curriculum, which, in spite of its many fine qualities, is still flawed and inaccurate and excludes most non-European perspectives and influences. The new multicultural curricula will also have to go through a process of evolution toward balance and accuracy. The appropriate role for aware white Americans is to participate in this evolution, rather than to attack it from the outside, as many critics of multicultural education have chosen to do.

Along with this honesty must come a healthy portion of humility. It is not helpful for white Americans to be marching out in front with all the answers for other groups. The future belongs to those who are able to walk and work beside people of many different cultures, lifestyles, and perspectives. The business world is embracing this understanding. We now see top corporate leaders investing millions of dollars annually to provide their employees with skills to function effectively in a highly diverse work force.[5] They are forced to make this expenditure because schools, frankly, have not done an adequate job. Diversity is a bottom line issue for employers. Productivity is directly related to our ability to deal with pluralism. Whenever power, truth, control, and the possibility of being right are concentrated in only a few people, a single perspective, one culture, or one approach, the creativity of an entire organization suffers.

Honesty and humility are based on respect. One of the greatest contributions white Americans can make to cultural understanding is simply to learn the power of respect. In Spanish, the term "respeto" has a deep connotation. It goes far beyond mere tolerance or even acceptance. "Respeto" acknowledges the full humanness of other people, their right to be who they are, their right to be treated in a good way. When white Americans learn to approach people of different cultures with this kind of deep respect, our own world becomes larger and our embrace of reality is made broader and richer. We are changed by our respect for other perspectives. It is more than just a nice thing to do. In the process of respecting other cultures, we learn to become better people ourselves.

But all of this is not enough. As members of the majority population, we are called to provide more than honesty, humility, and respect. The race issue for white Americans is ultimately a question of action: What are we going to do about it? It is not a black problem or an Indian problem or an Asian problem or a Hispanic problem—or even a white problem. The issue of racism and cultural diversity in the U.S. is a human problem, a struggle we are all in together. It cannot be solved by any one group. We have become embedded in the problem together, and we will have to deal with it together.

This brings us to the issue of co-responsibility. The way for us to overcome the denial, hostility, fear, and guilt of the past and present is to become active participants in the creation of a better future. As white Americans, once we become aware of the heavy weight of our oppressive past, our role is not to fall into a kind of morose confessionalism about the sins of our ancestors. The healing response for ourselves, as well as for those who have been the victims of oppression, is involvement, action, contribution, and responsibility. The healing path requires all of us to join our efforts, resources, energy, and commitment. No one group can do it alone. Together we are co-responsible for the creation of a new America.

THE SEARCH FOR AUTHENTIC IDENTITY

Before white Americans can enter fully into this active partnership for change, however, we need to come to terms with who we are as a people. One problem that arises from an honest appraisal of the past is that it sometimes becomes difficult for us as white people to feel good about our history. Where do we turn to find positive images for ourselves and our children? In the 1960s and early 1970s we saw a revolution in positive identity for blacks, American Indians, Hispanics, and Asians. During this period there was an explosion of racial and cultural energy—what James Banks refers to as the ethnic revitalization movement.[6] What were white youths doing at this time? There was a revolution happening with them as well: a revolution of rejection. As the civil rights movement, the anti-war movement, and the women's liberation movement were bringing to the public's attention many of the fundamental flaws of a culture dominated by white males, the youths of white America were searching for an alternative identity.

At this time in our history, white America was at war with itself. The children of affluence and privilege, the very ones who had benefited the most from membership in the dominant culture, were attacking the foundation of their own privilege. In creating a new counterculture of rebellion and hope, they borrowed heavily from black, Indian, Hispanic, and Asian traditions. Their clothing, ornamentation, hairstyles, spiritual explorations, jargon, values, and music defined an eclectic composite culture that symbolized identification with the oppressed. In their rejection of the dominant culture, they sought to become like those whom the dominant culture had historically rejected.

Thus we have the essence of the "wannabe" phenomenon: white Americans trying to be someone else. When the limitations of privilege, of affluence, of membership in the dominant group become apparent to us as white Americans, we often turn to other cultural experiences to find identity, purpose, meaning, and a sense of belonging. When the truth of our collective history is brought home to us, we turn to other traditions for a new place to be.

But there is another alternative for white identity, one that resides within our own cultural roots. It became clear to me during my sabbatical study tour around the world in 1990-1991. I began the trip with the goal of gaining some new insights about education from the First Peoples in several countries. During a seven-month period I was immersed in the rich contexts of the Navajo, Hopi, Maori, Australian Aboriginal, Balinese, and Nepalese culture. I gained much from my exposure to the traditional perspectives of these cultures, but the most powerful personal experiences came for me in the place I least expected them—my own ancestral Europe.

In the Basque country of northern Spain, in the Pyrenees Mountains near the French border, I entered a prehistoric cave that was one of the sacred sites of the ancient people of Europe. I was amazed by the beauty and the power this cave held for me. I had been in the sacred caves of the Anasazi, those people who preceded the Navaho and Hopi in what is now Arizona and New Mexico. I had been in the ceremonial caves of the aboriginal people of Australia. In both of these previous experiences, I had been drawn to the handprints on the walls, created there by ancient artists blowing pigment through a bone or reed to leave images of their hands on the surface of the stone.

When I discovered, in the deepest part of a cave in the Pyrenees, 21 handprints created by ancient Europeans in the exact style of the Anasazi and the Aboriginal people, I knew I had connected with a profound source of my own identity. There was a sense of the universality of all human experience. In the projection of our hands on stone walls, in the desire to express ourselves and find meaning in life, we are all one. And then came an even deeper lesson. In my journey around the world, I had been searching for meaning in other people's cultures. Here in a cave in Europe was a connection with my own. After leaving the Pyrenees, I spent the next three weeks exploring the ancient sacred sites of England and Scotland. In the company of Peter Vallance, a storyteller, dancer, and modern version of the old Celtic bard, I continued to grow more deeply into a sense of rootedness in my own past. I learned that the old Celts and other ancient ones of Great Britain were a fascinating people. They had spread over a large area in Europe and were, in fact, some of the people who worshipped in those magnificent caves in Northern Spain.

I also learned that the Celts became the victims of the imperialistic expansion of Roman Christianity. Their culture was overwhelmed by the twofold aggression of the Roman army and the church. Consequently, much of their history is lost to us today. The amazing stone circles, like Stonehenge, which are still evident throughout the British Isles, stand as powerful reminders of the Celtic vision of nature and of the people's sacred connection with both the earth and the sky.

What does my experience in Europe mean for us as white Americans? First, there is no need to look to other cultures for our own sense of identity. Any of us who choose to look more deeply into our roots will find there a rich and diverse experience waiting to be discovered. Second, the history of oppression and expansionism perpetrated by European nations is only part of our past. It is a reality that must be acknowledged and dealt with, but it is not our only heritage as white Americans. In fact, many of our own ancestral groups, like the Celts, have themselves been the victims of the same kind of imperialistic drives that have been so devastating to other indigenous populations around the world. And third, when we push the human story back far enough, we come to a place of common connection to this earth, to a place where people of all races are brothers and sisters on the same planet. It is in this recognition of both our uniqueness as European Americans and our universality as human beings that we can begin to make an authentic contribution to the healing of our nation.

WHO ARE MY PEOPLE?

As a result of my world tour and of my lengthy struggle with the issues discussed here, I have come to a new sense of my own identity as a white American. I have seen that I have deep connections with this earth through my own cultural ancestry. I have also become aware of a complex, painful, yet rich history of connections to all other peoples. I have seen that white Americans can be drawn together with people everywhere who are struggling with the questions of cultural and human survival. We can develop a deep commitment to and a strong stake in the preservation and strengthening of diversity at home and throughout the world. We can become aware that our energy and vision, along with those of other Americans of all cultures, are essential to the healing that must take place if we are to survive as a pluralistic and just nation.

It is time for a redefinition of white America. As our percentage of the population declines, our commitment to the future must change. It is neither appropriate nor desirable to be in a position of dominance. Even though we are undeniably connected by history and ethnicity with a long legacy of oppression, this identification with the oppressor is not our only means of defining ourselves. We can choose now to contribute to the making of a new kind of nation. Young white students need to see that they, too, can be full participants in the building of a multicultural America.

Because the music of the United States is propelled by such a rich mixture of cultural rhythms, it is time for all of us to learn to move with grace and style to the new sounds. The future calls each of us to become partners in the dance of diversity, a dance in which everyone shares the lead. And because we have been separated by race and ethnicity for so long, we may all feel awkward at first with the new moves. It will take time to learn to fully embrace our emerging multicultural partnerships. But with a little help from our friends in other cultures, even white folks can learn to dance again, as we one did among the great stone circles of ancient Europe. Rather than being isolated in the dance hall of the dominant, we now have an exciting opportunity to join with Americans of all cultures in creating a nation that actually tries to move to the tune of its own ideals. These are my people, and this could be our vision.

1. Andrew Hacker, *Two Nations* (New York: Macmillan, 1992).
2. Richard Alba, *Ethnic Identity: The Transformation of White America* (New Haven, Conn.: Yale University Press, 1990).
3. Peggy McIntosh, "White Privilege and Male Privilege: A Personal Account of Coming to See Correspondences Through Work in Women's Studies," unpublished paper, Wellesley College, Wellesley, Mass., 1988.
4. Diane Ravitch, "Multiculturalism: E Pluribus Plures, *"American Scholar,* Spring 1990, pp. 337-54; and Arthur M. Schlesinger, Jr., The Disuniting of America: Reflections on a Multicultural Society (New York: Norton 1992).
5. Roosevelt R. Thomas, Jr., *Beyond Race and Gender* (New York: Amacon, 1991).
6. James A. Banks, *Multiethnic Education: Theory and Practice,* 3rd ed. (Boston: Ally and Bacon, 1994).

How We Are White

Gary R. Howard
www.ghequityinstitute.com

Reprinted from: *Detroit and the Crisis in Urban America: Education, Incarceration, Segregation and the Future of U* *Multiracial Democracy.* (Rowman & Littlefield).

Original version appeared in: *Teaching Tolerance*, Fall 2004.

The break is over and I am ready to begin the second half of a four-hour multicultural curriculum workshop. Twenty-five teachers and staff are scrunched into 2nd grade desks, all eyes and white faces turned toward their one African American colleague, who has asked to address the group. He announces that he will be leaving this workshop immediately and resigning at the end of the year. He has lost hope in their willingness and ability to deal with issues of race.

After he leaves, a painful silence grips the room. I realize that my planned agenda is no longer appropriate. Gradually the participants begin to talk. Their comments are rife with guilt, shame, anger, blame, denial, sadness and frustration. It becomes clear there has been a long history leading to this moment. Together they are experiencing a collective meltdown over the realities of race and their own whiteness. One faculty member remarks, "I feel so helpless. What am I supposed to do as a white teacher?"

In my 35 years of work in multicultural education, I have encountered a seemingly universal uneasiness about race among white educators. Since the publication of my book We Can't Teach What We Don't Know: White Teachers, Multiracial Schools (Teachers College Press, 1999, 2006), many people have shared their stories with me. A white teacher from California reports, "I realize that I have contributed to the failure of my students of color by not being able to drop the mask of privilege that I wear." Another white teacher writes, "I thought I was going crazy. It was helpful to hear that other white teachers feel similar confusion."

As white educators, we are collectively bound and unavoidably complicit in the arrangements of dominance that have systematically favored our racial group over others. In my own family, the farm in Minnesota that I cherish as part of our heritage was actually stolen from the Ojibwe people only a few years before my great-grandparents acquired it. This is only one of the countless ways I am inextricably tied to privilege. I did not personally take the land, yet I continue to benefit from its possession.

But privilege and complicity are only part of the story. The police officers who brutally assaulted civil rights activists during the first Selma march in 1965 were certainly white, but so were some 500 of the marchers who stood on the Edmund Pettus Bridge two days later with Dr. Martin Luther King Jr. to protest the violence of that bloody Sunday. It is true that three white men dragged James Byrd to a horrific death in Jasper, Texas, but it is also true that many white townspeople and a predominantly white jury condemned this act of racist violence.

In the course of my work and personal reflection, I have discovered there are many ways of being white. Some whites are bound by a *fundamentalist* white orientation. They view the world through a single lens that is always right and always white. White supremacist hate groups represent one particularly hostile form of fundamentalist white identity, but there is also the Tea Party version that masks its racism with the guise of patriotism. They self-righteously flaunt the flag and the constitution under the banner of "I want my country back," which more accurately translates as "I want to keep the White House white." And there is yet another form of fundamentalist white identity, an uninformed and well-intentioned version, that simply has never been exposed to other perspectives nor questioned its own. This was my orientation from birth through my high school years, when I had never met a person who wasn't white. Fundamentalist white teachers often say things like, "I don't see color," or "I treat all my students the same," or "Why are they sending those kids to our school?"

Other white folks live from an *integrationist* white orientation, where differences are acknowledged and tolerated but still not fully accepted, appreciated, or respected. Integrationist whites are self-congratulatory in their apparent openness to racial differences, yet often paternalistic and condescending toward people of color. In this way of being white, we prefer to keep the peace, avoid confrontation and maintain control, rather than actually get to the core of our separate truths and unique racial perspectives. Integrationist white teachers say to students of color, "I know how you feel," even when we have no real connection to their reality. This was my orientation when I first began "helping" Black kids in the ghetto in the 1960s. I thought I was the solution, rather than the problem. Related to the work of eliminating racial achievement gaps, educators in the integrationist orientation often put the blame on our students of color and their parents, rather than questioning how our own beliefs and practices might be contributing to the educational disparities we see manifested in our classrooms.

Thirdly, there is the *transformationist* white orientation, which is a place of humility and active engagement in one's own continuing growth and reformation. Transformationist whites have acquired a paradoxical identity, which allows us to acknowledge our inevitable privilege and racism while at the same time actively working to dismantle our legacy of dominance. Transformationist white teachers know it is our place and our responsibility to engage issues of race and social justice in the classroom. We become allies and advocates for our students and colleagues of color and anti-racist change agents among our white colleagues. We know that the real work of school reform requires us to transform both ourselves and our practices and to challenge the arrangements of dominance that underpin school inequities. Transformationist white educators know that policies like No Child Left Behind and Race to the Top are tragically inadequate to address the deeply rooted social justice and racial disparities that continue to fuel school failure for far too many of our students of color.

White educators do have a choice to grow beyond our ignorance, denial, and guilt. Throughout the country and over many years I continue to meet transformationist white educators who have made that clear choice and that deep commitment to continue to work and grow personally and professionally in racially diverse schools, rather than fleeing to the white enclaves of suburbia. There is a journey for us, which I envision like a river that carries us through many confusing currents and treacherous rapids, but which eventually can lead to a place of authentic multicultural white identity. Ultimately, good teaching is not a function of the color of our skin. It is much more closely related to the temperament of our mind and the hue of our heart. We did not choose whether to be white, but we can effect how we are white. This is both our challenge and our hope.

In the last few years I have returned several times to work with the elementary staff that experienced such a painful meltdown over issues of race. With courage they have stayed on the river, chosen to look deeply into the reflective pool of their own difficult history together, and have come to a place of greater honesty and renewed commitment to a multicultural vision for their school. At our last meeting, when the painful event was alluded to in discussion, a newly hired Asian American teacher asked, "What happened?" A veteran white teacher responded, "It's a long story we need to share with you. It will help you know who we are."

School Improvement for All

REFLECTIONS ON THE ACHIEVEMENT GAP

Gary R. Howard
www.ghequityinstitute.com

Originally published in: *Journal of School Improvement,* Volume 3, Issue 1, Spring 2002.

INTRODUCTION

If we are to create effective schools that truly serve all children, then closing the achievement gap is certainly an essential priority for the 21st century. When school districts throughout the country disaggregate educational data related to student outcomes, a consistent pattern emerges. Race, culture, ethnicity, language, and economic status continue to be powerful predictors of school failure. Whether the measure is grades, test scores, attendance, discipline referrals, drop-out or graduation rates, those students who differ most from mainstream White, middle/upper class, English speaking America, are also most vulnerable to being mis-served by our nation's schools. Teachers, administrators, school board members, scholars, policy leaders, students, and parents are aware of this gap in educational equity, and numerous programs, initiatives, and strategies are now in place to address it.

My purpose here is to delineate the deeper issues that have caused and continue to perpetuate the achievement gap. How do we understand this phenomenon in ways that will help us address it effectively? If our analysis is inadequate, our responses will be as well. The stakes are high, both for the students we serve and for the nation we hope to fashion in freedom and justice. If race, ethnicity, language, and socio-economic status continue to be significant predictors of school failure, then we as a nation that is growing rapidly in these very dimensions of difference will certainly lose the productive engagement of increasingly larger portions of our young people.

THE LENS OF SOCIAL DOMINANCE

The achievement gap cannot be understood without honestly confronting issues of social dominance. The process of schooling is neither power-neutral nor culture-neutral. Through periods of slavery, Jim Crow, and segregation, Blacks have for centuries been either legally forbidden an education or systematically relegated to inferior schools. For Native Americans, schooling in the 19th and early 20th centuries was used as a tool for cultural genocide, the official federal education policy being to "kill the Indian and save the man" (Harvey & Harjo, 1994). It is no mere coincidence that those racial, cultural, linguistic, and economic groups who have for centuries been marginalized by the force of Western domination are the same groups who are now failing or underachieving at disproportionate rates. Schooling, like all other social institutions, functions as a system of privilege and preference, reinforced by power, favoring certain groups over others. This is the sad asymmetry of social dominance: the victors of history disproportionately thrive while the descendents of the vanquished inordinately struggle just to survive. Such inequities are perpetuated through three highly interrelated and mutually reinforcing dynamics of dominance: the assumption of rightness, the luxury of ignorance, and the legacy of privilege (Howard, 1999).

The assumption of rightness, as related to the achievement gap, often leads teachers to assume that the problem of school failure lies in the students and their families and not in the structure of schooling. We make assumptions about who can and cannot learn; and the more uncomfortable we are with difference, the greater the likelihood that we will relegate certain children to lower levels of expectation and academic opportunity. For example, an African American chemist working for a Fortune 500 company told me recently that he and his wife had to advocate every year for their two sons not to be placed in special education classes. In their small rural community, where their sons were among very few children of color, teachers would routinely refer these two boys to special classrooms. Strangely enough, this occurred in spite of the fact that both students performed well in regular and even advanced classes. Eventually, each of these young men went on to graduate from prestigious colleges and acquire lucrative positions, but one has to wonder what would have happened without the advantage of parents who could resist the assumptions of school personnel. For the 90% of educators who, like me, grew up in predominantly White suburban communities, it is natural to assume that school, as it is presently constituted, works well for all students. From our assumption of rightness, we can easily conclude that our professional judgements are correct and that those who don't achieve are either not sufficiently intelligent or inadequately supported by their home environment. The deficiency, therefore, lies in the child or the home and not in the system of schooling.

The luxury of ignorance allows many dominant culture educators to remain unaware of the intense "sociocultural misalignment between home and school" (Comer, 1988, p. 44) that is experienced by students from poor and racially diverse backgrounds. Even for those children of color who are successful, school is often experienced as a foreign environment. An African American athlete attending a predominantly White high school described his experience this way: "I can handle school, but it's just that every day seems like an away game." On the other hand, for me and most of my white, middle-class colleagues, the neighborhood school in the suburbs was a direct reflection of our home environment. For us, every day was a home game. We enjoyed the easy comfort of a smooth transition between home and school and have assumed that ought to be true for the diverse children we now teach. One of the dilemmas of dominance is that we are often blind to the negative impact our imagined goodness and normalcy have on others who do not share the demographic advantages of dominance that have favored our group.

The legacy of privilege refers to those advantages that flow to some and not to others, based solely on our membership in the dominant group. Privilege is illustrated in a story told by a Hispanic high school student entering her first day in an honors AP English classroom. She was the only student of color in the class, and the teacher pulled her aside the end of the session to ask, "Are you sure you want to be in here? This is going to be a very challenging course." The privilege comes in the fact that none of the Anglo students were asked that same question. Privilege is also exercised in the many strategies employed by families and politicians who seek to escape or abandon public education in communities that are urban, poor, and predominantly populated by children of color. For decades we have witnessed White flight to the suburbs, and "good schools" have in many people's minds become synonymous with "White schools." Today we see a more complex phenomenon, wherein families from all racial and ethnic backgrounds, once they have achieved a level of economic success, will follow the money to the suburbs, thus creating a kind of "green flight" that continues to drain valuable human and economic resources from our core cities and most challenged environments (Wilson, 1987). Another manifestation of privilege is the movement toward voucher programs that may save some students but actually exacerbates the concentration of poverty and failure in certain schools by creating enclaves of elitism for a privileged few.

I present this discussion of social dominance not for the purpose of casting blame, but for the hope of increasing our clarity and consciousness regarding the deeper dynamics underlying the achievement gap. If we understand how our assumptions about schooling have been shaped by the forces of social dominance, we are less likely to impose our narrow cultural lens on the experience of those who have not benefited from these dynamics of privilege and favored position. By acknowledging that race and class inequities in academic outcomes are a logical consequence of our system of education, and not an aberration, we are more likely to look for systematic changes rather than casting aspersions on the idiosyncratic failures of students, parents, or teachers. In reality, we are all socialized into a system of social dominance that is highly resistant to change, and it is that system that must be transformed.

A COLLAGE OF CAUSATION AND RESPONSE

The achievement gap has many faces and many voices. It is the Black high school junior in Indiana who asks her teachers, "Why am I the only Black student in the gifted program?" It is the Haitian student in New York who sadly reveals that, "Some teachers steal our hope." It is the White student in an impoverished rural community in Washington state who says, "None of my brothers and sisters have finished school, so why should I?" Educators who are passionate about closing the achievement gap must see the history of social dominance writ large in the lives of young people today. The dynamics that underlie these student comments and cause the achievement gap are myriad: generational poverty and families in pain, political cynicism that leads to the abandonment of urban public education, lowered expectations, stereotypes about race and poverty, teachers not prepared to deal with diversity, inadequate funding, outright racism, the unfortunate identification of school success with "acting White" (Fordham & Ogbu, 1986), and all the many other "savage inequalities" (Kozol, 1991) that flow from dominance.

Consciously or unconsciously, all students are asking themselves several critical questions related to identity, inclusion, and success: Who am I? What is my worth? Do I belong? Am I safe? Is school my place? Am I smart? Can I be successful? Who cares about me and who decides whether I succeed? These questions form the implicit curriculum that functions beneath the surface of schooling. How we as educators, parents, and policy leaders engage these questions and how we support young people in their journey to adulthood, will ultimately determine our success in closing the achievement gap.

Multiple Causes. The good news in this effort is that scholars, educators, and communities throughout the country have recognized many of the elements that comprise the complex collage of causation and are working toward curative strategies. James Banks and several colleagues working through the Center for Multicultural Education at the University of Washington and the Common Destiny Alliance at the University of Maryland (2000) provided one of the most comprehensive and useful summaries of variables relevant to the achievement gap. Funded by the Carnegie Corporation, a consensus panel of interdisciplinary scholars worked four years to identify the most salient factors affecting education and diversity. Their findings are organized into 5 categories, 12 principles, and 62 variables, evidence in itself that any attempt to address the achievement gap must be as multidimensional and varied as the causes of social dominance.

The five broad categories in the Banks study include teacher learning, student learning, intergroup relations, school governance, and assessment. Key selected principles and variables are: teachers' understanding of diverse ethnic groups, student access to equitable opportunities to learn, creation of super-ordinate groups that engage students in significant experiences with cultures other than their own, reduction of fear and anxiety in the school experience, administrative processes that emphasize shared decision making and collaboration, and the use of multiple culturally sensitive measurement and assessment techniques. I recommend that universities and school districts order the full report, which includes a checklist for assessing school improvement related to the 62 variables.

School District Initiatives. In addition to the Banks study, school districts throughout the country are developing their own comprehensive understanding of causal factors and possible strategies for addressing the achievement gap. Minneapolis Public Schools, for example, has a "Twelve Point Plan for Improving the Academic Performance and Graduation Rates of Students of Color" (2001). Selected elements of the MPS plan include: using student data to direct action, creating a more diverse workforce in the school district, targeting resources to needy schools, reducing over-referral to special education, investing in school readiness through pre-school programs, and increasing support for students with behavior related issues.

Minneapolis is also engaged in an inter-district process that brings the city together with nine suburban districts to share resources and students in an effort to improve the educational experience for all. The West Metro Education Program (WMEP) offers cooperative inservice opportunities for teachers and administrators in its 10 member districts. Working extensively with the WMEP district over the past two years, I have been heartened to learn that the issue of closing the achievement gap is perceived there as not only the responsibility of urban educators with high poverty and diversity among their student population, but is actually beginning to be embraced as the larger responsibility of all surrounding communities and school districts. Not everyone in the metro area believes this, of course, but there does exist a critical mass of committed people who share the vision and that is sufficient to initiate change.

In Federal Way School District, a large suburban community outside of Seattle, the student of color population has grown rapidly in recent years and is now 40%. Speaking with a long-time African American community activist, I was inspired to hear that their White male superintendent has become a trusted champion of effective schools for all students and has initiated creative ways to approach the achievement gap. He has funded a new position, Director of Equity and Achievement, to assure that the school district is continually attending to the issue of closing the gap. He has also personally interviewed students of color in each of the district high schools to gather first-hand data on their perceptions of their school experience. In one powerful aspect of these interviews, he asks bright and talented students of color why they are not participating in Advanced Placement classes. A consistent pattern has emerged from these interviews, with the following three responses being given, in order of frequency: (1) I didn't know I could, (2) I don't want to be alone, and (3) I don't want to fail. Clearly, the assumptions and self-perceptions underlying these responses are sad evidence of the lingering and debilitating power of social dominance in the lives of young people today.

In the East Ramapo Central School District, outside of New York City, students of color represent close to 80% of the school population. With a diverse and enlightened leadership group drawn from the school board, the district administrative team, and teachers, this district has taken on the achievement gap in a direct and encouraging way. When I first began my work with them, I was surprised and delighted to learn that one of their primary activities would be to focus on increasing the cultural competence of all school district employees. They had worked with the complex issues of the achievement gap long enough to realize that the problems lie not so much in the deficiencies of students as in the inadequacy of school culture to effectively serve all students. They are now working together in central office and building level leadership teams, including district administrators, principals, teachers, support staff, and parents, to find ways to help all employees grow in their ability to relate effectively with people who experience the world through different cultural frames. Their goal statement is: The East Ramapo School District offers an educational program that is open, inclusive, and welcoming of all students and families in our community. Working together to strengthen our cultural competence and benefit all students, each year we achieve a significant reduction in the achievement gap." Through dedicated leadership, committed teachers, and constant attention to the issue, they are documenting those reductions each year.

Leadership. One of the most influential factors in closing the achievement gap is the presence of enlightened leadership at the building level. Principals cannot do this work alone, but it is extremely difficult to do without them. If students and teachers are not empowered and inspired by their principal, they often languish under the pressures of the achievement gap. In Seattle, John Morefield (1996) exemplifies those principals throughout the country who are creating schools that work for all children. When Morefield became principal of Hawthorne Elementary School, located in one of Seattle's most racially diverse and lowest income communities, he promised that all entering kindergartners would graduate from fifth grade with skills at or above grade level competency. Over the years he and his dedicated staff delivered on their promise. Morefield summarized his approach in a report, "Recreating Schools for All Children," another resource I would recommend for all educators and policy leaders.

Some of the elements included in Morefield's vision of effective schools for all students are: strong leadership, unity of purpose, a caring and nurturing school environment, consistent and positive discipline, a multicultural curriculum, a belief in the importance and empowerment of parents, and a staff that believes that teaching is a calling and a vocation, not just a job. Morefield (1996) recognizes the necessity to shift schooling away from its Western dominant assumptions of competition and rugged individualism and toward a more egalitarian ethic based on cooperation and relationship. He states, " I have come to believe that a school designed to work for children of color, works for White children. The reverse, however is not true. Consequently, if we design schools to work for children of color, they will work for all children."

Research Findings. The research literature also has much to teach us about the salient factors related to closing the achievement gap. Comer (1988) has spent years documenting significant gains in student success through the work of strengthening the ties between schools and communities and actively engaging parents in every aspect of schooling. Gay (2000), in her inspiring new book, brings together extensive research and practical experience to demonstrate the power of classroom teaching strategies that are culturally responsive to the reality of students' lives. Steel (1999) has studied the impact of "stereotype threat" on the performance of Black students. He defines stereotype threat as "the threat of being viewed through the lens of a negative stereotype, or the fear of doing something that would inadvertently confirm that stereotype" (p. 46). Through the impact of stereotype threat, even the most talented students of color continue to experience the deleterious effects of past and present social dominance. The sad lesson of this work is that even if no one in the school is being overtly racist toward students of color, the strong presence of the threat is still internalized and often destructive. Because the achievement gap has resulted from a process as deep and pervasive as social dominance, it is important that we also view both the causes and our curative responses from an equally complex and multi-dimensional perspective. Meaningful progress toward effective and equitable schools will require all of the compassion, commitment, vision, and will that educators, parents, and policy leaders can direct toward this issue.

TESTING IS NOT TEACHING

Accountability and assessment strategies are certainly part of the complex collage of responses that must be applied to the achievement gap. Given the multidimensionality of the above discussion, however, it is perplexing that some politicians and educational leaders appear to believe that testing in itself will somehow lead us to the promised land of educational equity. In the 2000 Presidential debates, for example, it was unsettling to witness two privileged candidates playing political one-ups-man-ship with the issue of how often they would test our nation's students. Before any politician attempts to speak with authority on the efficacy of testing as a solution to educational inequities, he or she ought to be required to teach at least one year in a public school classroom.

More relevant to the actual realities of schooling, the father of a fourth grader in Texas recently told me about asking his daughter the perennial parent question: "What did you learn in school today?" Her response was, "We learned the TASS test (The Texas state-wide assessment). In sharing this story, the father was concerned that testing might be taking over the learning process in his daughter's school. In a different part of the country, a sixth grade teacher told me of verbally administering a portion of his state's test that asked his highly diverse and mostly low income inner city children to interpret the meaning of the western folksong, "Home on the Range." While giving the test, the teacher thought to himself. "How will any of my students know what is going on in this song? The cultural context is totally foreign to them." Indeed, an intelligent urban child might well wonder why anyone would have their home on the stove anyway, and why are all those animal in the kitchen? The teacher wisely concluded that this section of the test was not measuring his kids' ability to read and interpret, but rather their familiarity with white rural culture.

In a middle school in Washington State, I was in the principal's office planning future workshops when the state test results for her school were brought in. Her faculty had worked tirelessly the year before to raise the achievement level of their high poverty urban population, but the scores had actually gone down. Watching her review the numbers, there was much sadness in the principal's expression. We talked about how and when she would share this information with her dedicated team of teachers, who were just that day coming back from summer to ready their classrooms for a new year. We wondered together what these scores meant. Had teachers truly failed to improve the educational outcomes for their students? Or had the statewide test failed to measure what the children had actually learned?

Each of these stories raises serious questions about the current fixation on standardized testing as the *sine qua non* of educational reform. Issues like these cause many of us to wonder whether the politics of accountability are actually running counter to the best interests of our most at-risk students. In fact, the thing our students are most "at risk" from may be precisely the narrow politics that now frame so much of the accountability discussion.

Assessment and accountability are critical to the educational process. But the methods of assessment must be multi-dimensional, culturally and situationally appropriate, consistent with instructional goals, attuned to different learning styles, and balanced with other indicators and measures of student success. Testing is not teaching. It is one measure of educational outcomes, but not the only one. Just as the causal factors which have fueled the achievement gap are numerous and complex, so must our measure and assessment procedures be equally broad, multi-dimensional, and flexible. High stakes testing alone is a tragically inadequate response to the complexities underlying the achievement gap.

Certainly we as educators and policy leaders must hold ourselves accountable, but we have to ask, "To whom are we accountable?" Clearly, we are accountable to the children in our schools, to their families, and ultimately to the future of our nation. However, if we continue to trivialize our understanding of accountability to the point where it becomes synonymous with testing, then we will have failed our students and may discover 10 years from now that educational inequities have actually been exacerbated rather than reduced.

THE MEASURE OF OUR NATION

We have seen in the discussion above that a clear understanding of social dominance is the essential backdrop for our efforts to create effective schools that serve all students. As long time civil rights activist Bob Moses (2001) points out in his campaign for mathematical literacy for poor and minority students, the issue of academic achievement is for us today what the issue of voting rights was for our nation 40 years ago. He says, "If we don't get it, we are headed for a new form of serfdom" (p. 72).

Whereas the 20th century was an era of winning access for people who had theretofore been excluded from the full benefits of citizenship, so the 21st century must be dedicated to assuring success for the children of these same groups of people. Success begins with equitable educational outcomes, so the task of closing the achievement gap is essentially the task of unraveling the crippling effects of past and present social dominance.

If we are to move from social dominance to simple decency as a pluralistic nation, then public education must offer a broad and inclusive doorway to success. It is the responsibility of all Americans to champion our youth, especially those who have been most debilitated by the forces of unfairness, which for far too long have separated far too many from the full fruits of citizenship . The achievement gap is a crisis as great as any we have faced as a nation. It calls us to compassionate action and the generous outpouring of our personal and political will.

Speaking for my own position as a White educator, we cannot as a nation close the achievement gap until a critical mass of conscious White Americans begin to accept poor children, urban children, and children of color as our own children. High stakes testing is the easy strategy. It has the political advantage of a "get tough on education" rhetorical ring, but it is neither compassionate nor adequate. When White teachers, policy leaders, parents, and scholars join with families and communities of color and claim with a united voice that "all the children are our children," perhaps then we shall see the type of investment in quality education that our children deserve—the type of investment middle and upper class Americans presently demand for their children.

In less than nine months during 2001 our nation dedicated over a trillion dollars to tax relief and another trillion to aid for the victims of September 11. Would it be fair to say that the survival and success of our nation's youth require an equal investment? Politicians and bureaucrats often tell us we should not merely throw money at the problems of educational equity, but perhaps we should try it once. Perhaps we should actually fund the things we know will bring positive change: smaller class size, smaller schools, excellent well paid teachers, and inspired leaders with the resources to bring their vision into reality. The issue of educational equity is not about testing; it is about teaching, learning, funding, and creating relationships that work. The achievement gap is an unhealed wound on the heart of America. We are losing the lifeblood of future generations at a rate that is unsustainable and culturally depleting. How we respond, and the depth of our commitment to heal this wound, will in the decades to come be a critical measure of our worth as a democratic community.

REFERENCES

Banks, J., Cookson, P., Gay, G., Hawley, W. D., Irvine, J. J., Nieto, S., Schofield, J. W., & Stephan, W. G. (2001). *Diversity within unity: Essential principles for teaching and learning in a multicultural society.* Seattle: Center for Multicultural Education, University of Washington. The full report can be ordered through the Center for Multicultural Education at the University of Washington, 110 Miller Hall, Box 353600, Seattle, WA 98195-3600. Phone: 206-543-3600. Email: centermc@uwashington.edu. Web site: http://depts.washington.edu/centerme/cenpub.htm.

Comer, J. (1988). Educating poor minority children. *Scientific American,* November 1988.

Fordham, S. & Ogbu, J. U. (1986). Black students' school success: Coping with the burden of 'acting white.' *Urban Review,* 18(3), 176-206.

Gay, G. (2000). *Culturally responsive teaching: Theory, research, and practice.* New York: Teachers College Press.

Harvey, K. D. & Hrjo, L. D. (1994). *Indian country: A history of native people in America.* Golden, CO: North American Press.

Howard, G. (1999) *We can't teach what we don't know: White teachers/multiracial schools.* New York: Teachers College Press.

Kozol, J. (1991). *Savage Inequalities.* New York: Crown.

Minneapolis Public Schools, (2001). *Twelve Point Plan for Improving the Academic Performance and Graduation Rates of Students of color (With Particular Focus on African American, American Indian and Hispanic/Latino Students) Accessed: April 2002.* Available: (http://www.mpls.k12mn.us/about/twelve_point_plan.shtml).

Morefield, J. (1996). Recreating schools for all children. *New Horizons for Learning.* http://newhorizons.org/article_morefield.html.

Moses, B. (2001). Radical equations. *Time Magazine,* June 18, 2001, p. 72.

Steele, C. M. & Aronson, J. (1995). Stereotype threat and the intellectual performance of African Americans. *Journal of Personality and Social Psychology,* 69, 797-811.

Steele, C. M. (1999). Thin ice: "Stereotype threat" and Black college students. *The Atlantic Monthly,* p. 46.

Dispositions for Good Teaching

Gary R. Howard
www.ghequityinstitute.com

Originally published in: *Journal of Educational Controversy*, **an online publication of Woodring College of Education, Western Washington University, Volume 2, Number 2, Summer 2007, http://www.wce .wwu.edu/eJournal/.**

DISPOSITIONS FOR GOOD TEACHING

The central focus of my work over the past 30 years has been to struggle with two overarching and related questions. First, what are the qualities of personhood that the adults in our nation's classrooms must embody to be worthy of teaching our richly diverse students? And second, how do we best prepare ourselves and our colleagues for this work? In this article I reflect on the first of these questions[1], and do so in light of the fact that any discussion of "teacher dispositions," either in pre-service or in-service contexts, is best engaged from the perspective of the students who populate our nation's public schools. These children and young adults reflect a multi-faceted and increasingly broad spectrum of racial, cultural, linguistic, economic, religious, and sexual identities. The adults in these spaces determine, in large measure, both the tone and the outcome of schooling. On the one hand, we have teachers who are highly effective in working in diversity-enhanced schools, and on the other, we have those who are utterly unprepared and even destructive in their teaching. Having benefited from the former, an urban African American low-income student, upon receiving an academic award and scholarship at her high school graduation, acknowledged the work of her principal and teachers by saying, "You made us think we were smarter than we thought we were." And having suffered from the latter, a Jamaican immigrant student said in a town meeting I facilitated for a school district outside New York City, "Some of our teachers steal our hope."

Between these two extremes lies a highly diverse range of teacher attitudes, beliefs, and behaviors. It is essential that we talk about who we are as educators, precisely because our personhood, as well as our professional practice, is intimately connected to the quality of our students' experience. In highly diverse educational settings, the salient issue for us as professionals is one of cultural competence: Do I have the capacity and flexibility to be with my students in an authentic and effective way? From my observation and analysis throughout the country, there are four dispositions that characterize good teachers in pluralistic schools.

A DISPOSITION FOR DIFFERENCE

I often tell a story about a white male teacher in an urban high school who said to me after one of my speeches, " I have no Black students in any of my classes." I was curious how that could be true given that over half the students in his school were Black.

When I inquired about this, he said, "I don't see race, so all my kids are the same to me." I replied, "You may not want to acknowledge the reality of race in your classroom, but I can guarantee you that all of your Black students know you're white." I then shared my belief that race does not have to get in the way of our teaching, but when it is denied, it probably is in the way.

[1] For a discussion of the second question, see my article in the March 2007 issue of Educational Leadership, "As Diversity Grows, So Must We."

Since 90% of our nation's teachers are white, the business of achieving greater equity and excellence in public education is in large part of a process of transforming the beliefs and behaviors of white educators. The three stages of White Identity Orientation that I have identified in my writing (Howard, 2006), provide one conceptual framework for discussing teacher dispositions. Whites in the *Fundamentalist* stage, like the teacher mentioned above, are predisposed to avoid, deny, or rationalize racial differences, thus distancing themselves from any need for self-examination regarding the meaning or impact of their own racial being. Whites in the *Integrationist* orientation are somewhat more open. They acknowledge that differences are real and even worthy of celebration, but often tend to approach their teaching from a missionary mentality of "serving the less fortunate." Like their Fundamentalist colleagues, they resist any serious interrogation of privilege, power, or their own potential complicity in the dynamics underlying racial inequities in school outcomes. Whites in the *Tranformationist* stage, on the other hand, actively seek to bring difference into their lives, precisely because this engagement challenges them to grow both personally and professionally. They are sophisticated in their analysis of racism and vigorous in their efforts to undo the legacy of white privilege in their classrooms and schools. At the same time, they are not apologetic about their whiteness and can engage with students of color in authentic, strong, and effective ways.

The point is, our disposition toward difference makes a difference in the lives of our students. It is not *whether* I am white, but rather my *disposition toward* issues of race and whiteness that really matters. For example, Transformationist white teachers in the many schools I have observed issue fewer discipline referrals to students of color, not because they are afraid to discipline (that is an Integrationist behavior), but because they have the personal capacity and professional skills to prevent and diffuse most cross-race confrontations. And this is not just an issue for white educators. Similarly complex dynamics are at play for a religiously conservative Black heterosexual male teacher in his interactions with gay and lesbian white students. Or for a middle class Latina teacher in her work with a wealthy Muslim immigrant male student. A teacher who is culturally competent and comfortable in his/her own skin, and who can negotiate effectively across these multiple dimensions of difference, is simply a better educator.

A DISPOSITION FOR DIALOGUE

Dialogue is the process whereby differences become meaningful. It is through dialogue that we create the opportunity to discover how we are similar or different from others, and to build bridges of communication and understanding. I have observed over my many years of conducting professional development workshops that the one thing teachers most often mention as the highlight of these experiences is "the opportunity for open and honest conversation with my colleagues."

Teacher-to-teacher dialogue is the essence of professional learning communities and a key component of effective school improvement efforts. Professional dialogue is powerful precisely because it provides a reality check across our different perceptions, perspectives, and practices. Such exchange opens the possibility of growth. Unfortunately, I encounter too many educators who are predisposed *not* to engage in this kind of reflective professional conversation. For example, as I was inviting the faculty in a large urban high school to begin a dialogue on differences, a white male teacher proudly announced, "I have good relationships with all of my students, and so I have no more need for personal transformation." Many of his colleagues were aghast at this comment, especially given the existence of a huge gap in math achievement for students of color in their school. Lacking a disposition for dialogue or personal growth, this teacher was a detriment to his students' success and a hindrance to his faculty's school improvement efforts.

Teacher-to-student dialogue is equally important. In the dialogic process of teaching, wherein there is a healthy and authentic flow of conversation between teachers and students, everyone has an opportunity to learn, including the teacher. Visiting recently in a high school special education classroom, populated by "behaviorally disturbed" Black and Hispanic male students and one white male teacher, I was able to observe the power of authentic dialogue. As part of his unit on the Constitution, the teacher was discussing the intricacies of habeas corpus, a topic with which the students could meaningfully engage, given their personal familiarity with the juvenile justice system. At one point the teacher made an inaccurate statement about the interpretation of a legal procedure, and one of the Hispanic students turned away from the computer on which he had been searching for a used car (I had been wondering if the teacher was going to confront him about this) and interrupted the teacher: "Excuse me, sir, but that's not how it works in our state," and went on to explain the correct legalities. Rather than becoming defensive or chastising the student for apparently not paying attention earlier, the teacher merely remarked, "Thank you for that. You're exactly right; my mistake."

This exchange illustrates several elements of good teaching, but I was particularly impressed by the power of the teacher's humility, honesty, and professionalism in engaging only those elements of student behavior that would serve to continue the dialogue, rather than extinguish it. The entire classroom atmosphere was infused with a palpable sense of respect for the students' knowledge and for their lived experience. Working in the presence of students for whom school culture was not, for the most part, a safe or successful place, this teacher navigated the dialogue across differences in such a way that everyone in the room could find safe harbor, including himself.

This disposition for meaningful dialogue has profound implications not only for our classrooms, but also for our world. I was inspired recently to learn about a group of former Israeli and Palestinian fighters who have come together under the banner of "Combatants for Peace" (www. combatantsforpeace.org). Each of the members of this group has committed acts of violence in the name of their conflicting truths, in some cases having injured or killed members of each other's families. In what must be incredibly painful conversations, they confess their actions to one another and reinforce their common commitment to give up the way of past hatred and violence. Having met initially in secret, they have now come into the public arena to declare that dialogue rather than death is the only way to true and lasting peace in their part of the world.

In another example of dialogue across difference, a Jewish rabbi, a Christian minister, and a Muslim imam, all U.S. citizens from the Seattle area, have been meeting since 9/11 for "vigorous discussion," and have traveled together to the Middle East in search of healing responses there as well as at home. Says Jamal Rahman, the Muslim member of this delegation, "Interfaith [dialogue] is not about conversion, it's about completion. I'm becoming a more complete Muslim, a more complete human being" (van Gelder, 2007, p. 13).

This human capacity to engage the conversation rather than wage war across our differences is a skill we want our children to acquire, and that we teachers must embody. This disposition for dialogue is an essential feature of what it means to be an educated person. Imagine how our post-9/11 world would be different today if those in power in our country had acquired this capacity from their teachers.

A DISPOSITION FOR DISILLUSIONMENT

Authentic dialogue across differences is powerful precisely because it allows us to see beyond the barriers of our own culturally conditioned realities. Whatever mind-spaces we may have been socialized into, as teachers we are called to transcend our particular truths and perspectives and come to a place of greater breadth and cultural competence. We do this because our work requires it. As teachers we must be flexible, genuine, and effective in our relationships with students, having the capacity for empathy and respect for their multiple lived realities. Of course, we want to share our world with them, but first we must be able to respectfully enter theirs and insure that our world is one in which they will feel welcomed.

At a time of violent collision across our differences as a nation, Abraham Lincoln said in an address to Congress in 1862, "We must dis-enthrall ourselves" because "the dogmas of the quiet past are inadequate to the stormy present." With these words, Lincoln called himself and other leaders to a profound reckoning with our own illusions, challenging his fellow citizens to break through old images and hostilities, to claim a higher path to community. Likewise for us as teachers, we are called to dis-illusion ourselves from our own race-, class-, gender-, and religion-based assumptions about what is good, true, worthy, and right. This is a positive form of disillusionment, not one of despair or disappointment, but one of strength and reckoning. In Parker Palmer's terms, we are challenged to see truth as "an eternal conversation" across differences (2004, p. 127), rather than as a set of fixed and final conclusions. This kind of proactive disillusionment moves us from a smaller reality to a larger one, from a circumscribed world to a more open, complex, diverse, and ever-changing environment—precisely the kind of environments we find in our schools.

My wife uses a cultural immersion assignment as a way of inviting her pre-service teacher undergraduates into an experience with disillusionment. Students design for themselves an opportunity to enter a cultural context different from their own, a context that places them in the minority. One young white woman chose to attend an African American church in the Central Area of Seattle. She went alone, and from her perspective was "the only white face in the congregation." The traditional time came for guests to introduce themselves, but as her turn approached the student became distraught. She had never been in a Black cultural context; she had never had the experience of being the only one like her. In her anxiety she lost her capacity to speak and walked out of the church before the minister came to her.

One would hope that our teacher candidates might come to us with more cultural competence than this young woman exhibited, but we know that she is more the rule than the exception. In the end, the melt-down experience was positive for her. Debriefing her cultural immersion project with my wife and her fellow students, she came face-to-face with her own limitations, and in a preliminary way began the process of disillusionment from her racial and cultural naïveté. After this lesson in awareness and humility, her subsequent work on issues of cultural competence and culturally responsive teaching was much more reality-based. Fortunately, she was able to initiate her disposition for disillusionment in the rarified environment of the university classroom, rather than requiring that her eventual students would pay that price for her, which is too often the case.

Disillusionment is not a single event or even a stage we go through; it is a life-long process intimately tied to our dispositions for difference and for dialogue. In my own experience, from over forty years of conversations and friendships with people of color, and now with a family of multiracial children and grandchildren, I have become increasingly disillusioned from my former assumptions about race, privilege, and whiteness. Likewise, through my forty-year marriage to a woman and in dialogue and friendship with female friends and colleagues, I have grown continually more disillusioned from my former paradigms around maleness, gender, and sexism. Similarly, through my conversations with the gay and lesbian friends that my children brought home in high school, and now through my own network of friends and colleagues in the gay community, I have become disillusioned from my narrow images of relationship, sexuality, marriage, and intimacy. In addition, through my immersion in many spiritual contexts in cultures around the world, I have become deeply disillusioned from the single-dimensional truth and narrow assumptions that I held as an 18-year-old Christian fundamentalist. Echoing the sentiments expressed by Jamal Rahman in the above discussion of interfaith dialogue, I feel that the ongoing erosion of my dogmatic Christian belief structures has only brought me closer to the true meaning of Jesus' teachings. Happily, none of these personal transformations has reached an end point, and I look forward to a lifetime of continuing disenthrallment.

Kwame Anthony Appiah (2006) has a wonderful way of talking about the kind of people we can become through exercising our dispositions for difference, dialogue, and disillusionment. He describes the qualities of personhood that lead to "cosmopolitanism." The cosmopolitan is a person who maintains and treasures his/her own particular cultural identity, but is not limited by it. The cosmopolitan seeks out differences, is energized by the exchange of realities, and is always open to learn more, to see the world through different eyes. The cosmopolitan expects and even welcomes disagreement, yet values community over conflict, and mutuality over dominance. These are certainly the capacities we want our students to embody as they mature toward adulthood, so we as teachers are called to become cosmopolitans ourselves. With this in mind, we can welcome our various and ongoing disillusionment, knowing that behind each veil of illusion lies a greater truth and a better way of teaching.a disposition for democracy

Good teachers know we are preparing our students for something much more interesting, valuable, and profound than standardized tests. Participatory citizenship in a pluralistic nation and world requires a complex skill-set that looks very much like the three dispositions we have discussed so far. The strength of character to engage effectively across differences, the power of critical thinking to sustain meaningful dialogue, and the self-reflective capacity to be disillusioned from our narrow certainties; these are the life-blood of democratic citizenship. Good teaching and good democracy flow from the same heart-space of passion for both the *Pluribus* and the *Unum* of our shared humanity.

Also embedded in both teaching and democracy is a passion for justice. Good teachers work their hearts out simply to give their students a fair chance of success in life, particularly for those students whose families and ancestors have been marginalized by the realities of racism, sexism, classism, homophobia, and the many complex dynamics of social dominance that underlie school inequities. I define social dominance as "systems of privilege and preference, reinforced by the consolidation of power, and favoring the advantaged few over the marginalized many." In contrast, the social justice we are seeking to achieve in our schools is characterized by "systems of equity and inclusion, reinforced by shared power, and favoring the good of the many over the greed of the few.

In this context, school reform can be understood as a movement from social dominance to social justice, as a process of undoing those educational systems that have favored only the few and replacing them with institutional practices that will more effectively serve the many. This is the original meaning and visionary intent of Marian Wright Edelman's passionate plea to "leave no child behind." It is both a vision for democracy and a vision for social justice.

When we acknowledge who is caught in the achievement gap—the same racial, cultural, and economic groups that have been marginalized by the larger dynamics of dominance in our society—it becomes clear that "education for all" and "justice for all" are synonymous goals. The work of transforming public education in the service of equity, inclusion, and excellence for all of our children, is social justice work. It cannot be successfully carried out without the transformation of all other social, political, and economic systems. For example, with the exceedingly high correlation between poverty and school failure, it is clear that ending or significantly reducing poverty would be one of the most efficient and effective ways to eliminate achievement gaps. It is tragically ironic, however, that the same administration that has championed the virtues of NCLB mandates has also put into place economic policies that have exacerbated poverty and increased the gap between the rich and the poor.

This is how social dominance works: Those who have the power to hold educators accountable for raising test scores, also have the power to insure that they themselves remain unaccountable for alleviating the very inequities that render those test scores so resistant to change. Challenging this dynamic of dominance is the work of social justice, which is perhaps the reason some politicians and academics have worked so hard to decouple the education conversation from the justice conversation. Surely, the legitimate and productive question is not whether we can say "social justice" in educational settings, but rather how we might transform those and other social settings to actually achieve it.

TEACHING FOR A NEW HUMANITY

Speaking recently about issues of social dominance and social justice with a class in the MIT program at Seattle University, I was intrigued by a question raised by one of the students: "Isn't all of your talk about social justice really running counter to human nature? Aren't we predisposed as a species to seek power over others?" This was an insightful query, and I acknowledged the truth of her response. In large measure, our history has been a story of revolving dominances, with one group establishing hegemony over others only to be later replaced by the emergence of a more powerful group.

Having said this, I suggested to the class that we are perhaps moving into a new time in our evolution as human beings. On a shrinking planet with national and cultural boundaries being erased by both economics and immigration, each of us and our students are becoming more intimately touched by increasing degrees and dimensions of difference in our daily lives. For the sake of our common survival, we can no longer trust our future to the dynamics of laissez-faire social Darwinism, wherein single-dimensional truths continue to compete for power and control. Instead, we need to nurture in ourselves and our students a new kind of social imperative, wherein the survival of the fittest is still in play, but our understanding of "fitness" gradually evolves toward those qualities of personhood that favor community over control and dialogue over dominance.

Having said this, it remains true that all American citizens have a constitutionally guaranteed First Amendment right to remain imprisoned in their own conditioned narrowness and cultural isolation. This luxury of ignorance, however, is not available to us as teachers. Ours is a higher calling, and for the sake of our students and the future of their world, we are required to grow toward a more adaptive set of human qualities, which would include the dispositions for difference, dialogue, disillusionment, and democracy. These are the capacities that will make it possible for us to thrive together as a species. These are the personal and professional dispositions that render us worthy to teach.

REFERENCES

Appiah, K. A. (2006). *Cosmopolitan: Ethics in a world of strangers.* New York: W. W. Norton.

Howard, G. R. (2006). *We can't teach what we don't know: White teachers in multiracial schools* (2nd ed.). New York: Teachers College Press.

Lincoln, A. (1862). Annual message to Congress—concluding remarks. http://showcase.netins.net/web/creative/lincoln/speeches/congress.htm. From R. P. Basler (Ed.; 1953). Collected works of Abraham Lincoln. Springfield Il: The Abraham Lincoln Association.

Palmer, P. J. (2004). *A hidden wholeness: The journey toward an undivided life.* San Francisco: Jossey-Bass.

van Gelder, S. (2007, Winter). Abraham to descendants: "Knock it off!" *Yes! Magazine.* 12–15.

GUIDE FOR REFLECTIVE CONVERSATION ON ANY OF THE ARTICLES

Individual Preparation Before the Conversation

Read the article through and mark the following passages:

1. Something that you agree with:

2. Something that you disagree with:

3. Something that you wonder about or don't quite understand:

4. Something that moves your thinking to a new level:

Reflective Small Group Conversation with Colleagues

1. Go around the circle 2 times, giving each person a chance to share his/her responses to items 1 and 2 in t pre-read, one round of agreements and one of disagreements. Do not try to argue or change people's minds, just listen to the different responses.

2. Do another round of sharing, asking each person to respond to either item 3 or item 4 from their pre-rea Here you can open up to discussing different ideas and perspectives as each person shares, while still keeping it very open and not seeking a right answer or single truth.

After these rounds of sharing:

3. What did you notice or discover in your group about the way you responded to the article—your similarities and differences?

4. What lessons or insights have come out of your conversation?

5. What are some implications for understanding cultural competence and culturally responsive practice?

6. Are there some questions you would like to explore more together as a group?

References

Byrd-Blake, M., Afolayan, M. O., Hunt, J. W., Fabunmi, M., Pryor, B. W., & Leander, R. (2010). Morale of teachers in high poverty schools: A post-NCLB mixed methods analysis. *Education and Urban Society, 42*(4), 450–472.

Carter, R. T. (1995). *The influence of race and racial identity in psychotherapy: Toward a racially inclusive model.* New York: John Wiley.

Casey Foundation. (2014). *Race for results: Building a path to opportunity for all students.* http://www.aecf.org/m/resourcedoc/AECF-RaceforResults-2014.pdf

Christensen, L. (2000). *Reading, writing, and rising up: Teaching about social justice and the power of the written word.* Milwaukee, WI: Rethinking Schools.

Comer, J. (2013). Foreword. In G. E. Singelton (Ed.), *More courageous conversations about race* (pp. viii–xiii). Thousand Oaks, CA: Corwin.

Danielson, C. (2007). *Enhancing professional practice: A framework for teaching.* Alexandria, VA: ASCD.

Darling-Hammond, L. (2010). *The flat earth and education: How America's commitment to equity will determine our future.* New York: Teachers College Press.

Fullan, M. (2009). *Motion leadership: The skinny on becoming change savvy.* Thousand Oaks, CA: Corwin.

Gorski, P. (2013). *Reaching and teaching students in poverty: Strategies for erasing the opportunity gap.* New York: Teachers College Press.

Helms, J. E. (1994). Racial identity and "racial" constructs. In E. J. Trickett, R. Watts, & D. Birman (Eds.), *Human diversity* (pp. 285–311). San Francisco: Jossey-Bass.

Howard, G. R. (2006). *We can't teach what we don't know: White teachers, multiracial schools.* New York: Teachers College Press.

Howard, L. L. (2009). *Bright ribbons: Weaving culturally responsive teaching into the elementary classroom.* Seattle, WA: Megaperspectives Press.

Marzano. R. J. (2007). *The art and science of teaching: A comprehensive framework for effective instruction.* Alexandria, VA: ASCD.

Meier, D. (2012). Foreword. In N. Schneider & M. Sapon-Shevin (Eds.), *Educational courage: Resisting the ambush of public education* (pp. ix–xii). Boston: Beacon.

Mrydal, G. (1944). *An American dilemma: The Negro problem and modern democracy.* New York: Harper & Row.

Nieto, S. (2013). *Finding joy in teaching students of diverse backgrounds: Culturally responsive and socially just teaching practices in U.S. classrooms.* New York: Heinemann.

Noguera, P. (2008). *The trouble with black boys and other reflections on race, equity, and the future of public education.* San Francisco: Jossey-Bass.

Parents Involved in Community Schools v. Seattle School District No. 1, 551 U.S. 701 (2007).

Ravitch, D. (2013). *Reign of error: The hoax of the privatization movement and the danger to American public schools.* New York: Knopf.

Saifer, S., Edwards, K., Ellis, D., Ko, L., & Stuczynski, A. (2011). *Culturally responsive standards-based teaching: Classroom to community and back.* Thousand Oaks, CA: Corwin.

Schniedewind, M., & Sapon-Shevin, M. (2012). *Educational courage: Resisting the ambush of public education.* Boston: Beacon.

Shade, B. J., Kelly, C., & Oberg, M. (1997). *Creating culturally responsive classrooms.* Washington, DC: American Psychological Association.

Singelton, G. E. (2013). *More courageous conversations about race.* Thousand Oaks, CA: Corwin.

Steele, D. M., & Cohn-Vargas, B. (2013). *Identity safe classrooms: Places to belong and learn.* Thousand Oaks, CA: Corwin.

Tatum, B. C. (1992, Spring). Talking about race, learning about racism: The application of racial identity theory in the classroom. *Harvard Educational Review, 62*(1), 321–348.

Tienken, C. H., & Orlich, D. C. (2013). *The school reform landscape: Fraud, myth, and lies.* New York: Rowman & Littlefield.

Wexler, B. E. (2006). *Brain and culture: Neurobiology, ideology, and social change.* Cambridge: MIT Press.

CORWIN
A SAGE Company

Corwin is committed to improving education for all learners by publishing books and other professional development resources for those serving the field of PreK–12 education. By providing practical, hands-on materials, Corwin continues to carry out the promise of its motto: **"Helping Educators Do Their Work Better."**